*The Teacher Rebellion*

# The Teacher Rebellion

DAVID SELDEN

Howard University Press
Washington, D.C.     1985

Printed in the United States of America


Library of Congress Cataloging in Publication Data

Selden, David.
  The teacher rebellion.

  Bibliography: p.
  Includes index.
  1. Teachers' unions—United States—History—20th
century.  I. Title.
LB2844.53.U6S44     1983     331.88'113711'00973     83-4403
ISBN 0–88258–099–X

*For the Teachers of America*

# Contents

# Preface

As reliable as falling leaves, teacher strikes have become har-
bingers of autumn. It was not always so. For the first century
and a half of American history, teachers accepted poor wages
and working conditions with hardly a grumble. Then, as the
social changes following World War II impacted the schools,
America's teachers became militant. They demanded better
pay, smaller classes, improved teaching conditions and other
benefits. When they were not satisfied with what their school
boards offered, they demonstrated, picketed and even went on
strike.

Yet, the teachers have remained divided. If the more than
three million educators and related professional workers
should come together under progressive leadership in a unified
organization, the effect on American society would be momen-
tous. The "United Teachers of America" would be the largest,
most articulate and most influential organization in the nation.

This book is a memoir of the postwar decades, when the
spark of teacher militancy spread across the country. I was
a participant in that movement. My experience helps locate
the events of the rebellion in their time and social context. It
also invokes the attempt to build that "one big union" for all
teachers.

The main thrust of the teacher rebellion was carried by
elementary and secondary school teachers. With some note-
worthy exceptions, college and university teachers were late in
joining the movement. For this reason, and to avoid "meanwhile, back on the campus" digressions, The Teacher Rebellion
deals only with the spread of teacher collective bargaining in
public school systems.

The events described here all really happened. Conversations are as correct as my memory allows; their sense is entirely accurate. However, to emphasize their personal origin, most conversations are contained in the sections called "Memory Tapes." These "Tapes" allow the reader an insider's view of the rebellion as it began to unfold.

*The Teacher Rebellion* was a half dozen years in the writing. I am deeply indebted to many people for their help and encouragement. The most notable of these are John Schmid, Pat Strand and David Elsila, former members of the American Federation of Teachers national staff. Les Strand gave *Rebellion* a line-by-line reading for editorial errors while the book was in manuscript. David Darland, formerly head of the NEA's department of instruction, provided much valuable information about the Association.

Other friends who were particularly helpful include Edward Simpkins, dean of the College of Education at Wayne State University; John Herling, editor of Herling's Labor Letter; and David Issacson of the Western Michigan University faculty. Arnold Johnston, a member of the WMU faculty, also made helpful suggestions. My dear friend Robert Halbeisen was especially supportive over a long period of time. Gregory Kearse, my editor at Howard University Press, supplied vitally needed encouragement and many useful suggestions.

Above all, however, the assistance given by my wife, Bernice, was invaluable. In addition to the usual editorial corrections, Bernice was able to curb many of the excesses which are endemic to first-person narratives.

# Part I

---

# A MOVEMENT BEGINS

# Chapter 1

## CIRCUIT RIDING

MEMORY TAPE: GOING FULL TIME

It is the day after Thanksgiving, 1948. I am sitting before the fireplace in my small, newly acquired, 100-year-old cottage near Peekskill, New York. It is cold out but the fire is comforting. Its flickers create interesting patterns on the whitewashed ceiling. I am cracking walnuts and sipping sherry.

I had left my teaching position in Dearborn, Michigan, in 1943 to join the Navy. After the war I had taught school in Florida. Now, I am in my second year of teaching in a junior-senior high school overlooking the Hudson River valley. This is it, I believe, from here to retirement, twenty or thirty years down the road.

The telephone rings. It is Jessie Baxter, an old friend and president of the Michigan Federation of Teachers (MFT). She is calling from a meeting of the executive board. The union has managed to scrape together $3,000 to hire an executive secretary. She asks, "Would you be interested in the job?"

Jessie's words are electrifying. Full time for the union! I had dreamed of such an opportunity but I had not thought it possible. Still, the salary is less than I am earning as a teacher. How will my family and I get along?

I tell Jessie that I am interested in the job and that I will need some time to think it over. If she will send an application, I will fill it out and return it as soon as I can.

After a few days, an application arrives. It is an all-purpose, six-page form which can be purchased at office supply stores.

*I fill it out carefully and send it back to Detroit. Weeks pass with no word. I begin to believe that the position has been offered to someone else.*

*It is March when a telegram arrives from Washington, D.C. The message reads, "You are hereby appointed to the organizing staff of the American Federation of Labor." It is signed, "William Green, President."*

*I call Jessie Baxter, who apologizes. "Didn't anyone tell you?" she asks. "After I talked with you I found out about the AFL job, so I just passed your application along to Washington. You will be assigned to the AFT, but you will be paid by the AFL. Congratulations!"*

## ROOTS

Since the turn of the century teachers had made sporadic and isolated attempts to form unions. In 1916 a handful of leaders from New York, Chicago, and other scattered localities met in New York City to form a "national" organization. A year later the American Federation of Teachers (AFT) was granted a charter by the American Federation of Labor (AFL).

Some of the leaders of the fledgling union, including John Dewey, the educational pioneer and philosopher, considered the new organization a militant vanguard within the established National Education Association (NEA). However, this ecumenical view was brusquely rejected by the conservative administrators who controlled the NEA. Long before I became a union member in 1940, the antagonism between the two organizations had become a bitter feud.

The clash between the AFT and the NEA had an element of class conflict. The NEA and its state affiliates were dominated by school superintendents and other administrators who seemed afraid of antagonizing the business interests which held the budgetary purse strings. Though committed to expanding the system of education and improving its quality, the administrators were concerned that teachers not become embarrassingly aggressive. The Federation challenged this paternalistic attitude and called on teachers to take their destiny into their own hands.

It seemed preordained that I join the AFT. My parents were teachers, and I came of age in Michigan during the turbulent thirties. By the time I began teaching in Dearborn, I called myself a Socialist. Although I was not a member of an organized group, I had read much of Marx, Veblen, the Webbs and others. Socialism seemed a matter of common sense.

I was also interested in the labor movement. Soon after coming to Dearborn, I did volunteer work for the United Automobile Workers (UAW) at its West Side headquarters in Detroit. I had worked in the auto plants to help put myself through school, but that was before the sitdown strikes and the growth of the union. Being at the UAW headquarters and teaching classes for UAW Local 600 gave me my first direct union contact. Thus, by 1940, when friends asked me to sign an AFT charter application, I was ready.

My joining the AFT was not without misgivings. I had grave doubts about the compatibility of public employee unions and socialism. If the workers owned the enterprise, why should they unionize and strike against themselves? Later I came to realize that a public boss could be as tough and oppressive as a private one, and that *all* workers need unions.


A TASTE OF VICTORY

The AFT was not much of a union in 1940, certainly not much of a union compared to the UAW. The United Automobile Workers was only a few years old but it had many more members than the AFT had enrolled after thirty years. In fact, there were only a few school districts where the Federation was well-organized. The prevailing view among AFT members was that most teachers were too conservative or too timid to join the union. They felt that most AFT locals could never be more than small agitation groups. Feeble though it was, however, the AFT was headed in the right direction. When I was asked to become president of the tiny new local I accepted. Soon I was devoting my spare time to building the union.

I was involved in an internal controversy almost immediately. Some of the members in the local wanted to restrict membership to teachers whose views on social and economic ques-

tions coincided with those of the members of the founding
group. In contrast, I thought the union should recruit all teachers, even the coaches in the physical education department. I
believed that once these half-hearted members were admitted,
the union could educate them; otherwise, they were likely to
work against the union. It was a view that I retained throughout
my union career.

During those early days in Dearborn I also learned the value
of militancy. Teachers are generally aspiring members of the
middle class who become militant only after extreme provo-
cation. In Dearborn, the board of education provided that prov-
ocation by making three blatantly political appointments to
high-paying administrative positions. Teachers were outraged.
Weak as the union was, I sent the school board a public letter
of protest. It was printed by all three Detroit papers.

The board of education responded to the union's public protest by insisting that I appear at a special meeting to apologize.
I tipped off the papers and instead of apologizing I repeated
my charges. The controversy went on for months, but in the
end the board established a rudimentary civil service merit system for extra-pay jobs.

The union had won a victory. In the course of the struggle
teachers had become so enthusiastic that the Federation ran a
slate of candidates against three board members who were up
for reelection. Although the AFT candidates lost, membership
in the union increased dramatically.

## MEMORY TAPE: ELECTION NIGHT

There is a hubbub of excited activity throughout my home on
Payne Street in Dearborn. It is school board election night. The
leaders of the Fordson Federation of Teachers, forerunner of
the Dearborn Federation of Teachers, are waiting anxiously for
reports of the vote from the watchers at the dozen polling places. It has been a long, eventful campaign. It is over, and we
do not know whether we have won.

The union did not intend to challenge the school board—
at least not so soon. The local had been chartered less than
two years and still had only fifty or sixty members. But one

thing led to another, and the Federation was drawn into a two-pronged drive: to elect three new board members and to win adoption of teacher tenure. The new board members and the one friendly incumbent would give teachers a favorable majority. Tenure was a local option by Michigan law. Up to that time, Dearborn had not participated.

The campaign had been hard fought. With the help of others in the teachers union, I had set up a Dearborn branch of Labor's Non-Partisan League. The Dearborn league included four organizations: a bus drivers local (about 200 members); a painters union (about 20 members); UAW Local 600 (more than 50,000 members); and our little teachers organization. During the campaign my basement had been converted from ping-pong parlor to political headquarters. Election workers spent hours sorting the names of Dearborn residents from Addressograph tapes of the Local 600 membership. The names were further sorted so that canvassers could seek out all the union members on each block.

We had also run an intensive registration campaign. To participate in school board elections a voter had to own property or be the parent of a school-age child. For months before the election we hauled prospective voters to the registration office at the board of education headquarters. Because many teachers were single or did not own property, the union bought a vacant lot and sold quitclaim deeds for five dollars so all teachers could register to vote.

Suddenly the telephone rings. Everyone stops in mid-sentence while I pick up the phone.

"Yes, this is Dave. Go ahead."

It is a watcher from one of the voting places. I scribble vote totals on a yellow pad.

"Wow! We won!" I shout. "How about tenure?"

Tenure, too, has carried. Although it is only a report from one precinct, we are jubilant. Victory is at hand! People dash to their cars and race to get the ingredients for a celebration. A keg of beer is already in one of the basement washtubs. Soon, the suds are flowing.

Then, the disappointing truth is revealed as the totals come in from the other precincts. It is a close contest, but all three union-supported candidates have been defeated. There is good *news, though. Tenure has been approved. Still, this morsel of success is not enough to lift the spirits of the Federation members.*

*The party makers return with White Tower hamburgers, pretzels and drinks. The little house fills with scores of disappointed election workers. The party becomes a wake. By midnight it is a mean, sodden brawl. Beer is spilled. At any moment a fight could break out. We do not even know the union songs with which to boost our spirits. But in the future, few elections will be lost by the Dearborn Federation.*

## BACK DOOR COLLECTIVE BARGAINING

During the Federation's challenge to the board of education the Dearborn branch of the Michigan Education Association remained quiet. After the election I proposed that the union take over the Association. It was not unusual for AFT activists to provide leadership for their local associations. The association membership was a shelter against harassment by administrators. In this case, however, I had a different purpose in mind.

Our slate of AFT members challenged the Association's board of directors on a publicly announced one-plank platform. If the union slate won, the Association would be voted out of existence. Although fewer than a third of the members of the Association were members of the AFT, the union slate won. To ensure their mandate, the new officers conducted a referendum on disbanding. When that carried, the Association was disbanded, leaving the Federation the only teacher organization in the district.

The Federation had backed into the position of sole representative of Dearborn teachers. It would be thrilling to report, "and thus did teacher collective bargaining begin," but although collective bargaining was within the grasp of the Dearborn Federation, none of us dared think in such terms. It would take nearly two decades of Federation development before anyone could say that.

## MISSIONARY WORK

I spent three years in the Navy during World War II. I went back into teaching in 1947, and in 1949 I became an AFT organizer. Actually, the union was too poor to afford organizers. I was paid by the American Federation of Labor, which then had a policy of helping struggling unions.

I became the AFT's "Eastern organizer." Ted Snow, another activist, became "Western organizer." I covered the country east of Lincoln, Nebraska, and my colleague covered the rest. For several years I roamed the territory, following leads forwarded from the AFT national office in Chicago. It was a frustrating but valuable experience.

My first organizing attempt was in Kentucky. One of the teacher uprisings which periodically sweeps through that state was taking place. The only AFT local in the state was the Louisville Federation of Teachers. By the end of the school year I had chartered thirteen new locals. Organizing? Nothing to it!

But a few months later it became clear that things were not as simple as they seemed. When I returned to Kentucky after the summer recess, I found that few of the new locals were functioning. The legislature had enacted a modest across-the-board pay raise. Coupled with intensified antiunion pressure from administrators, the flames of rebellion were damped.

Even worse, the Louisville union, which had included more than two-thirds of the city's teachers, was now wracked by an internal dispute. Most of the members had quit in disgust. Furthermore, prominent members of the Federation had become involved in trying to oust the secretary-treasurer of the Kentucky Federation of Labor, on whom I depended for important support.

In Kentucky, I learned that young unions are highly perishable. They require a lot of care and support. Even then workers can defeat themselves by dissension and disunity. I tried several times during the next two years to revive the Kentucky locals. I also spent a lot of time shooting at new targets of opportunity. Despite hard work, the results were discouraging. I came to realize that unplanned, helter-skelter attempts to organize wasted precious time and money. We needed organizers to handle assigned territories where work could be planned and strongholds developed.

Just before the 1951 national AFT convention in August, I presented an "area organizing plan" to John Eklund, the AFT president. I proposed that national dues, per capita, be raised by ten cents a month to produce a special organizing fund of fifty thousand dollars a year. State federations in various regions would then be encouraged to band together to raise part of the money to hire organizers. Each organizing area would receive support from the special organizing fund to subsidize the organizer's salary and expenses.

Eklund listened to my exposition of the plan with growing impatience. When I finished he pointed out that he was running for reelection. Coming out for a per capita increase was tantamount to political suicide. He suggested that I present the plan to Irvin R. Kuenzli, the AFT secretary-treasurer, who was the operating head of the union. The secretary-treasurer was chosen by the executive council, unlike the president and the vice-presidents, who were elected by the convention.

Kuenzli was no more encouraging than Eklund. For the past ten years he had steered the union through a series of internal crises. Though he had held the union together, his enthusiasm for organizing had long since cooled. He looked at me with condescension and said he would think about my proposal.

I spent the week of the convention trying to interest other AFT leaders in my plan, but I had little success. At the convention's end, however, my organizer colleague and I were asked to give reports to the executive council. I took advantage of this opportunity to present an amended version of my organizing scheme. I suggested that the national organization match funds raised by any group of state federations that would voluntarily raise their national per capita. The "voluntary" was important, since only a convention could raise the per capita rate, and the convention had already adjourned.

Most council members were openly skeptical of convincing state federations to increase their payments voluntarily, but on the theory that it would not hurt to let me try, they gave their approval. With this dubious charter I set to work.

The state federations in Pennsylvania, New Jersey and New York were scheduled to meet in October. I visited each and found that the teacher unionists were eager for organizing help and willing to make sacrifices to get it. By the month's end, all three state federations had agreed to raise their dues in order to participate in the new plan. However, New York City, virtually a state in itself, would be omitted.

The new organizing area would include about 3,000 AFT members—there were only 50,000 nationwide. These dues payers would produce enough money from their new special per capita payments to permit the plan to function.

A few minutes after the vote in the New York convention I went outside for a breath of air. I ran into Secretary-Treasurer Kuenzli, who was just arriving. We went to a Chock Full O'Nuts lunch counter to talk things over.

"Well, how's it going?" Kuenzli asked.

"Pretty good," I replied. "They just approved a voluntary dues increase."

"They did?"

"Yup."

The secretary-treasurer was incredulous. "How about New Jersey and Pennsylvania?"

"Same thing," I answered smugly. "Looks like I'm in business."

But there was one more problem to be worked out. I had made it clear that I would be an applicant for the position of territory organizer even though I was well aware of the job's shaky financial footing. But before I went over to the new job, I wanted to make sure that the American Federation of Labor hired someone to take my place. Once I'd taken care of that detail, I formally applied for the new position. Within a month I was working in my new territory.


## MAKING MY ROUNDS

With my organizing area now reduced to New York, Pennsylvania and New Jersey—still large enough, certainly—I worked out three organizing circuits. Every Monday morning I left my home near Peekskill, New York, to begin the route for that week. I drove from school district to school district, met contacts and discussed tactics and strategy. I dropped into teachers' lounge rooms, left literature and picked up news of what was going on. I located the cheap places to stay. Sometimes I stayed in the homes of union members or slept in my car. I returned home late Friday night or Saturday or sometimes Sunday if I had to cover a weekend meeting.

My circuit riding was supplemented by a monthly newsletter I wrote, mimeographed, hand-addressed and mailed. I used the telephone a great deal, and any contact person could call me collect any time. I called home every day or so to check for messages.

The objective was to line up a dozen or so teachers in each school district who would apply for a union charter. Other teachers could then rally around the nucleus when the time was ripe. I would help the new locals draw up a constitution, set up committees, adopt an action program and get out a news-letter. We would also arrange a schedule of meetings at which I could give advice and encouragement.

Unconsciously I was trying to duplicate my Dearborn experience. But, although I chartered dozens of locals during this period, none of them ever achieved the success of my home local. However, after a few months, my efforts began to produce modest results. Membership in the special organizing area began to increase.

Nevertheless, I was dissatisfied. From the outset I regarded the organizing area as a prototype which would lead to the formation of others. As soon as I felt the plan was working, I convinced the leaders in Pennsylvania and New Jersey to split off and join with Maryland, the District of Columbia and Delaware to form a new area to which another organizer was assigned. I then tried to convince the AFT leaders in Connecticut and Rhode Island to join with upstate New York to make a viable area in that region. I foresaw a network of special organizing areas spanning the country wherever there were organizing opportunities. This vision of AFT expansion was disrupted by a change of political alignment within the national union.


ON TO NEW YORK CITY

In 1952 Carl J. Megel became president of the union. Before Megel, AFT presidents had continued to work at their teaching positions, leaving the management of the national office and most of the policy decisions to the secretary-treasurer, who was a full-time union employee. Megel set out to establish himself as president in fact as well as in name. Within six months Secretary-Treasurer Kuenzli had been dismissed. The new president then turned his attention to other problems.

The AFT, small as it was, had long contained three political factions. The largest of these was the Progressive Caucus. The second largest grouping, to which Megel belonged, was usually called the "National Caucus," or sometimes known as the "Classroom Teachers Caucus." The third faction was a relatively small leftist caucus with strength mainly in New Jersey and California.

Even though I had never been politically active in the union, I felt that Megel regarded me with suspicion. I had come from Michigan, home of the Progressives, and lived in New York, another Progressive stronghold. Since the cooperative governance of the special organizing area insulated me from direct presidential interference, it did not come as a complete surprise when the new president moved to abolish the special organizing area and place me directly under his supervision. But before this change in my status could be carried out, an escape hatch suddenly opened up.

Although New York City had been excluded from the special organizing area, I had developed friendly relations with several of the New York leaders. In the spring of 1953 the chairman of the city's organizing committee asked me to become the local's organizer. I was very excited by this offer. After making arrangements for an ongoing relationship with some of the new locals that I had chartered in the special organizing area, I accepted the position.

# Chapter 2

## THE GUILD

1953

When I entered the grimy fourth floor office of the New York Teachers Guild at Two East Twenty-third Street that hot morning of July 1, 1953, I had no idea that I was taking a step toward the teacher rebellion of the 1960s. I felt overwhelmed by the immensity of the task before me. New York City was the largest school district in the world. More than 40,000 teachers and 800,000 students were distributed through 600 elementary schools, 100-plus junior high schools and 90 high schools. The teaching staff was the best-qualified and best-paid in any big-city school system. How could this elite corps be unionized?

The Guild was the outgrowth of a bitter struggle in the original teachers union. A social-democratic faction which included all of the officers had waged a long fight against a more militant rank-and-file faction led by Communists, Trotskyites and other leftists. The leadership group, unable to control the local, broke away to form the Teachers Guild. About a thousand members of the union seceded with them.

"The Split," as it is known in New York City teacher union history, occurred in 1935. It was a bitter, scarring experience for all who went through it. The participants will talk about it as long as they live. The newly formed Teachers Guild immediately applied for an AFT charter. The application provoked seven years of struggle, which resulted in expulsion of Local 5—the original local—and the chartering of the Guild as AFT Local 2. By the time I became New York City organizer,

14

the Guild had only grown to eighteen hundred members. The old Teachers Union, under its leftist leadership, had dwindled to about the same number.

The divisiveness between the Guild and the Teachers Union was augmented by other rivalries among the dozens of teacher organizations in the city. In fact, an organization existed for each category of teacher, including borough, religion, grade level of teaching and subject area. Furthermore, unlike most school districts, New York City had not fallen under the hegemony of the National Education Association.

The Guild competed with its rivals by intense leafletting and by providing a range of services. It maintained an office and published a four-page monthly paper. It also offered retirement counseling, grievance service and preparatory courses for the teaching license examinations. Its legislative program in Albany was the center of its action program.

Soon after I came to the Guild, its executive secretary left for a better-paying job, and I assumed the responsibilities of that position in addition to my organizing duties. There were two other staff members—a bookkeeper and a secretary. We were assisted by a corps of dedicated volunteers who stuffed envelopes, made phone calls and performed other essential tasks.

Charles Cogen was president of the Guild. For the next 14 years we maintained a close working relationship, although we were certainly an unlikely pair. "Charlie" was unmistakably a New Yorker, a Social-Democrat and scholar. He had graduated from Cornell Law School with honors in the midst of the Depression and had turned to teaching to support his family. He had never left the security of the school system to try his luck in law.

Charlie was usually cautious to the point of timidity but courageous and stubborn on occasion. He had joined the Teachers Union and left with the other moderates to form the Teachers Guild. In 1952 he became president as a compromise choice in response to demands by a rebellious faction of younger Guild members. Throughout our long association, I often urged him to do things he did not want to do, and he frequently moderated my often abrasive proposals. Whether because of our differences or in spite of them, we made an effective combination.

## THE SUBWAY CIRCUIT

In filling the roles of executive secretary and organizer I turned my attention to improving the internal functioning of the union. The Guild members enjoyed each other's company, and there were many meetings. The administrative committee— "AdCom," I nicknamed it—composed of the officers and committee heads, met every Wednesday afternoon at four o'clock. The 35-member executive board met two evenings a month. The delegate assembly, made up of representatives from schools in which there were Guild members, met once a month. There were also more than a dozen committee meetings every month.

I attended all the meetings. More often than not I prepared the agendas and reproduced the minutes. I tried to use each meeting as a pretext for a news release, a flyer to the schools or a petition to circulate among the teachers. The purpose was to portray the Guild as a sleepless champion of teachers' interests.

In addition to attending functions at headquarters, I pushed my way onto the subway several times a week to journey to a school. Teachers brought their lunches to the library, the teachers' lounge or a Guild member's classroom, and I held forth on the latest issues the Guild was espousing. At the end of the lunch hour I distributed membership applications and hoped someone would sign up. Afterward, I returned to Twenty-third Street to cut mimeograph stencils or copy materials for the afterschool and evening meetings.

Even though this work was more rewarding than the lonely missionary journeys and the circuit riding had been, the results were only slightly greater. Knowing that thousands of teachers were ready to be organized was stimulating, but I was still doing "sign 'em up organizing." Despite my frenetic effort the Guild was only gaining a hundred or so members a year.

During my earlier days as an itinerant organizer, I had pondered the economics of union organizing. According to my calculations, I would have to increase the union by at least a thousand members each year to cover the cost of keeping me on the road. For every three new members who joined, two others were backsliding. Progress was agonizingly slow.

While riding the subway circuit, I made similar calculations about organizing in New York City. At the rate the union was growing, it would take more than a hundred years to enroll a majority of the teachers. Even assuming that the growth rate would accelerate as the union became larger and more credible, the job could not be done in fewer than twenty-five years.

As one year and then two passed, I found such thoughts increasingly discouraging. Even though Cogen and other Guild leaders seemed satisfied with my performance, I could not justify merely "working for the union." Organizing was more than a job—it was a mission.

My dissatisfaction was deepened by a growing disillusionment with the labor movement. I had been attracted to unionism because I saw it as a lever to change society. I believed that most unionists were committed to the same idealistic goals that I had accepted. But after half a dozen years of contact with union leaders, little of that mystique remained. I was shocked to learn that most of them were not Socialists and that many were not even liberals. George Meany, president of the American Federation of Labor, so I read, openly supported capitalism.

The contrast between reality and my idealized version of unionism caused me intense pain. At a union legislative conference in Albany, delegates from the International Brotherhood of Electrical Workers (IBEW) objected to public ownership of the power plants along the St. Lawrence Seaway on grounds that it was easier to negotiate with private employers than with the government. I guiltily withheld comment because I did not want to appear foolish to these experienced unionists. Nevertheless, I felt that my silence betrayed my beliefs and principles.

In New York City I attended the Central Trades and Labor Council, which was controlled by a coalition of conservative Teamster and building-trades locals. Most liberal unions did not send representatives to this body. The Teachers Guild had almost no influence on its policies, even in matters affecting education.

Those were also the dismal years of McCarthyism, the cold war and Eisenhower. Liberalism was on the wane. A reactionary bipartisan coalition ruled in Congress. College campuses were "beat." The promise of racial integration offered by the

Supreme Court in *Brown v. Board of Education* remained un-
fulfilled.

If I could have comforted myself with assurances that unionism was increasing or that the Federation was moving ahead,
my morale might have been fortified. But there were no twitch-
ings in the liberal community to encourage me. I became more
depressed about the future of the Teachers Union, unionism
and American liberalism.

After five years of organizing teachers—two years in New
York City and three in other parts of the country—I was ready
to quit. I applied for a teaching position in a Westchester County
school district. Then, so subtly that I hardly noticed, things
began to change.


## ELY TRACHTENBERG

One of the first things I had done at the Teachers Guild was to
reorganize the organizing committee. The Guild's charter members had not been very good organizers, so I turned to the
younger, more militant members teaching in the junior high
schools.

I kept the office open evenings and scheduled organizing
committee meetings at night instead of after school. Once a
month there was a beer and peanuts party. I led sudsy rendi-
tions of labor songs with a cheap banjo. We viewed labor films
from the International Ladies Garment Workers Union and from
Rutgers University. I was trying to develop the camaraderie
which had carried the leadership group in the Dearborn local
to success. Gradually new young activists emerged within the
staid Guild, and unionism began to be fun again.

Ely Trachtenberg was a member of the new group. He was
in his early thirties, broad-shouldered and handsome. Well over
six feet tall, Trachtenberg taught in a Manhattan junior high
school and was on the Guild's executive board. He had belonged to the Trotskyist Socialist "party" led by Max Schachtman, the gifted Marxist intellectual. Schachtman insisted that
his followers take jobs in industry so that they could give socialist leadership to the workers at the work place. Following

this dictum, Trachtenberg had worked in an automobile plant and had joined the United Auto Workers.

Although I called myself a Socialist, I had had very little contact with other Socialists. Ely Trachtenberg, however, had grown up in the hurly-burly of left-wing debate in New York City, where socialism and union theory were constantly discussed. He was skilled in Marxist dialectic yet he had a pragmatic attitude toward the Guild's problems. He became chairman of the organizing committee.

I had realized that alone I could not organize 40,000 teachers. Neither could they be organized solely by propaganda emanating from the Guild's central office. Accordingly, I developed a school-by-school approach. The members in each school—even if there were only two or three—were to regard themselves as a little union. Each chapter was asked to elect a chairman, hold weekly meetings and develop a program to improve working conditions throughout the school. Trachtenberg added the principle of "chapter life" to this chapter structure.

This concept meant that the Guild chapter would give leadership to the *entire* faculty. Chapter meetings were open to nonmembers. They would be encouraged to participate in discussions and decision making. In the sectarian organizational atmosphere of New York, this lack of distinction between members and nonmembers was unheard of. The idea of letting nondues payers vote on Guild policy seemed strange, but Trachtenberg convinced me that teacher unity at the grass roots was absolutely essential. He was certain that dues paying would inevitably follow involvement.

We carefully analyzed the Guild's position among competing organizations. We prepared two lists. One included those items which tended to keep teachers from joining the Guild. The other listed those items which made the Guild attractive. From these lists we developed a report to the executive board and called it "Big Guild, Little Guild."

The thesis of "Big Guild, Little Guild" was that the union should regard itself as a "candidate for public office"—the office of bargaining agent. It should therefore do things which would gain teacher support. It should also avoid actions which would alienate any group of teachers. For instance, the Guild had always taken strong stands on issues involving separation of church and state. It had vigorously opposed efforts to establish prayer in the schools. The Guild had also protested the board of education's adoption of a policy statement on teaching moral and spiritual values because the statement seemed to be based on belief in a Christian God. We asserted that following a liberal line on such matters made the Guild vulnerable to attack by persons who were not so much interested in the issues as in discouraging teacher unionism. If Guild leaders wanted to take positions on such questions, they should do so in other organizations—at least for the time being. The Guild should emphasize the bread-and-butter issues of salaries, fringe benefits and working conditions. Once the union had become the bargaining agent, it could more safely turn its attention to broader issues.

## A CRUCIAL VOTE

"Big Guild, Little Guild" got a cold reception. It challenged deeply felt values which had guided the leaders of the Guild through their careers. Not surprisingly, our report was referred to a study committee, where it languished for months. Although most old-timers had been offended by our report, a few, including President Cogen, agreed with many of its recommendations. So did most of the younger members of the executive board.

Even though we could not persuade the board to adopt the recommendations of "Big Guild, Little Guild," we kept trying to gain acceptance of our ideas. We believed that if the Guild adopted a "candidate for office" attitude, it would soon launch a campaign to become the exclusive bargaining agent for the city's teachers.

At first the idea of collective bargaining for teachers seemed outlandish. Public employees had been excluded from the Wagner Labor Relations Act and the Taft-Hartley amendments, and besides, teachers were "professionals" who did not need bargaining rights.

Trachtenberg and I realized that one of the first tasks in moving toward collective bargaining would be gaining the assent, if not the support, of the Guild leadership. We made our move in the spring of 1956. We urged the delegate assembly to declare collective bargaining to be the Guild's highest priority. After lengthy debate the delegates voted approval.

Because the Guild's membership was less than five percent of the total teaching staff, a representation election would have destroyed the union. Few of those voting thought that such an election would be held. Had they known that such a vote would take place within five years, they might not have approved the collective bargaining motion.

The delegate assembly vote gave me a sense of embarking on a perilous voyage to an uncertain destination, but Trachtenberg's steady confidence was reassuring. He felt that if the Guild were defeated in an election, the winning organization would be forced to become a union because of the conflict inherent in the collective bargaining process. He maintained it was not the Guild that was important; it was the movement.

Today, having seen many unions merely operate as vending machines that dispense benefits to their members—or agree to "givebacks"—I am much less confident about the triumph of the working class. Collective bargaining is not an automatic mechanism; insight and leadership are needed too, but at the time, I found Trachtenberg's argument convincing.

With as much trepidation as hope, collective bargaining became the Guild's overriding concern. Every flyer, every report and every statement issued from the union's headquarters said that collective bargaining was the cure. Salary too low? Collective bargaining will increase it. Your principal giving you a hard time? The Guild will take care of him when it wins collective bargaining. Under this new drive membership began to grow.

Early in the struggle for collective bargaining, there was a victory in the school system's Bureau of Child Guidance (BCG). The BCG was a unique, semiautonomous agency of more than 400 psychologists, social workers and psychiatrists whose mission it was to help children and teachers overcome psychological and environmental obstacles to learning. These professionals were not the most likely group to lead the way to collective bargaining. Yet, under the subtle influence of Lou Hay, a dedicated social reformer and psychologist, the BCG employees conducted their own collective bargaining election. As a result the Guild was recognized as the bargaining agent for the unit.

# Chapter 3

---

# THE ROOTS OF REVOLT

TEACHER MILITANCY RISES

The social conditions which followed World War II had an unsettling effect on the schools, particularly those in the big northern cities. The postwar baby boom pumped hundreds of thousands of "extra" children into the school systems. The northward migration of blacks and other minorities added thousands of pupils who had attended segregated schools in the South or who had been excluded from schools altogether. Soon classrooms overflowed. Many of the entrants were ill-prepared to cope with school routine.

At the same time, the increasing turbulence in American society was reflected in the overtaxed classrooms. The controls which had enforced social order—family authority, community pressure, religion, racial repression and economic pressure—had weakened or disappeared. No new institutions of a more positive nature had emerged. As a result the nation experienced a rising tide of crime, violence and social disintegration.

Teachers bore the brunt of the deteriorating social conditions in the schools. Even in smaller, less urban districts, schools were becoming storehouses of highly combustible social conditions. Furthermore, teachers' salaries were lagging further behind the rising cost of living.

Before World War II, teacher protest was relatively mild. Strikes were practically unheard of, even during the Depression, when teachers' salaries were slashed and paid in scrip. In 1936 Chicago teachers marched on the board of education because the board had defaulted on their salaries. They chose a Saturday. The "walk," as it came to be known, was not a "walkout."

After World War II, spontaneous teacher protests and work stoppages erupted in scattered areas. But in New York City, a strike by public employees was considered too risky to contemplate. Even the valiant Mike Quill, leader of the subway workers, managed to settle with the city in time to avoid walkouts.

But although teachers seemed unlikely to strike, teacher militancy had escalated steadily in the late 1940s and early 1950s. The annual demonstrations at city hall became larger and louder. The "marches" on Albany via bus and train attracted more participation as city and state officials failed to improve salaries and working conditions.

In addition, the state legislature took an action in 1947 which served to agitate New York City high school teachers for the next ten years. For many years high school teachers had been paid $1,100 a year more than elementary school teachers. The lawmakers abolished this salary differential in an effort to recruit more elementary school teachers.

High school teachers were outraged. They felt that they had been grievously injured. The High School Teachers Association (HSTA), long somnolent, was aroused to angry reaction. After searching for an appropriate way to express their displeasure, they called for a boycott of extracurricular activities by coaches and other teachers. The Guild had long opposed the salary differential and had applauded its abolition. But after some hesitation it voted to support the boycott.

The real strength of the after-school work stoppage lay in the high school coaches, who were members of a semiautonomous organization loosely affiliated with the HSTA. In the summer of 1952, the coaches received a special salary increase and they decided to resume their duties. The board of education also voted a general salary increase, but it refused to restore the differential.

In 1954, two years after the boycott of extracurricular duties, the HSTA again tried the same tactic. Not to be outdone, the Guild, on my recommendation, called a slowdown. I euphemistically dubbed it the "Minimum Service Program (MSP)."

A committee drew up a list of things teachers would no longer do, such as put displays on bulletin boards, bring materials from home, patrol the halls between classes or write on the blackboard.

The MSP project was an utter failure. Critics sourly asserted that teachers could not work any slower anyway. But the MSP failed because teachers could not bring themselves to sabotage their work. After a month of unsuccessfully promoting the scheme I quietly let it die. Teacher anger and frustration continued to mount.

## THE RIGHT TO EAT

While Guild organizing in the high schools was severely handicapped by its stand against the salary differential, the junior highs were prime territory. Teaching in the junior high schools was more difficult than teaching elsewhere, mainly because of the students' unruliness. Furthermore, half of the junior high school teachers were full-time substitutes who were paid less than regulars and received no fringe benefits. My slogan was, "Show me a junior high school teacher and I'll show you a union member."

Teachers in the elementary schools, however, seemed uninterested in joining anything, let alone a militant union. Therefore, the "Right to Eat" campaign surprised me completely. As a routine agitational exercise in the spring of 1958, a petition calling for the school board to grant a half-hour, duty-free lunch period every day was sent to all elementary schools. High schools and junior high schools had this privilege in addition to free periods during the day; elementary school teachers were required to supervise their students throughout the 35-hour school week; hence, the "Right to Eat."

The petitions were standard Guild tactics. They were circulated in response to almost every complaint. Most of them garnered scarcely more than two or three hundred signatures. Surprisingly, the "Right to Eat" petition attracted thousands of names during the first month of its circulation.

## ONE DAY AT A TIME

Emboldened by the response to the "Right to Eat" petition, I drew up a more inclusive list of demands that included a salary increase. To reinforce these demands I persuaded the executive board to call for a one-day demonstration work stoppage and rally at city hall on the day of the annual budget hearing.

After-school city hall rallies were a budget hearing ritual for teachers in New York. Two or three thousand people would go to city hall, picket for an hour or so, listen to a few speeches and go home to hear the budget hearing on radio. I had been searching for a more dramatic but "safe" form of protest against the city's education budget. A one-day work stoppage would certainly have the desired shock value without exposing teachers to reprisals. I knew that few teachers would actually walk out of their classrooms in defiance of the authorities. Most would call in sick or would take a day of unpaid personal leave. The demonstration would violate the state Condon-Wadlin Act, which prohibited strikes by public employees, but I thought it was unlikely that school officials would invoke the law for such a limited infraction.

Some of the old-timers in the Guild feared that the demonstration might get out of hand and turn into a full-fledged strike. When a reporter asked me about that possibility I replied that the union was "taking it one day at a time." In fact, President Cogen and many of his friends were afraid that the union would be destroyed by the stoppage. In order to reassure them, I drew up a "pledge of support," a petition-like sign-up sheet, so that I could estimate the amount of teacher support for the stoppage. Copies of the sheet were sent to the school chapter chairpersons, who were asked to report to the Guild office each week. But response to the pledge call was so poor that I had to pad the totals or risk cancellation of the walkout.

Fortunately, the success of the one-day work stoppage was aided by a provocative action by school and city officials. The school budget is prepared each fall. After approval by the board of education, it is sent to city hall and then submitted in revised form to the board of estimate and the city council. The 1958–59 budget had passed through several steps in the attenuated process when the school board president told a reporter that teachers would receive a $300 raise, a not inconsiderable amount at that time.

I began to consider ways to call off the stoppage in order to avoid an embarrassing debacle. Before I could take action, however, the actual budget was made public. Instead of the anticipated $300 increase, only $200 was provided. A hundred dollars does not seem crucial, but it angered teachers, and thousands of angry teachers signed the pledge of support.

## MEMORY TAPE: SCORE ONE FOR THE GUILD

I am sitting in my cubbyhole in the dilapidated home of the New York Teachers Guild. A telephone is pressed to my ear and I am scribbling notes on a yellow pad. There is a stir of excitement throughout the headquarters. People are checking lists of names. A Guild member at another phone is receiving reports from chapter leaders. In a corner Ely Trachtenberg is earnestly explaining something to a group of teachers. It is the night before "D-Day"—the day of the demonstration work stoppage.

I look up to see a grim-faced man glaring at me. It is Harry Van Arsdale, president of the Central Labor Council. In the two years since he had taken over the leadership of the council, its functioning has vastly improved. Van Arsdale, a veteran of many rough and tough organizing campaigns, is known as a progressive leader. I also know that he works closely with the city Democratic machine.

"I've been trying to get hold of you for hours," the union leader growls. "Is this the only phone you got?"

I have been trying to arrange a meeting with the central labor president for weeks, but he has been evasive. I wanted him to use his political influence to arrange a meeting with school officials. Now, when it seems too late, Van Arsdale is here. "No," I answer. "We have another."

"Two phones for 40,000 workers!" Van Arsdale snorts, and I try to hide my chagrin. I had wanted to install emergency phone lines, but the Guild could not afford the added expense.

"Where's Cogen?" Van Arsdale demands.

I explain that Cogen is on his way to appear on an eleven o'clock television news broadcast.

"Get him back," Van Arsdale snaps. "We're going to Brooklyn to meet with the school superintendent."

A break at last! I phone the television station. Cogen has not yet arrived.

"Tell them to send him to the superintendent's office as soon as he shows up," Van Arsdale directs. I leave the message, and the labor leader hustles me out of the office and into a waiting taxi. Soon we are racing down East River Drive, Brooklyn-bound.

Dr. John J. Theobald, the superintendent of schools, is waiting for us. Theobald is the son of a former high official in the school system. He is an adventurer in education. He has used his political connections, in addition to his other skills, to become head of the world's largest school system. He leads us into his inner office. A television set flickers in a corner.

"I've been listening to the news," Theobald says. "You've got the whole city up in arms. Where's Cogen?"

"He's on his way," I answer, more confidently than I believe. I know that the thrifty Cogen will be coming by subway to save taxi fare, and that could take a while. I hope that nothing has gone wrong. We have already entered the countdown to what may be the first citywide strike in New York City history. But, I am far from confident about the outcome. A small turnout would be a defeat for teachers and a setback for Guild organizing. I am hoping that this last-minute meeting will end in a settlement.

The eleven o'clock news comes on. The camera zooms in on two men sitting at a desk. One is the special events broadcaster for the program. The other is Charlie Cogen. In the superintendent's office we are aghast. "My message must not have gotten through," I explain.

Van Arsdale snatches a phone, dials information and gets the number of the TV station. He places the call and barks, "This is Harry Van Arsdale. Let me speak with Cogen. No, Cogen, the president of the teachers union. I know he's there because I can see him. This is an emergency." There is a pause. Then, "OK. Tell him to come to Superintendent Theobald's office right away."

*"Tell him to take a taxi,"* I interject, and Van Arsdale relays the message.

We watch the scene on the tube. In a minute or two we see someone hand a paper to the reporter. He glances at it and gives it to Cogen. "Mr. Cogen," he says, "Perhaps you would share this important message with our viewers."

Charlie reads the note. "Dr. Theobald would like to see you in his office as soon as possible. Take a taxi." Cogen looks uncertainly at the television reporter. "Excuse me," Cogen says and he walks out of the camera's view. A half hour later he joins us.

It does not take long to find the money for the $300 raise the teachers had been expecting. The word goes out to the news outlets. The one-day teacher demonstration work stoppage has been averted.

## THE FRUITS OF MILITANCY

The aborted one-day work stoppage was not a sensational victory, but it was enough to demonstrate the organizing value of militancy. In the remaining two months of the school year, Guild membership soared past the 3,000-mark. Charles Cogen was on his way to becoming a folk hero.

Over the summer, I made plans for an intensive organizing campaign to maintain the momentum. I asked the AFT national president, Carl Megel, to provide extra organizing assistance. He agreed to finance an additional organizer—to be designated by me—and I asked Ely Trachtenberg to take the job. But Trachtenberg wanted to stay in the school system.

My second choice was George Altomare, one of the junior high school activists who belonged to the union's executive board. But Altomare turned down the organizing position. I then turned to another member of the activist group, Albert Shanker.

Shanker and I were close friends. We lived in the same apartment complex in upper Manhattan and visited constantly. Shanker had joined the Socialist party as a student at the University of Illinois. After Shanker became a union staff member we rode to work together every day. Our friendship became a pupil-teacher relationship—I was fifteen years older, more experienced in union organizing and head of the union staff.

During the next school year union membership continued to grow, but in January growth was accelerated by a major event in the history of New York City teacher union organizing—this was the 1959 strike of the evening high school teachers.

## A STRIKE IN THE NIGHT

Most of the thousand teachers who taught in the night schools also taught full-time during the day, and many were members of the High School Teachers Association. They were led by two officers of the HSTA, Roger Parente and Samuel Hochberg, both of whom had organizational backgrounds. Hochberg had been a member of the original Teachers Union in his early days of teaching, while Parente's father was an officer in a building-trades local. In spite of their commitment to the salary differential for high school teachers, their views on most union issues were far more progressive than those of other HSTA leaders. In fact, their views were more progressive than those of many Guild members.

Working with the HSTA's free-wheeling attorney, Harold Israelson, Parente and Hochberg demanded that the superintendent of schools raise wages and improve conditions for night school teachers. They threatened a shutdown of the night schools to begin in early January. Israelson had devised a scheme to get around the state antistrike law. He pointed out that while strikes by public employees were illegal, resigning was not. If everybody resigned at the same time, the effect would be the same as a strike. Sign-up sheets were distributed among the evening high school faculty. Signing the sheet indicated one's intent to resign on January first if there was no settlement of the demands.

As the deadline approached, it became clear that the conflict in the night schools would not be settled. Guild leaders were in a quandary about proper union policy. A victory for the HSTA-led group would be a setback for the Guild in the race for organizational dominance in the city. Most Guild leaders believed, therefore, that nothing should be done to assist our militant competitor. On the other hand, the effect would be worse if the night school teachers should succeed despite Guild opposition.

Ely Trachtenberg convinced the Guild executive board, as he had convinced me many months before, that it did not matter which organization sponsored a particular militant action. What mattered was that the workers, in this case the teachers, advance. It was the struggle that was important, not the organization. It was heresy, but it was true, and I strongly supported Trachtenberg's position. The Guild could only win the organizational war by fighting the teachers' battles.

The Guild gave complete support to the strikers in the night schools. Pickets carrying Guild signs marched side-by-side with the other high school pickets in the frigid January darkness. When Hochberg and Parente called a rally at city hall, the Guild telephone network, mimeograph machine and chapter structure were used to turn out a crowd. Every night, Shanker and I made the rounds in our station wagons, which we called "Guild Coffeemobiles." We dispensed coffee and donuts to the shivering demonstrators.

By the end of the strike, the Guild and the high school militants had established strong bonds of comradeship. The strike was a success. Collective bargaining had come to the evening high schools. More important, teachers were taking their first steps toward unity.

# Chapter 4

# THE UFT

## TALKING UNITY

The strike by the night school teachers was a triumph for teacher militancy and union solidarity. Hochberg and Parente, however, considered it a mere skirmish before the main battle for the high school teachers' salary differential. They therefore turned to trying to revitalize the High School Teachers Association. Ten years had passed since the legislature had wiped out the high school differential, but high school teachers still rankled. As a result the HSTA had become a one-issue organization. That issue was a powerful unifying force for the 10,000 high school teachers, but it alienated them from the 30,000 teachers in the elementary and junior high schools. Obviously, the HSTA needed reinforcements.

On the urging of Hochberg and Parente, the association changed its name to The Secondary School Teachers Association (SSTA) in order to recruit junior high school teachers, who were promised a special differential of their own. An open meeting was called to kick off the organizing campaign.

I regarded the junior highs as the Guild's exclusive territory, and I particularly wished to repel the high school invasion. It was just possible that the lure of a special salary increase and the aura of high school teacher militancy might attract a following. I therefore decided to flood the meeting with Guild loyalists.

Hochberg later told me that when he looked out at that crowd of young, militant junior high school teachers—many of whom he knew to be members of the Guild—he realized that the SSTA, with its conservative, older leadership, would never appeal to them. The meeting was a failure. Hochberg and Parente were forced to search for a new way to achieve the goal of restoring the salary differential.

It was now time for the Guild to take the initiative. Supporting the evening high school strike had proved to be more than a defensive maneuver. The nighttime picketers had developed a feeling of solidarity which transcended organizational demarcations. Representatives from the Guild and the SSTA began meeting secretly to explore the possibility of merging the two organizations.


## THE PROMOTIONAL INCREMENT

From the outset the SSTA's insistence upon restoration of the high school salary differential stood in the way of a merger agreement. The Guild's opposition was based largely on expediency, since there were more elementary and junior high school teachers than there were high school teachers, but for the SSTA, the differential was the Holy Grail.

Support for the differential was more than a matter of some people wanting to make more money than others. The high school license examinations were more difficult than the others. One must also have completed five years of college and have earned 36 credits in an academic field before taking the tests. Elementary school teachers needed only four years of college with a major in education. It was common for high school teachers to teach in the elementary schools while they completed their course requirements for the high school license. Thus, going to teach in a high school was a step up in status.

Almost everywhere except New York City, however, the single-salary system was the rule. Before the adoption of single-salary schedules, women were paid less than men. Frequently, single men were paid less than married men. Married women, if they were hired to teach at all, were paid less than single women. Relatives or friends of school officials were often treated more favorably than those without such connections.

These "special" arrangements undermined teaching standards and depressed salaries.

The solution to the conflict between the "single-salary Guild" and the "differential SSTA" turned out to be simple and rational. Under the single-salary system, teachers with more years of service and greater academic preparation were paid more than their colleagues. Therefore, paying high school teachers more because of their greater academic qualifications would not violate the single-salary principle. It would only be a violation if other teachers with equivalent qualifications were denied the same extra payment.

The city had recognized this principle long ago. The basic salary schedule for teachers with minimum qualifications had fifteen annual steps. There were also two extra salary increments, one for 30 college credits above the baccalaureate, and another for 30 credits beyond that. Why not have a third differential for high school teachers and all others who had equivalent qualifications? Call the new differential the "promotional increment" in order to give it status.

Once the salary issue had been resolved, the rest of the merger plan speedily fell into place. All that remained was to gain the official approval of the two organizations. However, although the secret negotiators from the Guild had a quasi-official standing, the SSTA operatives were entirely on their own.

By coincidence, the SSTA and Guild executive boards were scheduled to meet on the same day, the SSTA in the afternoon and the Guild in the evening. Soon after the SSTA board adjourned, I received a telephone call from Sam Hochberg. He was dejected. The SSTA officers had been shocked and outraged when they learned about the merger plan. They charged that Hochberg and Parente had betrayed the SSTA's basic policy by accepting the promotional increment concept, because it would permit elementary and junior high school teachers to qualify if they met academic standards the equivalent of those for high school teachers.

At the Guild executive board meeting that night I took the position that there was nothing for the Guild board to discuss because the SSTA had rejected the merger plan. Furthermore, since the Guild's position in any future negotiations might be undermined if the merger terms were to leak out, I refused to disclose any of the details. Although annoyed, the Guild's board members were forced to accept my silence. The Guild-SSTA merger plan was shelved for the time being.

But the urge to unite was a powerful force. Once set in motion, it was difficult to confine.

## CATU

Rumors about the attempted merger reverberated through the giant school system. Under increasing pressure from their members, the SSTA leadership went through the motions of discussing unity. Several official but secret meetings between SSTA and Guild officers were held in some of the most unlikely places in Manhattan. One meeting was in Toffenetti's restaurant, a bustling establishment below Times Square. Another was held in the august Columbia University Faculty Club. But agreement could not be reached.

Beginning in the fall of 1959, two important steps were taken to move the merger talks off dead center. First, in order to arouse teacher support for the unity idea, the Guild made a public offer to join the SSTA. Second, in order to put pressure on the reluctant leaders of the SSTA, a merger support group called the Committee for Action Through Unity (CATU) was set up in the high schools.

CATU consisted of three young militant members of the Guild executive board and the three chief SSTA militants, Sam Hochberg, Roger Parente, and their associate, John Bailey. Sign-up sheets were mimeographed in Guild headquarters and mailed to Guild high school chapter chairpersons and to friends of the three SSTA militant leaders. The Guild-SSTA merger idea soon gained widespread acceptance among high school teachers.

Recruiting for CATU was given a powerful boost by an advertisement which mysteriously appeared on the School Page of the *World, Telegram & Sun*. The ad revealed the hitherto secret details of the aborted merger plan of the previous spring, including the compromise salary schedule and the promotional increment. It strongly implied that a $1,000 salary increase was within the grasp of high school teachers if the Guild and the SSTA would amalgamate.

The *World, Telegram & Sun* ad was the work of John Bailey. Within a few days, more than 2,000 high school teachers had signed the CATU support sheets, and there was no longer any doubt that the time had come for united teacher action.


*MEMORY TAPE: THE UNITED FRONT*
*FROM BELOW*


*President Cogen calls the Guild executive board to order. The minutes of the previous meeting have been distributed. He calls for corrections, and the minutes stand approved. The board then moves to a special order of business: CATU.*

*Many board members are perturbed by the formation of what they think is a rival group. I am called on for an explanation. Most of the board members do not know the depth of my involvement.*

*"I felt I was carrying out our policy," I say. "CATU is just a way to force the SSTA to move. It is not a permanent organization."*

Q: *Did you consult with Charlie before going ahead?*

A: *I didn't think it was necessary. We were already on record favoring merger between the Guild and the SSTA.*

As a matter of fact, I had avoided talking with Cogen until after the CATU ad had been published. Cogen would have insisted that an action as far-reaching as CATU be debated thoroughly before proceeding. That would have defeated the whole scheme. The new committee would have been revealed as a Guild plot.

After the ad had appeared I had received an urgent phone call from Cogen. He wanted to see me immediately. I drove to Charlie's apartment in the upper Bronx and found him lying on a couch. Two of his old friends were also present. In the discussion that followed I heard the term "united front from below" for the first time.

During the tumultuous days of "The Split" in the original New York City Teachers Union, the "united front from below" designated the left-wing membership caucus which had gained control of the union over the opposition of the elected officers. Cogen and some older executive board members see CATU as a possible plot to destroy the Guild.

Q: This group is backing a salary differential for high school teachers, isn't it?

A: Yes and no.

The executive board had not known the details of the compromise salary plan until the CATU ad appeared. Many of them had not yet grasped the significance of the promotional increment. I point out that the promotional increment is really a single-salary plan because the extra pay differential would be based on educational qualifications which all teachers could acquire. Many board members still object to it but they are through with me for the time being. They want to question the three board members who were a part of CATU. These are George Altomare, Milton Pincus and Louis Heitner.

Altomare follows my line: he felt he was carrying out Guild policy. Pincus tries to minimize the situation: he says the CATU matter is being blown out of proportion. Heitner is the last to be quizzed. So far, the board is still unaware that I am the architect and chief carpenter of the CATU project.

Heitner strips away my anonymity. "Listen," he says. "When my organizer calls me and asks me to do something, I do it!"

I try to look unconcerned during the vigorous discussion that follows. "The united front from below" is frequently heard. Shanker takes the floor. He has retained his seat on the board even though he is a full-time union employee. I had told him that union staff members usually do not run for political office. He had insisted that by continuing on the board he could support positions the two of us had discussed privately. He tells the rest of the board members that thousands of teachers have already signed the CATU petitions. The teachers want unity, he says, and there is no way the sign-up sheets can be called back. He finishes his speech and looks mockingly at first one member and then another. He demands, "Well, what are you going to do about it?"

Shanker holds the floor for a long moment before sitting. There is nothing the executive board can do, and he has left

*them no way to cover their impotence. I am embarrassed. I wish*
*he had let them work their own way to the inevitable conclu-*
*sion.*

*After futile efforts to revive the dying meeting, the board*
*adjourns. CATU has survived, but I am acutely aware of lin-*
*gering resentment among the board members.*


## THE GUILD NO MORE

As the CATU movement continued to gather force, the Guild
renewed its public demand for merger talks with the SSTA.
Two meetings were held, but the SSTA officials had no intention of uniting with the Guild.

The rejection of the Guild's offers opened the way for further
negotiations with Hochberg and Parente. The enthusiastic response to the CATU sign-up sheets had convinced the two leaders that breaking away from the SSTA to establish a new organization would be a step toward leadership of the city's
teachers. By vote of the Guild executive board, the CATU representatives were invited to enter into direct negotiations with
Guild representatives, by-passing the SSTA officers.

The negotiations were as hard fought as if Hochberg and
Parente had headed a functioning organization rather than a
phantom created by the Guild. When asked by members of the
executive board what the Guild had to gain from the CATU
merger, I replied, "We are buying the franchise to organize in
the high schools."

Once the salary differential issue was settled, the chief problem in the "merger" talks became the distribution of power
within the new organization. In private, Charlie Cogen was far
from the tiger he often appeared to be in public. Other Guild
leaders seemed equally vulnerable. At one point, the CATU
leaders tried to assure me that I had nothing to fear from their
possible accession to power in the new organization.

In the end, the twelve officerships provided in the UFT constitution were evenly distributed among Guild members and
the newcomers. Cogen remained president, and Hochberg became "deputy president." The executive board was expanded,
and Hochberg and Parente were allowed to choose a third of

the members. Safeguards were designed to prevent high school teachers—who comprised less than a third of the teaching staff—from being overwhelmed by other teachers.

When the merger plan was complete, a special meeting of the Guild delegate assembly was called. The most effective speech of the occasion was made by the leader of the Guild veterans, Rebecca Simonson. She had been president of the Guild for the ten years preceding Cogen's presidency. Simonson reminded the Guild leaders of the many crises they had survived to establish a liberal, "responsible" organization. Now, she said, the time had come to take a bold new step into the future.

The reorganization plan was approved overwhelmingly. The New York Teachers Guild ended, and the United Federation of Teachers emerged.

# Chapter 5

# YES IS FOR THE TEACHERS

## A FALSE SETTLEMENT

Two themes pervaded the negotiations which led to the formation of the United Federation of Teachers (UFT). One was the dedication of the new organization to collective bargaining; the other was its commitment to teacher militancy, including a willingness to strike if other methods of achieving the union's objectives failed.

Soon after the UFT was established, six demands were presented to the board of education. A call for a collective bargaining election headed the list. The other demands were: a $1,000 promotional increment; a substantial across-the-board raise; duty-free lunch periods; ten days a year paid sick leave for full-time substitutes; and the deduction of union dues from pay checks. Each of the demands was carefully chosen to arouse the greatest possible support from the teaching staff. However, it soon became evident that the school board was not going to meet the UFT demands. The union then set May 16, 1960 as a strike date.

Again, the pledges of support were circulated in the schools. The response was far from overwhelming, but it was more successful than the petition for the one-day work stoppage of the previous year. I again sought the aid of Harry Van Arsdale. The central labor body president arranged a conference with Superintendent Theobald on the day before the strike date just as he had the year before.

The superintendent was accompanied by a committee of school board and staff members. After several hours of haggling, the negotiations came to a standstill. The school board representatives agreed that a representation election should be held, but they refused to set a date. They had agreed to a modest across-the-board raise but rejected the promotional increment. They also had granted five paid sick days a semester for substitutes. But no concessions had been offered on the demands for duty-free lunch periods and the dues checkoff. These partial gains were far short of the brave program the UFT had started with. Furthermore, the school officials refused to put their token offers in writing.

The UFT representatives decided to caucus. The committee consisted of Cogen, Jules Kolodny and me from the former Guild. Hochberg and Parente represented the CATU newcomers. We went into a nearby room, and Van Arsdale joined us. We discussed compromise formulas for advancing the negotiations. The labor council president became increasingly impatient. Finally, he said, "Look! We aren't getting anywhere. When I get to this point in my negotiations with employers I say, 'Gentlemen!'" Here he slammed his palm on the table for emphasis. "'Your shops will not open tomorrow.'" He stopped and glared at the committee before continuing. "If you can say that and make it stick, all right. You have my support. But if you don't have the troops we might as well stop wasting time. You've got all you're going to get."

The committee members avoided looking at each other, but each of us knew that Van Arsdale was right. Cogen took a vote. I was called on first. I pointed out that only 7,500 teachers had signed the pledge-of-support sheets—not enough to conduct a successful strike. I voted to accept the board's terms. Kolodny also voted to accept. Cogen then called on Hochberg, who responded hesitantly, "Yes." Parente was last. The vote stood at three to zero. When his turn came Cogen would undoubtedly also vote to accept, but Parente voted no.

At the time I believed Parente's seemingly meaningless negative vote was a political gesture intended to lay the groundwork for a campaign for more militant leadership later on. After observing Parente's coolness under fire in other situations, I came to believe that his vote had probably been an honest expression of his opinion.

The UFT returned to the bargaining table, and Cogen reported our acceptance of the board's terms. I made a last ditch effort to get the terms in writing, but I had to be satisfied with a joint press release. I had little faith that the superintendent would carry out the settlement terms, but the teachers were not yet ready for a strike. If the board and the superintendent reneged on the terms of the settlement, perhaps the teachers would be angry enough to carry out a citywide walkout. For possible future reference I carefully preserved my penciled notes of the negotiations.


## COLLISION WITH THE LABOR MOVEMENT

While the Teachers Guild was developing into the United Federation of Teachers, important events were taking place in the labor movement. In 1955 the American Federation of Labor and the Congress of Industrial Organizations merged after two decades of bitter conflict. The merger ended what had come to be a meaningless competition. I assumed that the more dynamic and progressive CIO forces would soon become dominant in the merged organization.

Under the terms of the AFL-CIO merger agreement, the state and local labor bodies were to settle their differences and unite within a year after the national merger. In many states the amalgamation was accomplished quickly, but in New York, months passed with no visible movement. The city's central labor body remained in the grip of the Teamster and building-trades machine. The city CIO unions continued to go their way under the leadership of Mike Quill, head of the Transport Workers. The situation was much the same at the state level.

Well past the merger deadline, the city and the state labor bodies were unified. The mergers followed the deaths of both the local and the state AFL presidents. Harry Van Arsdale had become president of the New York City Central Trades and Labor Council.

Van Arsdale had achieved a reputation as a progressive unionist. He stood in sharp contrast to most of the other labor leaders I had known. He was certainly no Socialist, but he was daring, imaginative and tough. He was a skilled organizer and union administrator. As leader of Local 3 of the International Brotherhood of Electrical Workers, one of the largest unions in the city, he had solid membership support, giving him great political power. Furthermore, he understood and supported the UFT's drive for collective bargaining despite some uneasiness about teacher militancy.

Van Arsdale spent a great amount of time trying to work out mergers between the UFT and other New York City teacher organizations. But eager as he was to bring the city's teachers into the AFL-CIO, he carefully protected the interests of the Democratic party.

As head of the New York City central labor body, Harry Van Arsdale had strong influence throughout the labor movement. He was close to AFL-CIO president George Meany—also a New Yorker—and to many prominent people in the Democratic party. As a result he was an important figure in the 1960 presidential election campaign. The labor movement, sensing its chance to recover from its decline during the 1950s, was solidly behind John F. Kennedy. The New York City unions were doing everything possible to turn out a large enough Democratic majority to overcome anticipated Republican votes from upstate. Van Arsdale, therefore, wanted the election to go smoothly in the city, without being disrupted by a major labor dispute such as the UFT's wrangle with the board of education.

## BROKEN PROMISES

My doubts about the good faith of School Superintendent John Theobald and the board of education in the settlement of May 16, 1960 were justified by subsequent events. Throughout the summer I watched grimly for some sign of compliance with the agreement, but none came. In fact, the legality of collective bargaining had been questioned by the school board and referred to the city attorney for an opinion. Also, Superintendent Theobald, speaking to a meeting of community school board members in the Bronx, had stated that he was not sure that the

school board could carry out the sick-leave-for-substitutes provision.

At a meeting of the UFT's collective bargaining committee
in September, I expressed my misgivings about the actions of
the superintendent and board of education. I suggested that the
UFT might have to set a new strike date if the May 16 agreement
was not implemented. I received strong support from an unexpected quarter.

During the summer, the UFT had retained the services of
Henry Mayer, an outstanding labor attorney. Mayer was a dis-
tant relative of Cogen. All during the collective bargaining committee meeting Mayer stoutly reinforced my cautious reference
to another strike vote. In measured tones he opined, "You will
never get collective bargaining unless you strike for it."

Henry Mayer's portentous pronouncement had the force of
holy writ. Hochberg immediately took up the cry. Within minutes the committee voted to recommend to the executive
board—which would meet that evening—that a new strike date
be set for November 7. The choice of that date was deliberate.
The committee believed that no punitive action would be taken
against strikers on the eve of the national election for fear of
alienating potential Democratic voters.

Cogen had not attended the collective bargaining committee
meeting, but I managed to warn him before the executive board
meeting began that evening.

"Was Henry Mayer there?" Charlie asked.

"Yes, he was there. He agrees with me."

"He agrees with you?" Cogen was incredulous.

"Yes. The vote in the committee was unanimous."

Cogen was stunned. He called the executive board to order.
The strike recommendation was the first order of business. The
debate was long and heated, but the board voted to send the
strike recommendation to the delegate assembly for final approval. In the notice of the meeting sent to the delegates, I listed
only one item: "Appropriate action in response to the broken
promises of the superintendent and board of education."

The cryptic meeting notice had prepared the delegates to
vote for a strike. Many questions were asked. Some of the veterans from the Guild, drawing on their years of dialectical de-

bate, advised delay, saying, "The time is not yet ripe," a formula transposed from Marxian writings.

I was usually unruffled in meetings, but as I listened to the temporizing tenor of the discussion I became infuriated. Suddenly I leaped to my feet and seized the microphone. In a choked, intense voice, I declared, "You have been treated with arrogance and contempt by the board and the superintendent. If you let them repudiate last May's agreement without doing something about it, you have no right to call yourselves a union! Let's cut out this nonsense and vote!"

Shocked by my unusual display, the delegates quickly approved the strike. This time no pledge-of-support sheets would be circulated. Everyone knew that if school officials made no move to comply with the May 16 agreement the teachers would be walking out.

Nevertheless, because the UFT membership was still less than ten percent of the teaching staff, I stepped up the propaganda barrage and bought a half hour of television time to appeal directly to the teachers for support. The main feature of the television program was Henry Mayer, whitehaired and Moses-like. He solemnly assured teachers that they need not fear reprisals from the board of education because the state antistrike law was unconstitutional.

Cogen, who was worried about the legality of the impending walkout, was especially comforted by Henry Mayer's dictum, inaccurate though it proved to be. A few months later, the New York State Court of Appeals upheld the antistrike law's constitutionality in a case involving a strike by another union. Cogen indignantly asked Mayer if he had not stated that the law was unconstitutional. "Sure," the lawyer replied glibly, "and I still believe it is unconstitutional, but no court would ever rule that way."

*MEMORY TAPE: MEANY IN PERSON*

*There are seven of us in a room in the Commodore Hotel on an afternoon in October, 1960. George Meany's massive bulk fills the overstuffed hotel chair. Sitting astride a straight chair turned backward is Harry Van Arsdale. His posture seems cho-*

sen to demonstrate that he is only a disinterested observer, even though he had called the meeting. Carl Megel, an unexpected visitor, is seated on another straight chair. Cogen, Sam Hochberg, Roger Parente and I are perched on the bed, a foot-stool and the desk.

It is the first time I have seen Meany up close. I am aware of his low opinion of teachers unions in general and the New York teachers organizations in particular. This judgment stems from his experience as president of the New York Federation of Labor in the 1930s and 1940s. He had suffered through the years of ideological warfare connected with "The Split" in the old Teachers Union. The experience had made him highly skeptical of the capacity of teachers to organize at all.

Following the AFL and CIO merger, the Guild had invited Meany and Walter Reuther to receive the Guild's John Dewey Award at its annual spring conference-luncheon. Although both leaders accepted, neither appeared. Reuther sent a staff person as a substitute, but Meany did not even send a message. To conceal Meany's snub, I sent a telegram in Meany's name. In all innocence, Cogen read the wire to the assembled guests, who applauded lustily.

Now Meany takes his cigar out of his mouth and demands, "Who's doing the talking?"

"I am," I reply with a quick admonitory glance at Cogen.

"How many members you got?" Meany inquires.

"Five thousand," I lie.

"How many teachers are there?"

"Forty thousand." There were now really forty-five thousand, but I shaded the number downward to improve our odds.

"How many will strike?"

Had I a fraction of Meany's audacity I would answer by saying, "Most of them." Lacking that boldness, I hedge. "At least ten thousand, maybe twenty," I say.

Meany grunts contemptuously. "They won't pay dues to you but they'll strike for you. Is that it?"

Hochberg and Parente watch me for any sign of wavering. I stick by my guns. "That's about it." I feel like an impudent schoolboy.

Van Arsdale takes up the attack. "Megel," he asks, "Don't they have to get permission from the International?"

*Megel squirms uneasily. The UFT is already the second largest local in the AFT, and it is still growing. The AFT president is an artful politician. He does not want to antagonize the New York local. "Well, you see, Mr. Meany and Mr. Van Arsdale," he replies deferentially, "we have local autonomy in our union, and . . ." His voice trails off as he realizes that the two labor leaders are not impressed.*

*Meany takes a heavy puff on his cigar.*

*Suddenly he blurts, "For Christ's sake, Harry. Can't somebody blow the whistle on these guys?"*

## THE 1960 STRIKE

Van Arsdale made the ritualistic effort to work out a settlement of the strike before the November 7 deadline. The night before the walkout was to begin, he called us together to see if some compromise could be devised. We knew that the teachers were determined to march. The committee held firm. The next morning the picket lines went up, and the strike was on.

The official figures show that only 5,000 teachers responded to the UFT's call, but actually, more than 10,000 took part in the strike. Officials at school board headquarters reported only the number of regularly appointed teachers who went out. They omitted the more than 5,000 full-time substitutes who answered the call. The union's claim of more than 10,000 strikers was conservative.

Two or three hours after the strike began Van Arsdale called. "Well, how many do you have out?" he asked.

I replied evasively that it was too soon to tell. He replied that he had driven by several schools and had not seen any pickets. I believed him. I had just returned from doing the same thing, but I stoutly maintained that the strike was a success.

"Looks pretty thin to me," the labor leader said bluntly, and he hung up.

At four that afternoon there was a rally at St. Nicholas Arena, a big barn of a building used for boxing and wrestling matches. That afternoon it was packed with roaring, screaming teachers. They had done it! They had struck. They had struck back at the board of education, the administrators and the indifferent politicians who had ignored and humiliated them.

There were emotional speeches, and the rafters shook with cheers. Nevertheless, the walkout seemed to have evoked no official response other than the false figures released by Superintendent Theobald. As the St. Nicholas meeting was breaking up, someone tugged at my arm and told me that I had a phone call in the basement.

I pushed my way through the excited crowd and descended the iron stairs. Outside one of the fighter's dressing rooms, the receiver of a wall phone dangled by its cord. I lifted it and said hello.

"Who's dis?" a peremptory voice demanded.

"Dave Selden."

"Vere's Cogen?"

"He already left."

A pause followed by "OK. Listen; vill you take mediation?"

"Who is this?" I ask.

"Dubinsky. I vant to meet with you."

It was David Dubinsky, legendary president of the International Ladies Garment Workers Union (ILGWU).

"What time? Where?" I say. It was an opening which could not be ignored.


THE LABOR COMMITTEE

On the evening of November 7, 1960, the day of the first New York City systemwide teachers strike, Cogen, Hochberg, Jules Kolodny, and I met in Dubinsky's Manhattan apartment.

The garment workers union president had started his working life as a baker in Poland. Just before World War I he had migrated to New York and started working in the garment industry. He joined the union and began to rise in its hierarchy. He led the union's Social Democratic faction in the ideological wars of the twenties and thirties and emerged as the powerful union's undisputed leader. He helped organize the New York Liberal party in opposition to the American Labor party. The Liberal party's dependence on ILGWU financial support gave

Dubinsky an independent political organization and great bargaining power within the labor movement and the Democratic party.

When the committee left Dubinsky's apartment after four hours of intense discussion and phone calls to city hall, a plan had been worked out for ending the strike. The mayor would appoint a fact-finding committee consisting of Dubinsky, Van Arsdale and Jacob Potofsky, president of the Amalgamated Clothing Workers. An announcement of the "labor committee" would be made the following morning—Election Day. The UFT would call off the strike, and in due course, the committee would report the "facts" it had found. Because the committee members were union leaders, there was every reason to believe that their report would be favorable to the UFT.

None of the UFT committee members was enthusiastic about the scheme Dubinsky had worked out, but we felt that we had little choice. Many members of the UFT's executive board were outraged by the labor committee proposal. They were still flushed from the excitement of the rally and they wanted to continue the strike until the board of education surrendered unconditionally. After two hours of histrionics and debate the plan was finally approved. The next hurdle was the delegate assembly.

The mood of the delegates when they met the following afternoon was even more angry than the executive board's. Their resentment had been aroused by public statements by Van Arsdale and Dubinsky. Anxious to offset any adverse effect of the strike on voters, the labor leaders and the mayor had called a press conference at city hall. They had declared the strike over—before the delegate assembly had voted. Van Arsdale had even pledged that there would be "no recurrence."

Cogen and I and a few others tried to explain away the "betrayal" by the labor leaders. Our efforts were met with boos, whistles and cries of "sell-out!" Considering the fact that the delegates had been summoned to decide whether to call off the strike, their rage at finding the decision taken for granted was understandable. Finally the tumult died, and the first New York City systemwide teachers' strike became a part of history.

## THE TRUCE

The strike, though it lasted only one day and produced no immediate benefit for teachers or the union, resulted in great gains. The teachers had proved that they would walk out if pushed far enough and they had gained new confidence in their strength. Next time, the union would be stronger. Meanwhile, the outcome of this strike would depend on what the labor committee did.

The UFT was in a difficult position following the strike. Van Arsdale and the other members of the committee were as much attuned to the needs of the city administration and the Democratic party as they were to the needs of the teachers union. As Hochberg wryly put it, "The UFT was in the hands of receivers."

In order to preserve some sense of the militancy teachers had felt and to mitigate Van Arsdale's "no recurrence" statement, UFT flyers and press statements revealed that the union had entered into a "truce" with the board of education.

A special edition of the *United Teacher*, the UFT monthly paper, extolling the virtues of Van Arsdale, Dubinsky and Potofsky was published. It reiterated the original demands of the UFT. As a reminder I made sure that the three members of the labor committee received copies of the paper.

The truce dragged on for two months. There were extensive undercover negotiations throughout. First, a small committee from the UFT met with the labor committee. I produced my notes from the negotiations of the previous May and convinced the labor leaders that Superintendent Theobald and the board of education had reneged on the original agreement as the union said they had. Then, with the support of the labor committee the UFT negotiators met with the superintendent. This meeting proved as unproductive as a secret meeting which Parente and I attended in Theobald's home on Long Island.

Still another undercover meeting with Theobald and three school board members was arranged during the truce period by David Dubinsky. This conference was held in a midtown Manhattan hotel. The UFT was represented by Cogen, Hochberg and several other UFT officers. Bottles of Chivas Regal were on the table.

As soon as the first round of scotch was poured, Theobald began telling ribald stories as though he were at a fraternity party. Aided and abetted by the Chivas Regal and a few of the other participants, the entire evening was passed in this way. There was no discussion of the dispute between the union and the management representatives. Dubinsky finally called a halt to the party and left abruptly.

The labor committee produced a report in January, 1961. It recommended that substitute teachers get their sick leave—effective February 1 instead of the beginning of the school year. The promotional increment and other salary increases were only vaguely hinted at. The long-sought collective bargaining election was referred to a special committee of experts headed by Professor George Taylor of the University of Pennsylvania.

As an ironic aside, it should be noted that Dr. Taylor later headed another New York commission which produced the "Taylor Act." This law imposes heavy penalties on public employees who strike. Another member of the Taylor collective bargaining commission was Professor Archibald Cox from Harvard, who was a victim of the Watergate "Saturday Night Massacre."

Although I was greatly disappointed by the recommendations of the labor committee, I had no choice but to "tough it out" before the delegate assembly. After a bitter debate the committee's recommendations were accepted. In the weeks that followed I desperately tried to persuade the Taylor Commission to hold the promised collective bargaining representation election promptly.


THE REFERENDUM

The Taylor Commission displayed no sense of urgency in setting about its work. The first move was to schedule a series of hearings on the questions related to the collective bargaining election. I had naively assumed that the election could be held in a few weeks' time. Because there was no statute covering the matter, there were many questions to settle before the teachers could vote. There was even a question as to whether the election could legally be held. Many lawyers argued that granting exclusive bargaining rights to one organization would violate the constitutional rights of members of other organizations. This was the position taken by the National Education Association and some of the other teacher organizations at the commission's hearings.

The Secondary School Teachers Association and the Elementary School Teachers Association also took the position that there should be three bargaining agents—one for high school teachers, one for junior high school teachers and one for elementary school teachers. This divisional bargaining idea was tempting. The UFT would be a sure winner in the junior high schools and would have a good chance of winning in the other divisions. But, teacher unity had been the main theme of the UFT's drive for collective bargaining. Changing policy in favor of three bargaining agents would confuse UFT followers and extend an already attenuated process.

The Taylor Commission made its report four weeks before the end of the 1960–61 school year. It recommended that a referendum be held to ascertain whether teachers wanted collective bargaining. Although I was initially angered by what I took to be another stalling tactic by city and school authorities, I later realized that the referendum would serve the purpose of authenticating the representation election when it was held.

The referendum put the other teacher organizations in a difficult position. Some of them—including the NEA—urged teachers to vote "no." The UFT was much better organized than any of the other groups. With the slogan, "Yes is for the teachers, no is for the board," the schools were flooded with UFT literature. The result was a stunning victory for the union. More than 85 percent of the teachers voted in the mail poll. Nearly thirty thousand voted for collective bargaining, and fewer than six thousand voted against it.

# Chapter 6

## "CB" AT LAST

### SHOCK WAVES

The UFT's victory in the collective bargaining referendum sent shock waves throughout the education world. Skeptics had doubted that teachers could organize to win collective bargaining rights. But the referendum indicated that collective bargaining for teachers was close at hand—at least in New York City. If the new relationship between teachers and their employers were to expand, control by administrators, school boards and educational associations would be weakened.

Even within the AFT, reaction to the UFT's triumph was not entirely jubilant. Many AFT leaders were convinced that the New Yorkers were endangering the entire teacher union movement because the associations might call for representation elections. The old AFT nucleus locals would be overwhelmed. Some long-time AFT politicos saw the New York upsurge as an unwelcome harbinger of a shift in AFT internal politics.

Soon after the UFT victory in the collective bargaining referendum in the summer of 1961, I attended the AFT convention for the first time in many years. I was seeking additional financial aid. My quest was met with flinty suspicion by the executive council. President Megel stiffened the resistance by accusing the New York local of not paying proper per capita dues to the AFT. Using a common organizing tactic, I had exaggerated the UFT's membership claims in order to make the union appear stronger than it was, and Megel seized on these inflated figures as an indication of cheating.

I readily admitted that there were discrepancies between the publicized claims and the real totals. I pointed out that this difference would cease in the fall because we would begin collecting dues through monthly payroll deductions. UFT membership would then be a matter of public record. During the course of this explanation, however, I said that the union would have to pay five cents per member per month for the checkoff privilege, prompting one of the council members to object.

"Are you saying we should reject the dues checkoff until we can get it free of charge?" I demanded angrily. "I'd rather not pay for the checkoff, but if I can't get it any other way I'll pay."

Despite its initial hostility, the executive council voted to give the UFT $5,000. It was a generous and wholly unprecedented action. Many of the council members came from impoverished locals to which $5,000 was a fantastic sum. Yet, they were true believers, and the lure of a possible victory for the teacher union movement conquered their doubt and timidity

As a matter of fact, I had not even dared to let Cogen or other local leaders know the true state of the UFT's finances for fear that they would want to call off the collective bargaining campaign. Thus, the UFT and the national union were committed to the drive for collective bargaining without knowing exactly where the next step would lead.

ENTER THE NEA

Meanwhile, in NEA headquarters in Washington there was little comprehension of the revolution which was developing in New York. The city had long been an organizational backwater for the Association. Its membership in New York City had never exceeded a thousand or so. A good number of these members were administrators and college teachers. Thus, in its complacency, the NEA saw no cause for alarm in the drive of the city's teachers for collective bargaining.

Soon after the 1960 strike, at the request of highly placed New York City school official Bernard Donovan, NEA representatives met with a group of antiunion city administrators and teachers. From this meeting came a new NEA policy called "Professional Negotiations."

As I saw it, the new scheme was an attempt to adapt collective bargaining to the paternalistic mode of the associations. NEA policy makers conceded that raw collective bargaining might be all right for blue collar workers, but teachers, they thought, were part of a professional team to which everyone in the educational structure belonged: teachers, principals, superintendents and staff specialists such as psychologists and guidance counselors. "The profession" would negotiate—not bargain—with board of education representatives, and the superintendent would act as advisor to both sides. I nicknamed the NEA plan "pro-negs" to highlight its obvious internal contradictions. For example, it would have been impossible for the superintendent, who is under contract to the board of education, to act as impartial advisor in the bargaining process.

In reality, standard collective bargaining suits the educational enterprise very well—even better than it does many private enterprises. Though school systems do not operate for profit, their organizational structures are much like those of private manufacturing firms. There is the same conflict between teachers and administrators as there is between workers and bosses elsewhere. Even though administrators believe policy making should be left to them, teachers must participate in the policy-making process if they are to be truly professional. The NEA tried to convince teachers that "professional negotiations" was more appropriate than collective bargaining, but the concept failed to catch on, and the term was finally abandoned.

There were a few NEA leaders who realized that adding 45,000 members to the struggling 60,000-member Federation would provide the money, credibility and inspiration which the union needed in order to grow. After some initial hesitation, an NEA office was opened in the Time-Life Building in midtown Manhattan. The NEA headquarters contrasted sharply with the UFT's dingy loft on Twenty-third Street. Following the collective bargaining referendum, the Association expanded its New York staff. It also effected a coalition between the Elementary School Teachers Association and the Secondary School Teachers Association, a move I had predicted.

The NEA called its new coalition the Teachers Bargaining Organization (TBO). The New York City school system had be-

come a David and Goliath battleground for a fight between the
two national teacher organizations.


## MEMORY TAPE: JOE BROWN

*A paper cup half full of cold black coffee stands among the
disarray on the desk in my gritty, five-by-eight office at UFT
headquarters. I am listening to a voice on the telephone. The
voice belongs to "Joe Brown."*

*Joe Brown had first phoned me a month ago. He had said
that he was working at the New York NEA headquarters and
that he wanted to talk with me privately. Fearing some kind
of trap, I had arranged a rendezvous in a Twenty-third Street
bar. Shanker followed me into the bar and was not to acknowledge me unless I signaled to him.*

*My precautions had proved unnecessary. Joe Brown, except
for his name, turned out to be genuine. He had claimed to be
a member of the Masters, Mates, and Pilots Union and because
of marital problems he was not shipping out. To support himself, he had signed on with an agency that supplied temporary
office help. Now he was managing the NEA's new Time-Life
Building office.*

*He had said that he wanted to help the UFT because he
believed in unionism. To prove his good intentions he had offered me the key to the NEA office. I hastily rejected Brown's
offering but I expressed interest in knowing what the Association was doing. It was then that I had learned that Brown's
interest was more than a fraternal wish to help a fellow unionist. What he needed, he had explained, was a card in the
motion picture operators union. He would also need some
money for "expenses."*

*After arranging a way to communicate by using code
names—that was where "Joe Brown" came from—we parted.
Back in my office I had called Lane Kirkland, then George
Meany's assistant. Kirkland, I knew, was a member of the Masters, Mates, and Pilots Union. I had told him Joe Brown's story,
and Kirkland called back the next day. Brown's story checked
out. Getting the union card had not been easy but it had been
accomplished, and the card was being sent to me. From then*

on, Joe Brown had kept me informed of every move of the NEA, sometimes within minutes of the time the decision had been made.

Now, I sip my cold coffee and listen to the telephone. Joe Brown is saying, "Somebody important is here—a Dr. Lieberman. A big shot. They went into the inner office and closed the door, so I don't know what they're talking about. I'll call you after he leaves."

It can only be Dr. Myron Lieberman, the well-known educational writer. Lieberman had come to New York several years ago to be dean of the graduate school of education at Yeshiva University. His reputation as an educational "futurist" had preceded him. Cogen had eagerly sought him out and offered him a place on the Guild executive board. He had accepted but he had attended meetings only occasionally. He had usually been more a critic than a participant.

As the collective bargaining campaign was getting underway, Lieberman and I had lunch together. I had explained in detail my HSTA-Guild merger strategy and ended with "So for the HSTA it will be 'merge or split,' and I don't care which way it goes!"

Lieberman had been impressed but skeptical. His final comment as we parted on the Fifty-seventh Street sidewalk in front of Yeshiva University had been, "Utterly bankrupt! Utterly bankrupt!"

Lieberman wrote frequently for Saturday Review, Nation, Phi Delta Kappan and other periodicals. He very often wrote about teacher organization problems and he maintained friendly relations with both the NEA and the AFT.

An hour passes between Joe Brown's first report on Lieberman's visit to the NEA office and Brown's second call. He tells me that he could not overhear any of the conversation between Lieberman and the NEA official, but he says that Lieberman left minutes before.

I become aware that someone is standing in my doorway. I return the phone to its cradle and look up. It is Myron Lieberman.

"Hello, Mike," I say. "What were you doing in the NEA office?"

*Lieberman's jaw drops. How did I know where he had been?*
*Recovering, he says he is working on a magazine piece and*
*was gathering material. I accept the explanation and never*
*mention the incident to him again.*


## THE GOLDBERG VARIATION

After the 1961 AFT convention, I took a week off to drive to
Michigan for a family gathering in observance of my parents'
fiftieth wedding anniversary. Ours is a large family, and the
celebration was a memorable occasion. In the midst of the fes-
tivities, I telephoned Cogen in New York.

"How are things going?" I asked.

"Fine. How are things with you?"

"Great. Anything new?"

There was a pause. "No. Nothing special. We had a meeting
with the mayor yesterday."

Although Cogen and I had already worked together for nearly
ten years, we had not become reconciled to each other. Privately, he was critical of my rambunctiousness; in return, I was
disdainful of his caution and conservatism. I scrupulously de-
ferred to him in public, but I frequently disagreed with him in
the inner councils of the union. Understandably, the UFT president usually took advantage of opportunities to assert his independence. Very often repairs and corrections had to be made.
Consequently, when Charlie off-handedly mentioned meeting
with the mayor I was alerted.

"What did the mayor want?" I inquired.

"Arthur Goldberg set it up. He wanted to talk about the bargaining election."

Arthur Goldberg was the United States Secretary of Labor.
Originally from Chicago, he had become the attorney for the
United Steel Workers and then the CIO. I had known since the
prestigious Taylor Commission's creation that top-level Democrats were interested in the New York City teacher bargaining
election.

The first instance of high-level intervention in UFT affairs
had come the preceding spring. One of Goldberg's partners had
asked that I supply him with a complete list of teacher griev-

ances. Over a weekend, Shanker and I had drawn up an outline and split it in half. Shanker wrote the first part and I the other. We had produced a vivid justification for the UFT's position. I thought Goldberg's personal interest in the New York election stemmed from the document that Shanker and I had produced.

When I pressed Cogen for details about the meeting with the mayor, I discovered that Goldberg had advised reverting to the three-unit election plan. This would allow junior high teachers to vote first, and high school and elementary teachers would vote at some later date. Apparently, Cogen had given a favorable reaction to Goldberg's plan.

Although I had once been tempted by the three-phase election plan, the overwhelming UFT victory in the referendum had convinced me that the best strategy was to go for broke and press for a citywide election to be held as soon as possible. I accused Cogen of messing up the entire collective bargaining election campaign and demanded that he call a meeting of the UFT officers to discuss the situation. Cogen agreed. I left the wedding anniversary celebration and drove back to New York.

When the UFT administrative committee met, it flatly rejected Goldberg's plan and voted to demand that the mayor set a systemwide election date. The mayor, up for election that fall, agreed to hold the vote before the end of the year. For good measure, he endorsed the principle of the promotional increment.

From then on it was "winner take all." The election was held December 20.


## STAFF AND MONEY

In the fall of 1961 the collective bargaining campaign began in earnest. The mayor named Ida Klaus to lay down the rules for the election. She had many years of service in the federal government, where she had virtually created collective bargaining for federal employees. Klaus selected Nathan Feinsinger, a well-known arbitrator from Wisconsin, to hold hearings and establish the boundaries for the bargaining unit.

The UFT campaign proceeded at a gallop, pushed along by hundreds of volunteers. The jerry-built TBO, however, even though it lacked neither money nor staff, could not enlist much grass-roots support. The slogan, "UFT Gets Things Done!" constantly reminded teachers that it was the UFT which had led the fight for higher salaries and other benefits, including collective bargaining.

The NEA had only recently come to the city in force. It had no record of achievement, and lacking activist members, it had to rely on out-of-town staffers. In an attempt to recruit indigenous workers, the Association asked school principals to designate TBO representatives in their schools, opening the organization to the charge of being dominated by administrators.

The union's paid campaign staff was never large. In the final phase it consisted of seven full-timers. John O'Neill, a Brooklyn junior high school teacher, had been hired in the fall of 1960. Several months later, AFT president Megel assigned Henry Clark and Sally Parker to New York. They were the AFT's only organizers, aside from Shanker, who had been working since the fall of 1958. The Industrial Union Department in Washington sent Harold Ash, a seasoned organizer, and Lucille Swaim, a graduate student. I was the seventh. There were also six part-timers, New York City teachers who worked the telephones in the evening.

Considering the size of the campaign, the equivalent of 900 shops in private industry, its costs were very low. Still, lack of funds was a constant problem. Money was needed for newspaper ads, pamphlets, flyers, postage, extra telephones, extra working space, new equipment and many other unavoidable costs. I was shameless in cadging funds from other unions. Many gave amounts varying from $100 to $5,000. The latter amount came from the New York City Central Trades and Labor Council, thanks to Harry Van Arsdale.

## MEMORY TAPE: DUBINSKY TO MEANY TO REUTHER

*I am on my way to meet with David Dubinsky at the headquarters of the International Ladies Garment Workers Union (ILGWU), a few blocks from Times Square. I have been urged many times over the years by older Guild members to make* this journey. They know Dubinsky has given ILGWU funds to many worthy causes. Why not teacher organizing? Until now I have resisted because I believe garment workers should not have to pay for organizing workers who make much more than they do. But now I am desperate. The campaign still has three months to go, and the union is flat broke.

I know Dubinsky from his days on the labor committee. He welcomes me into his office, and I begin explaining the union's need. He has already given $2,000 to the campaign, and he sees he will be faced with a recurring problem unless some ongoing solution can be found. He begins to pace behind his desk as I keep talking.

Abruptly, Dubinsky flips on his intercom. "Get me Meany," he barks. When the connection is made he picks up the phone and shouts gleefully, "Hallo, Chief!"

After some badinage, Dubinsky gets down to business. He explains that I am sitting in his office, and that the teachers need money to keep the campaign going. He listens for a moment to Meany's reply and then interjects.

"Yeah, I know, Chief. But listen, this is a big one, and they got a chance . . ."

The phone crackles with Meany's comment.

"I know, Chief. I know the AFL-CIO don't have money. I'm not asking you for money, see? I was thinking of our friend, your vice-president." He cackles sarcastically.

The ILGWU head is talking about Walter Reuther. Under the merger agreement between the AFL and the CIO, Reuther had become vice-president of the merged organization and chairman of the organizing committee. He was also president of the Industrial Union Department. The CIO had been allowed to transfer its $3 million treasury to the IUD. Reuther and other CIO leaders had long been contemptuous of Meany's laissez faire attitude toward organizing. They planned to use the IUD fund to show the AFL-CIO president how to build the union. They also hoped they might organize enough new members to swing the balance of power within the Federation in their favor.

Meany and Dubinsky drift off into random talk. The plot has been hatched.

When I get back to the UFT office I write a letter to Reuther. I am only slightly acquainted with him even though I have attended many meetings where he was speaking, but in due course a check for $15,000 arrives. Later, Reuther produces $10,000 more, and still later a loan of $50,000 is arranged through the Amalgamated Bank, which is owned by the Amalgamated Clothing Workers.

Each new infusion of money was doled out to the most pressing creditors. Without Reuther's help I don't know how the UFT could have made it.

## MEMORY TAPE: BROTHER MEANY

A week after receiving the second gift from the IUD, Henry Clark, AFT organizer, is sitting in my office. He is a big, vociferous man, and he is haranguing me about the need for more funds.

"God damn it, Selden," he says. "We just gotta get more money in here."

"Yes, Henry," I reply wearily.

"God damn it," he expostulates. "How can you sit there so calm? If I was you I would pick up that phone and call Meany and I'd say, 'Brother Meany, we just gotta get some more money in here.'"

Clark knows little of my previous encounters with the labor federation president. Nor does he know of Meany's past relations with New York City teachers.

"You may think I can call Meany any time I feel like it and get some money," I protest, "but it's not that easy."

"You haven't got the guts," Clark taunts.

Without another word, I pick up the phone and dial the AFL-CIO number in Washington. "This is Dave Selden with the teachers in New York," I intone. "I'd like to speak with Brother Meany."

The fraternal form is an attempt at irony for Clark's benefit. I rarely use it because I consider it hypocritical in many cases. To my astonishment, a gruff voice comes on the line. "Yes?"

It is Meany! It is too late to back out. Half-mimicking Clark, I plunge ahead. "Brother Meany, we just gotta get some money in here."

With hardly a pause, Meany replies, "I just sent you $25,000."

"What? Oh. You mean the IUD money?"

"That's right. They're still a part of the AFL-CIO, ain't they?"

"Thanks," I mumble and hang up.

## FINALE

The collective bargaining marathon came to an end a few days before Christmas, 1961. Ida Klaus, managing the step-by-step advance toward the election with exquisite precision, had hired the Honest Ballot Association (HBA) to conduct the vote of the 45,000 teachers by mail.

I had discovered the HBA two years earlier, mouldering away in a decrepit downtown, hole-in-the-wall office. I had the idea of circulating a petition for a representation election, even though teachers, like other public employees, were excluded from the rights provided under labor laws. A way was needed to provide credible verification of the number of signatures on the petition, and the Honest Ballot Association filled the bill.

The petition attracted more than enough signatures to have required a collective bargaining election if labor board rules had been applicable. I filed the petition with the secretary of the board of education with great fanfare. Later, although the petition had been conceived only as an elaborate public relations exercise, Ida Klaus agreed to credit it as fulfilling the show-of-interest requirement for listing the UFT on the ballot.

The Teachers Bargaining Organization also produced the proper number of signatures for a place on the ballot. The old Teachers Union, reduced to a tattered remnant but determined to enter the election, barely made it.

The final effort of the UFT campaign was a carefully orchestrated extravaganza. A large advertisement appeared in the New York Times. It featured endorsements by Eleanor Roosevelt; A. Philip Randolph, president of the Brotherhood of Sleeping Car Porters; Herbert Lehman, former governor of New York; and several other prominent New Yorkers. The ad appeared on the day most teachers received their ballots. In the day's mail was a reproduction of the ad with a message from Charles Cogen on the back.

The teachers had ten days to return their ballots. More than a hundred UFT volunteers staffed telephone banks every afternoon and evening and urged their colleagues to "vote for the organization which won the right to vote!"

On the night the ballots were counted, my secretary, Mavis Smith, and I went to the UFT office to answer the phones. Cogen, Shanker, Altomare, Hochberg, Parente and the organizers and everybody else who had been closely identified with the campaign all went to the midtown high school where the thousands of ballots were being counted. I felt that my work was over. The only thing that mattered was the outcome of the election.

From time to time someone called from the countingplace. The vote had been heavy. It would take a long time to finish the count. There were fewer phone calls than I had expected. I chatted with Mavis and thought of the future. I had learned a lot in my eight years in the city, but I had come as an organizer. If the UFT won the election, as I was confident it would, collective bargaining would spread. A new national movement would begin, and I wanted to be part of it.

After a while I put paper in my typewriter and wrote a letter to AFT president Carl Megel. I suggested that the AFT establish the position of national director of organization. If that were done, I wrote, I would be an applicant for the job.

Finally the count came in. The UFT had won a smashing victory, defeating the Teachers Bargaining Organization by more than three-to-one. The old Teachers Union, going down with all guns blazing, had polled less than ten percent.

## Part II

---

# THE MOVEMENT GROWS

# Chapter 7

# *BARGAINING BEGINS*

## CRITICAL MASS

For American teachers the 1960s began December 20, 1961. On that date the United Federation of Teachers was elected sole bargaining agent for the 45,000 members of the New York City teaching staff. During the 1960s the rebellion which began in New York spread throughout the nation. It spread because the conditions in the schools required strong corrective action, but it also spread because rebellion was in the air.

Blacks in the South demanded racial desegregation on buses and trains. Black college students had sit-ins at segregated lunch counters. At the University of California, students demanded "free speech"—the right to criticize university policies in their own terms. At the University of Michigan, a new organization called Students for a Democratic Society (SDS) was formed. The SDS demanded "participatory democracy" for everybody. The political left, which had been suppressed during the 1950s, sprang to life with renewed vigor. The dissatisfied and the disgruntled, lulled by the apathy of the Eisenhower years, began demonstrating, marching and picketing, and the teachers joined the parade.

At first, the uprising of the New York City teachers was considered a local phenomenon, even by the participants and members of other AFT locals. It was thought that while collective bargaining might be acceptable for New York liberals, it would never do for Chicago, Detroit, Philadelphia, Boston or other cities. Some of the veteran AFT leaders felt threatened when

it became clear that the New Yorkers intended to export the
new doctrine to other school districts. They feared that the
teachers union could never win in a nationwide struggle against
the educational establishment.

The defeat of the hastily contrived Teachers Bargaining Organization was received with surprising equanimity by the
leaders of the NEA. Most of them felt that the UFT would not
be able to carry out its grandiose intentions. Its failure would
open the way for the Association to come to the rescue of the
New York teachers. In the meantime, demands for collective
bargaining by militant teachers in NEA strongholds could be
quieted with "professional negotiations."

For me, achieving collective bargaining in New York City
had never been an end in itself, but there was only one New
York. The New York triumph was not like a victory in some
lesser city. The more than forty thousand new AFT members
which would result from the UFT victory would nearly double
the size of the teachers union. It would increase its credibility
and provide additional income for organizing drives in other
cities. New York had critical mass.

Slowly, a coherent national union strategy was beginning to
take shape. I never doubted that the New York City victory
would be a springboard for victories elsewhere. There were
more than three million teachers and other educational workers. If they could be organized into a union it would be the
biggest in the AFL-CIO. With that kind of base it would be
possible to join with other liberal unions to reinvigorate the
entire labor movement. It could become the force for social
change I had originally believed unions to be.


## THE PACKAGE

New York City teachers returned to their classrooms with am-
bivalence after the collective bargaining election. Many were
looking forward to the new era. They had been intrigued by the
promise of collective bargaining, but they had no understanding of its reality. As a matter of fact, I was none too sure myself
about how to go about it. But I was convinced that the process
should be as much like that in private industry as possible.

There were few guidelines. Ten years earlier the Wagner administration had ostensibly established collective bargaining for employees in some city departments. When I asked the leaders of these unions for copies of their contracts I found that there were none. Most of them negotiated on a piecemeal basis, benefit by benefit. The specifics of these understandings were usually set forth in letters of understanding. Even the contract for the transit workers, who had also achieved collective bargaining in the late 1930s, was sketchy.

Within the AFT, the locals in Butte and Anaconda, Montana, a suburban Chicago local, and the union in Pawtucket, Rhode Island, had won written agreements, but these were little more than recognition statements. I wanted a written contract covering not only salaries, hours, fringe benefits and a grievance procedure, but many other items so that copies could be sent to teachers in other school districts.

The first step toward obtaining a comprehensive contract was to draw up a list of demands to be presented to the negotiators for the board of education. During the election campaign, as a campaign tactic, all teachers had been invited to submit proposals for inclusion in the contract when the UFT had won. This list was designed to appeal to all classifications of teacher voters. In preparation for the UFT's first negotiating session with the representatives of the board of education, I recommended that the entire list of UFT election promises become the union's demand package. As a result the Federation submitted more than 150 demands to the board at the outset of the bargaining.

A minor incident related to the demand package sticks in my mind because it forecast things to come. When the UFT executive board was about to approve the package, Shanker suddenly moved to change the definition of the promotional increment so that anyone with a master's degree would qualify for the new promotional salary differential. The differential would be extended to thousands of elementary and junior high school teachers who had majored in "education" rather than in a "hard" academic subject area.

The change was worthy enough; many teachers felt that the education majors should not be discriminated against. Hochberg, Parente and other members of the CATU group were out-

raged, however. The requirements for the promotional increment had been carefully negotiated. Changing them without
consulting both parties to the agreement was a breach of faith.
Nevertheless, backed by the Guild majority on the executive
board, the change was approved. The action marked the beginning of Shanker's political base in the union.


THE NEGOTIATING COMMITTEE

Every organization has its own internal political life. During
the UFT's collective bargaining campaign the struggle to build
an organization that could contend with school and city authorities was of such importance that potential organizational
politicians largely set aside their ambitions and rallied behind
Cogen. Even so, there were many militants who were dissatisfied with Cogen's mild brand of unionism.

Before formation of the UFT there had been relatively little
factionalism, mainly because there were no political prizes to
strive for. The Guild was a protest group at best. More often it
seemed to be little more than a debating society. Furthermore,
most members were in agreement on matters of fundamental
policy, and the union functioned most of the time by consensus.

However, when the Guild became the UFT, the spirit of the
organization changed dramatically. With the UFT acting as the
sole bargaining agent, the city's teachers union offices, which
had formerly gone begging, became prestigious and eagerly
sought after. Whereas veteran members had been contented to
maintain the Guild as an organization of influence, and carried
this attitude over to the UFT, the newcomers from CATU regarded the UFT as an organization of power.

When it became necessary to choose the first negotiating
committee, Guild-CATU tension increased. A relatively large
negotiating committee would permit the main groups within
the huge school system to be represented, but political factionalism complicated the choice of committee members.

When I came to New York I had made it clear that I would
maintain the organizer's traditional nonpolitical stance. I had
even refrained from joining the local to show that I had no
political ambitions. But I had also reserved the right to partic-

ipate in policy formulation. After formation of the UFT I was careful to keep good relations with both the veteran members and the new CATU group. By siding with one faction or the other, depending on the issue, I was able to "manage" the union's development. I even brokered the first two elections of UFT officers, working out bipartisan slates which ran unopposed.

After much discussion of the make-up of the negotiating committee, it was decided that it would be composed of the 12 officers. I would act as an advisor. Shanker was admitted to the negotiations as a nonvoting secretary. Cogen was chairman and chief spokesman, although he frequently let me handle specific points. Parente, who was then secretary of the union, had also been chosen chairman of the salary committee and had responsibility for negotiating all salary matters.

The negotiating committee was split seven to five along political lines, with the veterans in the majority. Divided as it was, the committee just barely managed to maintain a united front when it confronted the board of education negotiating team. Discussions in caucuses were always acrimonious, and voting more often than not was seven to five. It was an absurd situation, but somehow the negotiations were carried on.


## SOAP COUPONS

The school board and the union groped through new territory. The UFT negotiating team was not alone in facing internal problems. Superintendent John J. Theobald had decided to head the board's negotiating team. Although he was a longtime personal friend of Mayor Robert F. Wagner, and a former deputy mayor, his flamboyant style had led him into various difficulties. He undoubtedly hoped that he could emerge from the negotiations with the support of the teaching staff to bolster his tottering tenure.

Collective bargaining involves two types of union demands: those that seek new rights and privileges and those that seek new economic benefits. A skillful union negotiator will try to keep progress in each category balanced. Once one category is settled, there is less leverage for settling the other. Such niceties of technique were not possible in the first New York City teacher negotiations. The budgetary process on which monetary gains depended was far along when the bargaining began. After a review of the UFT's complete package, it was decided to deal directly with the salary problem.

Roger Parente was a superb negotiator: pragmatic, intelligent and articulate without being verbose. Unlike Cogen and the rest of the "Old Guilders," who regarded a strike as a revolutionary act, Parente considered a work stoppage as the logical result of a breakdown in negotiations.

Theobald handled the bidding with Parente's encouragement, and the school board's salary offer soon approached an unprecedented $1,000 a year per teacher. Then, it was discovered that Theobald was only talking about the board's budget *request*. The superintendent's proposal, therefore, would not be binding on the city.

Theobald's view had a certain logic. It was the board of education which had held the representation election and which had recognized the UFT as bargaining agent, not the city. Although the board was legally autonomous, it was a fiscal prisoner of the city because city approval of the education budget was required. As the superintendent put it, once the board and the UFT agreed on a settlement they could go hand in hand to city hall and to the legislature in Albany to get the funds needed to put the agreement into effect.

Cogen tended to agree with the superintendent, as did most of the other Old Guilders. Insisting on negotiating for hard cash would almost certainly result in a head-on clash and a strike which the union might lose. But Hochberg and Parente and their followers tried to harden the UFT's position with a motion in the UFT delegate assembly that the board of education and the city be held accountable for Theobald's highest offer.

The Hochberg-Parente motion was defeated by a narrow margin, but a substitute motion was passed which warned the board and the superintendent not to make any offer which could not be redeemed in hard cash. In a statement to the press after the meeting—a statement which I attributed to Cogen—I paraphrased the union's position as refusing to bargain for "soap coupons." Cogen did not care for the saucy words which I had put in his mouth, but they were in keeping with the mood of the teachers.

As anticipated, rejection of Theobald's proposal to negotiate for a budget request changed the nature of the negotiations. Faced with having to bargain for real money, the board's attitude stiffened. The UFT countered by setting a strike date of April 11, 1962. The date was chosen because the mayor's budget would be recommended to the board of estimate and the city council at that time.

During the two or three weeks before the strike deadline, many "friends" from the labor movement and the Democratic party, locally and nationally, volunteered to work out under-the-table settlements. However, none of the would-be peace makers was able to produce the extra three or four million dollars needed to work out a satisfactory contract. The emerging militant teacher movement needed more than merely a passable settlement to demonstrate the value of collective bargaining.


## MEMORY TAPE: THIRTEEN MILLION DOLLARS

It is three o'clock the morning of Sunday, April 3, 1962. I have just returned home after a busy night, and the phone is ringing. The previous afternoon had been taken up by a negotiating session between the UFT team members, the board of education and the superintendent of schools with his staff. The talks had reached an impasse.

While Cogen advanced fruitless arguments to the board's negotiating committee, I wandered into a side room where the acting business manager of the school system was killing time with several other staff members. I doodled with some of the budget figures and bantered with the staff members. Then, suddenly, I thought I saw a way to make another $13 million available.

In the depths of the Depression, the school system had been allowed to borrow against the following year's state aid. This expedient had been continued. The current legislature had taken a step toward eliminating the practice by advancing the state aid payment date by three months. The intent was to "catch up" on the state aid payments over the next four years so that the city would not have to borrow. The result, however, allowed the city to borrow five quarters of aid instead of the four it had budgeted.

"Look!" I exclaimed to the business manager. "Show me where I'm wrong!" The school official looked at me for a long moment. Then he turned away without a word.

I went back into the negotiating room and asked Cogen to call a recess. When the UFT team assembled in its caucus room I tried to convince them that I had found $13 million. None of them understood budgets—not even Parente. They could not believe that there would be that much loose change lying around.

Finally Parente said with a sly smile, "Dave, there is no $13 million and you know it."

"Charlie," I had pleaded, "let me argue this with the board." Reluctantly Cogen and the rest of the committee agreed, but it was no use. I could not make the board or the superintendent see my $13 million. The best I had been able to do was to get them to say they would check with the mayor, who was week-ending in East Islip, Long Island.

The phone keeps ringing.

The negotiating session broke up after my futile effort to explain my discovery. I went to Ratner's Restaurant on the Lower East Side with a member of the CATU faction. I made phone calls to my "friends" in the Democratic party and learned that there was a chance the city could find another $13 million. It might cover a minimal settlement, and I spent a lot of time trying to convince my companion to accept a settlement based on that amount. At the same time I was still trying to think of ways to reveal the elusive $13 million dollars.

I finally pick up the phone.

"Is this Dave Selden?"

"Yes. Who is this?"

"This is Abe Beame. The mayor asked me to call. What's this about $13 million?" Beame is the city controller. I try to explain my concept to him. He listens for a moment and then interrupts. "No. You're wrong. There is no $13 million. It's just some kind of mathematical trick. An optical illusion."

I try again with the same result. Finally, I say desperately, "Abe, you could do it if you wanted to."

"Yes," he replies, "and I would be the one who went to jail.
I'm the controller, not you!" He hangs up.

I fall into bed and manage to get a few hours' sleep.

The following morning Shanker comes by to have a cup of
coffee before we ride downtown to the office. I am phoning a
telegram to Governor Nelson Rockefeller. I tell Shanker about
the three o'clock phone call. "If Wagner and Beame won't do
it, maybe Rocky will," I mutter grimly. "The Democrats had
their chance. Now let's see what the Republicans can do."

## THE SECOND STRIKE

Strikes by public employees violate a principle of common law
known as "the sovereignty doctrine." A strike by public employees is considered to be the same as a revolt against the king
in Blackstone's day. Hence, public officials can easily obtain
court injunctions against employees who strike, and the penalties for disobeying such orders can be heavy fines and im-
prisonment.

Days before the Wednesday strike deadline I went from one
public official to another, trying to make them understand the
"found" $13 million. I wanted Democrats to intervene with the
city and I wanted Republicans to get some action from the state.
But no one seemed interested.

A meeting of the delegate assembly was held the day before
the strike deadline. Cogen and the Old Guild majority on the
executive board tried to win a week's postponement of the
strike. The Hochberg-Parente faction dissented. In support of
the official position Shanker gave a graphic description of what
would happen to pickets and strike leaders. But there was no
holding back the teachers. They were going out!

More than 25,000 responded to the call. Almost all senior
and junior high schools were shut down in addition to
hundreds of elementary schools. In the late afternoon the teachers gathered at city hall. The streets were jammed for blocks
around the historic building. Traffic throughout Manhattan was
disrupted. Cogen and other leaders spoke to the crowd from a
sound truck.

While the rally was in progress, process servers searched the crowd for union leaders to give them copies of the injunction which the school board had obtained only hours before. By the time the rally ended, Cogen had called an executive board meeting for that evening to consider the union's response.

The board of education's countermove had been anticipated, and this strike, in contrast to its predecessor, was overwhelmingly supported by the teachers. Still, UFT leaders were uncertain about what to do. They debated for hours. The UFT's new lawyer, Wilbur Daniels—an assistant to David Dubinsky—pointed out the consequences of disobeying the injunction, and the executive board finally voted to end the strike. Cogen and other board members were in tears.

## FOUND MONEY

Collective bargaining for teachers might have ended in those bleak predawn hours following the 1962 New York City teachers' strike had it not been for a spectacular turn of events. When I dejectedly unlocked and opened the door of the UFT office a few hours after the executive board's surrender, I found a telegram. The yellow message inside was pure gold.

The telegram was from Governor Rockefeller. It summoned UFT representatives and school and city officials to a meeting later that morning. I felt a surge of joy. At last someone in Albany had believed what I had been trying to tell them. Rockefeller had intervened. The call to the meeting had been sent out before the executive board had capitulated, and it was too late to call the meeting off.

Everyone had gathered in the governor's New York City office: Mayor Wagner; Controller Beame; Superintendent Theobald; School Board Chairman Anna Rosenberg Hoffman; other board members; and all the members of the UFT's negotiating committee. Nelson Rockefeller, governor of the Empire State and owner of who knows what portion of the Earth, entered like a latter-day Apollo, blonde hair shining and bluff chin jutting. He moved around the room shaking everyone's hand, patting shoulders and beaming briefly on each of us.

The governor invited the mayor and the controller to join him and the state budget director in another office. A half hour later, the officials reappeared. Rockefeller announced that they had discovered a way to make another $13 million available to the school system. Mayor Wagner was buddha-faced, but Abe Beame winked at me.

There are probably many—even among the participants— who believe that the April 11, 1962 New York teachers' strike was called off because UFT leaders had advance knowledge of the governor's intervention. Others may believe that the strike forced the city to produce the extra $13 million. Neither assumption is entirely true. But without the crisis created by the strike, no one in authority would have intervened. For teachers and the world at large, collective bargaining was a success.

# Chapter 8

---

# COMPLETING THE DESIGN

## NO CONTRACT, NO WORK

A new salary schedule incorporating a $1,000 promotional increment was negotiated. The teachers were ecstatic, but completion of a comprehensive written agreement had become more difficult than before. There were still scores of nonmonetary issues to be resolved. The teachers, happy with their promised money, were in no mood to pressure the board of education.

The board smarted from its defeat in the strike and wished to prevent a repeat action. It suddenly produced a no-strike clause to be made part of the contract. The wording of the proposed clause declared that strikes were not only illegal but "contrary to public policy." The union was willing to foreswear strikes during the life of a contract, but the board seemed to demand a blood oath renouncing strikes in perpetuity.

September came. No additional gains were made, but under the guiding hand of Ida Klaus the contract began to take shape. A draft agreement was completed. Although far from ideal, it was a document unprecedented in American education.

With great reluctance, because of the obnoxious no-strike clause, the negotiating committee decided to take the draft contract to the 55-member executive board without recommendation. A bitter debate ensued. The moderates, led by President Cogen and other Old Guilders, argued that the negotiating committee had done the best it could. They proposed that the contract be approved and recommended to the delegate assembly.

The militants, led by Hochberg and Parente, asserted that accepting the no-strike pledge would be worse than having no contract. The union would be wise to wait until budget time the following year, when teachers might be more willing to "get tough" with the board of education. Some of the more militant speakers, perhaps drawing on leftist theory, advanced what I called the "cataclysmic theory of unionism." They asserted that the UFT would never amount to anything until it went out on a *real* strike which would continue until the school board surrendered unconditionally.

I did not want to go through another year without a contract, and I did not think the UFT was ready for a final showdown with the board. I wanted to consolidate the gains the UFT had made and regularize union functioning through use of the grievance procedure and other parts of the contract. Most of all, I saw close at hand that written document which could be distributed throughout the nation to make other teachers receptive to militant action. Yet, the board's no-strike clause seemed too much to swallow. Furthermore, failure to sign a contract would open the New York union to criticism from the NEA and even locals in the AFT.

As I listened to the debate and mulled over the predicament, I saw a way out: let the union accept the contract, with the no-strike clause. At the same time, the union should publicly adopt a no-contract, no-work policy. In other words, the UFT could concede that it would not call a strike during the life of the contract. But, if the contract ended before a new one had been negotiated, a strike would take place.

I was attacked by both sides in the argument. The Old Guilders were afraid of provoking the board of education; the militants called it sophistry. Nevertheless, the idea was adopted. In a single stroke the union had turned the tables on the board of education. Instead of renouncing the right to strike, the union had reasserted that right and strengthened it.

When the board of education members learned of the union's action they were furious. Withdrawing the salary and other concessions would stir a storm of teacher protest. Withdrawing the salary concessions might provoke another strike, and the board did not want to go through that experience again. The contract was approved by both sides, and no-contract, no-work became an integral part of the teacher bargaining process.


## MULTI-YEAR CONTRACTS

The no-contract, no-work policy led to the adoption of two corollary practices that became a part of the standard teacher bargaining process: September strike dates and multi-year contracts.

In the debate over acceptance of the first New York City contract, the militants favored an April 15 termination date. If a strike became necessary, it would occur in time for the settlement to be funded and included in the city budget. If the union's desire to set such a date became obvious to school officials, they might insist that the union's no-strike pledge carry through the budget-making period. It was not likely that the board would agree to a termination date that would only be timely for the union, however.

I believed there were advantages for the union in having the contract terminate in the summer. It seemed only logical that a contract should cover a full school year. Termination in April would come months before the school year was finished. Students and teachers should be able to look forward to a full, uninterrupted school year. If a strike became necessary, it should occur at the beginning of the school year in September. A strike in September would merely extend the summer vacation.

The more I thought about the contract termination problem, the more I became convinced that end-of-summer termination was best. In that event, however, how could money for salary increases and other benefits be included in the budget? Budget adoption had a psychological finality, but was it legally final? Could a supplemental budget be passed? I studied the city charter and consulted with experts but could get no definitive answer.

I finally concluded that contracts would have to stretch over more than one budget year. Typically, as the end of a contract approaches, the no-contract, no-work policy exerts pressure on negotiations. It is possible to win modest gains before the budget is adopted, but in a two-year contract, gains which cannot be included in the first-year budget can be charged to the second. It might be easier, in fact, to negotiate benefits falling due in the future than those which have to be paid for immediately.

The board of education was eager to sign a multi-year contract, if only to get some respite from union pressures. The UFT militants objected. They did not want the teachers to "cool off."

The second New York City contract was negotiated exactly according to plan. In June of 1963, the union voted to reject the board of education's "last best offer." The expiration date of the current contract came and passed. Under the no-contract, no-work policy a strike was due to begin on the first day of the new school year in September. The bargaining continued all summer. At the last moment an agreement was reached. The schools opened on time. This progression of events became a familiar sequence in district after district as the teacher collective bargaining movement spread across the nation.


SCOPE OF BARGAINING

One other piece of the basic design for teacher collective bargaining evolved during negotiation of the first two New York City contracts. This was the union's insistence on an unlimited scope of bargaining—the right to bargain on *anything*.

"Scope of bargaining" has received much discussion among labor lawyers and other collective bargaining professionals. Established doctrine has it that there are three general bargaining categories: mandatory subjects, permissive subjects and forbidden subjects. Employers are required to bargain on mandatory subjects such as wages, hours, and working conditions. They *may* bargain on other subjects such as the product design and the nature of the production process if they wish, but there are certain subjects which cannot be bargained at all. At the time, none of us on the UFT bargaining committee knew about these distinctions.

One of the demands put forward by the UFT in the first round of negotiations called for limited class sizes: 25 pupils in regular classes; 20 pupils in specialized classes such as shops or art studios; and no more than 15 pupils in classes for children with retarded mental development. Ida Klaus, speaking for the board of education, maintained that the size of classes was a matter of educational policy to be decided only by the administration and the board of education. She said the union had no right to bargain in the area of class size except to prevent teachers from being "sweated"; that is, forced to undergo undue hardship.

The UFT might have responded that collective bargaining concerns the price workers are paid for their labor. Because the amount of labor that a teacher supplies is directly related to the number of pupils taught, I felt that class size should be a part of the bargaining area. However, I feared that this argument might lead to discussion of teacher productivity, a negotiating swamp to be avoided, and I justified negotiating class-size limits on grounds of teacher "professionalism."

The AFT had long been attacked by the NEA as "unprofessional." However, I viewed the professionalism espoused by the NEA as a euphemism for snobbishness and elitism. Professionals were upper class; nonprofessionals were working class. Professionals received salaries or fees; nonprofessionals worked for wages. Professionals worked with their brains; nonprofessionals used their hands and bodies. Professionals were clean; nonprofessionals were dirty. In short, professionals belonged to professional associations, and nonprofessionals belonged to unions.

Of course, if there is any distinction between professionals and nonprofessionals, it lies in the assumption that professionals are self-directed and use their judgment in their work. Under the traditional paternalistic structure of American schools, teachers had very little to say about educational policy. I wanted to demonstrate that collective bargaining and unionism were essential to achieving professional status.

Ida Klaus espoused the doctrine of management rights normally conceded by unions in private industry. Private sector contracts usually contain a section granting management the right to determine product design, the nature of the production process, and the level of production. Applied to education, this doctrine meant that teachers—individually or collectively— could not participate in the determination of curriculum or academic standards. Further, they could not share in the choice of teaching methods or have a voice in policies affecting class sizes, enrollment and issues involving student attendance.

The philosophical point underlying the class-size controversy was never settled in the negotiations between the board of education and the UFT. The fact that the contract contained limits on class sizes constituted acceptance of the UFT's position. From that time, the Association's claim of sole possession of the essential ingredient in professionalism had a hollow ring.

### MEMORY TAPE: A RAINY DAY ON RANDALLS ISLAND

*Charles Cogen, several other UFT leaders and I are jammed into a car on East River Drive. We are trying to get to Randalls Island, located in the East River opposite 125th Street in Manhattan. It is September, 1963. Rain falls intermittently. We are coming from a meeting of the UFT delegate assembly in the former Tammany Hall auditorium at Union Square. The delegates have just approved the UFT's second collective bargaining contract. Now the agreement is up for ratification by the membership.*

*The school year is scheduled to begin tomorrow. The bargaining had continued "around the clock" for the past two weeks as both sides tried to reach agreement before the no-contract, no-work deadline. The negotiators had been sequestered in the Statler-Hilton Hotel. There had been occasional two- or three-hour breaks during which I had walked to Gimbel's and bought fresh shirts, socks and underwear. At one point, one of the mediators—Simon Ryfkind, a former federal judge—stretched out full-length on the green felt negotiating table and went to sleep. But now the negotiations are over, and it is up to the membership.*

*The new contract is more comprehensive than the first one, even though the salary gains are smaller. It is for two years, and the class size limitations have been improved. Nonteaching duties have been restricted, new fringe benefits have been added and the basis has been laid for "More Effective Schools."*

This last reference is intended to improve educational quality in the elementary schools. With this contract, collective bargaining for teachers has come of age.

Traffic is stop-and-go as three lines of cars edge toward the Triborough Bridge exit, the only access to the island stadium where the meeting will be held. Why does the slightest bit of rainfall always precipitate a traffic jam? Then I recognize teachers in the cars on either side. That's it! The Drive is jammed with the cars of teachers going to the meeting!

It has not been easy to complete the arrangements for the contract ratification process. I had kept the printers on standby so that the members could have copies of the agreement in case last minute pressure should produce a settlement, but where do you hold a meeting of fifteen to twenty-five thousand people in New York City on a rainy Sunday afternoon? There was no indoor meeting place of sufficient size, so we had opted for the old Randalls Island soccer stadium.

When the teachers in the cars recognize Cogen they make room for us to go by. Inside the stadium we see hundreds of umbrellas. Thousands of UFT members are seeking shelter from the rain. The other officers and the people who have helped work out the agreement are gathering on the infield where microphones have been set up—Harry Van Arsdale; Brendon Sexton, from the UAW; Nick Zonarich, the director of organization of the IUD; and many others.

I am one of the speakers. My voice is thick from the fatigue of marathon bargaining, but my message is clear. I speak of a movement of teachers which will sweep the cities of the nation. Boston! Philadelphia! Detroit! . . . All across this land!

# Chapter 9

# GOING TO CHICAGO

## SPREADING THE NEW GOSPEL

While the UFT was continuing to develop the teacher collective bargaining concept, teachers in other school districts began to push for adoption of the new system. AFT president Megel did not adopt my suggestion that a national director of organization help shape and guide the movement, but he did confer with the officials of the AFL-CIO Industrial Union Department in Washington about a nationwide organizing campaign. As a result, Walter Reuther expanded IUD support for the teachers union and used his authority as vice-president of the AFL-CIO and as president of the UAW to give additional aid.

Funds were made available to hire two young, activist teachers in New York to sign up the thousands of prospective new members. The two IUD organizers who had assisted in the New York campaign, Harold Ash and Lucille Swaim, were sent to Philadelphia and to Boston to stimulate campaigns in those cities. I traveled to Detroit once a week at UAW expense to help plan and direct still another campaign. The IUD also added several AFT organizers to its regional staffs in Chicago, Newark (New Jersey) and Milwaukee.

In addition to carrying out my duties for the UFT I found time to help AFT locals on Long Island and in other adjoining areas in New York, Connecticut and New Jersey. The New York state teachers federation, which had been virtually suspended during the long New York City campaign, was also brought back to life.

In the spring of 1963, the UFT conducted a conference on collective bargaining for the nearby AFT locals. Invitations were sent to President Megel and the members of the AFT executive council. Many of the union's officials attended. They were uneasy about the UFT's initiative, which they suspected was an effort to extend New York's influence within the union. They were also worried about the changes that collective bargaining would bring. I was called on repeatedly to answer the charge that representation elections would result in losses for many Federation locals.

The fears of the AFT officials were partly justified, particularly in smaller school districts. However, these losses would be more than offset by victories in large districts, and the increased dues income from these victories could be used to finance "re-run" campaigns in losing districts. Losing the first election would not necessarily be fatal, since the union could challenge again later on.

Actually, in Connecticut the state association seized the initiative under a biased procedure worked out in collusion with the state superintendent of education and won more than a score of representation elections before the Federation won one. That single AFT victory, however, was in Hartford, the state capital, giving the union a credible beachhead from which to recoup its losses.

One positive result of the UFT collective bargaining conference was a commission from Megel to write a collective bargaining handbook for use by other locals. I finished the booklet in a few weeks. It was called *Winning Collective Bargaining*. For the first time, ideas and tactics which became integral parts of the theory of the new movement were described in how-to-do-it terms. Because teachers, like other public employees, were specifically excluded from the scope of the National Labor Relations Act, they would have to "shoot their way" to collective bargaining, I wrote. That is, teachers would have to depend on their collective strength, as did auto workers in the 1930s. School boards had the power to hold representation elections. Teachers would have to force them to act.

If AFT locals assumed leadership of the collective bargaining movement, teachers would rally behind them, just as they had in New York. Most local NEA affiliates could be counted on to discredit themselves by opposing collective bargaining. They had nothing to gain from changing the status quo. This sequence was repeated until the associations began calling for elections themselves. Even then, in areas where the AFT was not a threat most of them continued to operate in their time-honored way.

*Winning Collective Bargaining* also stressed the importance of involvement of teachers at the grass roots, not only in the campaign for collective bargaining but in campaigns for specific benefits as a prelude to the bargaining campaign. For example, the "Right to Eat" campaign involved all the New York City elementary school teachers in a drive for duty-free lunch periods two years before the collective bargaining campaign began.

Finally, I cautioned against pressing teachers too hard to join the union. What the union wanted was their votes when the election was held. Too aggressive recruiting might alienate some teachers.

*Winning Collective Bargaining* was not used for mass distribution. Its new, militant approach might have frightened off some AFT members. In many school districts, too, the union had become so alienated from the mass of the teachers over the years that a collective bargaining election would have been disastrous no matter what kind of a campaign was mounted. But where conditions were right and local leadership had credibility the basic formula in *Winning Collective Bargaining* worked extraordinarily well.


## MEMORY TAPE: THEY SAY SOMEBODY SHOT THE PRESIDENT

*I take the elevator down to the lobby of the building where the new headquarters of the UFT is located. I am on my way uptown to the Americana Hotel, where the AFT executive council is meeting. In a half hour the council is scheduled to consider the question of choosing a national director of organization.*

*More than two years had elapsed since I had suggested that a national director of organization be appointed. Because of the AFT's delay and my increasing involvement in UFT projects, I had given up thinking about the idea. But the IUD, as* it had become more involved in the teacher collective bargaining movement, had become dissatisfied with the haphazard functioning of the AFT campaign.

In the summer of 1963 Nick Zonarich, the IUD director of organization, demanded that the AFT executive council put someone in charge of promoting collective bargaining, and at last, three months later, action is being taken.

A small crowd is gathered around the newsstand near the subway entrance. A transistor radio is crackling, and people are listening intently. The newsdealer is an acquaintance. "Why is everybody standing around?" I ask.

"Oh, they say somebody shot the president," he answers with a deprecating grin.

I grin back. Impossible. We don't shoot presidents, do we?

I turn and enter the subway. In a few minutes I reach the Americana. I enter the lobby and I know immediately that it is true. President Kennedy has been shot. People are gathered in small, somber groups.

I take the elevator to the floor where the executive council is meeting. Everyone is there: President Megel, the 15 vice-presidents and the usual staff members.

". . . and we don't know the extent of the injuries," Megel is saying.

No one speaks. All eyes are downcast. One of the vice-presidents hesitantly points out that there is nothing we can do, so we may as well go ahead with the meeting. No one objects, and Megel says, "All right, then . . ."

There are three candidates for the position to be filled: Charles Smith, from Gary, Indiana, James Mundy, from New Jersey, and me. The three of us leave the room. We will be called back one at a time. Of the three, I have the most organizing experience. Smith, however, is the main leader of his local and a civil rights activist and an effective unionist, although he has no collective bargaining experience.

Mundy is a recent law graduate, but he has not yet passed the bar exam. He has been teaching in Woodbridge, New Jersey. Megel had picked him to go on the IUD payroll as an organizer assigned to Newark. I have been coaching him for many months, giving him ideas and meeting with him to discuss the Newark campaign.

*My interview with the council does not go well. I am iden-
tified with the Progressive Caucus within the AFT, and only
six of the 15 council members are Progressives. I am asked to
explain my organizing strategy for the AFT. I say that the union
must develop new dues income quickly so that collective bargaining campaigns can be mounted throughout the nation.
Thus, the Federation should concentrate first on the larger districts. I know that my ideas will not gain the support of those
council members from small locals but I push ahead.*

*The council recesses until evening. I arrange separate in-
terviews with Megel and John Fewkes, the leader of the Chicago
local since 1936. Megel and Fewkes are evasive. Each says I
should seek the support of the other. Later that night I receive
a phone call from Megel. He tells me the council has voted for
Mundy by a straight caucus vote, nine to six.*

*Lyndon Baines Johnson is president. Kennedy was sup-
ported by most liberals. Johnson's reputation among liberals is
bad. I call Jack Conway, executive director of the IUD and a
chief advisor to Walter Reuther. I want to know what Reuther
is going to do about the situation in Washington. Conway has
already been working. He says Johnson will be more liberal
than people think. I am somewhat reassured. As an after-
thought I tell him about Mundy's selection.*

## POLITICS

As membership within the UFT had increased, the Guild and
UFT factions had continued their bickering. Chiefly prompted
by Shanker, the Guild faction had formed the Unity Caucus.
The CATU group, still under the leadership of Hochberg and
Parente, had formed the United Action Caucus.

Although my relationship with Shanker was still close, he
had not discussed his political activity with me. I was surprised, therefore, when, in the spring of 1962 he told me that
he was not going to run against Cogen for the presidency of the
union and that he would run for secretary instead. I had not
known that he was going to run for anything, even though we
spent many hours together every day.

At the national level the political effect of the growth of the New York local was felt soon after the bargaining election. AFT politics continued to be under the shadow of the Chicago local, still the Federation's largest, but all union politicos knew that it was only a matter of time before the UFT gained the ascendency.

At the 1962 AFT convention, Carl Megel ran for national president for the last time. He was backed by the Chicago Teachers Union and the National Caucus. His opponent from the Progressive Caucus was Myron Lieberman, by then well-known in educational circles. Although Lieberman had long questioned the need for teacher affiliation with the labor movement, he suppressed his doubts and ran an aggressive campaign. Megel, however, trounced his erudite opponent.

The 1963 AFT convention was held in New York City. It was first scheduled for Miami, but the switch was made in response to strong protests raised by the UFT because trains, buses and motels throughout the South were still segregated. Black delegates coming to the convention would be subjected to discrimination.

In early 1964 Shanker told me that he was going to run against Cogen for president of the UFT. I had been expecting this declaration, but it made me extremely uncomfortable. Charlie Cogen and I had been partners for more than ten years, and during that time the union had steadily advanced. I had persuaded him to take positions and actions that he fundamentally opposed in temperament and philosophy. At times I had found his resistance maddening, but in spite of our conflicts I felt that failure to support his reelection would be a betrayal. On the other hand, Shanker was my friend.

A solution to my dilemma occurred to me. If Cogen ran for *national* president, Shanker could run for president of the local. If Cogen won, I could go with him to the national headquarters in Chicago and I would be able to guide the course of the national teacher collective bargaining movement.

I do not know whether Cogen fully understood that Shanker would have run against him if he had insisted on running for reelection as president of the UFT. I do not know how such a contest would have come out either. Cogen was immensely popular, known to the rank and file, and had a reputation as a militant leader. Shanker was less well-known but he was strong within the Unity Caucus where the contest would have been decided. If Cogen had stuck to his guns, he might well have won the caucus nomination and reelection to the UFT presidency.

It was not easy to persuade Cogen to run for national president. He would be "going for broke," because the UFT election was in May and the national election was not until August. He was never eager to take such chances, but I assured him that he would be a sure winner in the national election, and he gave his consent.

Shanker had originally suggested holding a testimonial dinner for Cogen to ease him into retirement. With the change in political plans, this affair was converted into an occasion for Cogen to launch his national candidacy. Many out-of-town AFT leaders attended. It also turned out to be a celebration of Shanker's election as UFT president.


## THE 1964 CONVENTION

When Cogen announced that he intended to run for the AFT presidency, he and I assumed that his opponent would be Carl Megel. Megel had been a good president in many respects, but he had accumulated the usual quota of enemies over the 12 years of his incumbency. He was also not a good public speaker. His conversation and speeches were studded with "down home" provincialisms and grammatical errors. Although he was a cunning politician, he was unable to develop large issues which could command the allegiance of teachers.

On the other hand, Cogen's national image was that of a successful strike leader and pioneer in the collective bargaining movement. He was an accomplished speaker. More practically, the growth of the UFT had given him a solid political base. Because organizing was the number one concern of every local leader, Cogen inspired confidence in the union's future. I was quite sure that he would be more than a match for Megel.

A month before the convention, however, the national president arranged with the executive council to be given a five-year contract as the AFT's Washington representative. Although he was no longer a contender for the presidency, he allowed the national staff to go all out "to prevent a New York takeover." I later learned that some on the national office staff believed Cogen was merely a stalking horse for me, and that I would become the candidate just before the election.

Cogen's first task as a candidate was to gain the endorsement of the Progressive Caucus. My connection with the members of the Michigan locals, who were mostly Progressives, stood me in good stead in my quest for votes for Cogen. I also gained the support of some of the other important caucus leaders.

The National Caucus—with the Chicago Teachers Union as its center of strength—chose Charles Smith as its candidate. Smith, the leader of the Gary local, was a strong candidate.

AFT conventions start on a Sunday afternoon and end the following Friday. Officers are elected on Thursday. Until the system was changed in 1972, the number of votes given to each local was weighted to reduce undue influence by the larger locals. All locals represented at the convention can cast the total number of votes to which they are entitled, regardless of how many delegates are actually in attendance.

The UFT ran an effective campaign. At the direction of George Altomare, who had become a vice-president of the local, a careful check was made of every delegate. By Thursday morning, it was clear that the election would be close.

Cogen was elected by 28 votes. But if the only delegate from the Los Angeles local had not fallen asleep in his room and failed to cast his local's votes for Smith, as intended, Cogen would have lost.

MEMORY TAPE: BIRTH OF CO-ORG

*It is Friday morning, August 23, 1964. In Chicago, at the Pick-Congress Hotel overlooking Lake Michigan, the AFT convention is grinding to its conclusion. Cogen has won the presidency by a narrow margin. The convention will adjourn in the early afternoon, and the new executive council of 15 vice-presidents and the president will meet to establish the direction of the new administration.*

I run into James Mundy in the lobby. His selection as national director of organization a year before had been one of the incidents that led to Cogen's candidacy.

"Jim!" I call. He turns toward me uneasily.

"Hi, Dave."

"Could I see you in my room in about half an hour?" I ask.

He thinks I am going to tell him he is fired, but he says, "Sure. What's your room number?"

I tell him and add, "Bring along a copy of the budget for next year and any other financial stuff you have, will you?"

"Sure."

Until this moment I have not decided what to do about Mundy, but now a plan is taking shape in my mind.

When he arrives in my room I make him welcome. "Sit down, Jim. First, let me relieve any concern you may have about your status," I say. "As far as I am concerned, you can remain in your present position."

Mundy is visibly relieved. I wait a moment and then state flatly, "I will become Cogen's assistant and you will report to me."

Mundy looks at me steadily as he assimilates what I have outlined.

"OK," he finally says. "What do we do now?" We shake hands. Then we go to work on a new organizing plan. It will revolutionize AFT financing and greatly increase organizing activity. I call it "Co-Org"—short for "Cooperative Organizing Plan."

It had been a matter of pride and political prudence for Megel and his predecessors to finish in the black every year. Although this conservative fiscal style suited most of the hard-bitten, Depression-scarred AFT leaders, it would prevent the Federation from capitalizing on the great organizing opportunity which the collective bargaining movement had opened up. A vastly expanded effort was needed and it would require huge amounts of money.

Fortunately, the interest of Walter Reuther and his aides in the teachers union had steadily increased since their early involvement in the New York campaign. IUD funds were flowing into AFT organizing at the rate of $200,000 a year. Two days earlier, Nick Zonarich, IUD director of organization, who spoke

at the convention, had offered a startling new proposal for AFT-
IUD cooperation. Speaking with Reuther's authorization, Zonarich had announced that the IUD was prepared to help raise
a $1 million organizing fund—half to be given by the IUD,
provided the AFT could produce the other half.

I refer to Zonarich's challenge and ask Mundy if he has any
ideas about where the AFT's half of the organizing fund can
come from. He points out that the union is now spending about
$150,000 a year of its own funds. He thinks that another
$100,000 might be squeezed out of other areas in the budget.
He thinks that is the limit until the next convention, which
might be persuaded to increase per capita dues.

"How about shaking down the big locals and the state federations for more money?" I ask.

Mundy laughs sarcastically. Most state federations did not
have enough income to even maintain an office, and the locals
were not apt to give money voluntarily to the national union.
"How are you going to do that?" he inquires.

"We'll put the IUD money up for matching and we'll require
the state federations and big locals to set up special collective
bargaining budgets—and maybe raise their dues, too," I reply.

Mundy shakes his head dubiously. "That will take time."

"Yes, I know," I answer, "but in the meantime we will lend
them the money to pay their share. All we have to do is convince the IUD to go along. With their guarantee we can go to
the bank and borrow $250,000 and then lend it to the state
federations." I am thinking of the Amalgamated Bank, which
helped finance the New York City campaign.

Later that day the executive council approves everything. I
become assistant to the president, the budget shifts are approved and the Co-Org Plan becomes official policy.

Three days later, Mundy and I fly to Washington to meet
with the top IUD staff members. They are dumbfounded by our
boldness, but they agree to go along.

# Chapter 10

---

# TALES FROM THE TEACHER WARS

## MEMORY TAPE: MOBILIZING THE TROOPS

In Chicago's Allerton Hotel, nearly fifty state federation presidents and executive secretaries are gathered. The tumult of the AFT convention has scarcely ceased. Mundy and I have returned from our meeting with IUD representatives in Washington. But because IUD funds are conditional on matching funds from the AFT, and these depend on what we can get the state federations to do, the meeting is crucial.

Cogen opens the meeting and gives me the floor. I launch into a description of the Co-Org plan.

"The state federations have a vital role in what we plan to do," I assure the state leaders. "The plan has three parts. First, we will be dealing directly with big city locals to finance representation election campaigns where we have a chance to win because we must increase our income quickly. Second, we will be working with you to help state federations handle campaigns in the middle-sized and smaller districts. The third part of the plan involves special situations which don't fit either category."

They are watching me intently. This is something new. The state federations have always been the weakest level in the union's structure. Now it seems they are going to get help.

"You will all have a big job to do," I tell them. "We will give each of you a subsidy, provided you are willing to help your-

*selves. If you want money from Co-Org you will have to hire
an organizer, someone we can work with."*

I watch the face of my old friend Eliot Birnbaum, president
of the New York state federation. I see open skepticism. Now
he speaks up. "Dave, you're risking everything on collective
bargaining. We're all in favor of collective bargaining, of
course, but first we have to organize. I know that in Syracuse,
where I teach, the AFT would be wiped out if we had a collective bargaining election."

I know he expresses the fears of many of those present. "Yes,
Eliot," I reply placatingly. "I know we aren't going to win collective bargaining in lots of places overnight, but we must keep
showing teachers that bargaining is our goal. We have to be
willing to push ahead even though we aren't sure of winning.
Don't forget, we won in New York City with barely ten percent
of the teachers signed up."

This reference to New York is a direct thrust at Birnbaum.
He had opposed the move for bargaining in the city because
he thought it was too risky. During the last year of the campaign
the UFT had made only token per capita payments to the state
federation, forcing it to virtually suspend its operations. At the
time Birnbaum had accused me of leading the state AFT to
destruction.

"You were lucky," Eliot now says. "What if the UFT had
lost? Besides, what worked in New York isn't necessarily going
to work everywhere."

"That may be true," I concede. "But I'm not saying we should
rush into elections where we know we are going to lose. Sure,
we will lose some, but even if we lost two out of three we would
still be gaining on the Association because they outnumber us
ten to one as things stand. A membership a third the size of
the NEA's would put us over the three hundred thousand mark.
For now, I'd settle for that!"

"How about the losers?" Birnbaum interjects.

"For years we have been saying that it is fear that keeps
teachers from joining the union. But they don't have to be union
members to vote for the union in a bargaining election. In secret
ballot elections we are going to draw many more votes than we
have members. The bigger we get, the faster we will grow."

Another hand goes up. It belongs to James O'Meara, the long-time leader of the Cleveland Teachers Union. I had invited him to the meeting because the big Cleveland local was the controlling force in the Ohio Federation of Teachers.

"Did you say we would have to hire an organizer?" he asks.

"Yes," I answer bluntly. I wait for the inevitable follow-up question.

"Where is the money coming from?" he asks.

I try to keep the edge out of my voice as I reply. "We're going to give you part of it and we're going to help you borrow part of it if you need it. But you're going to have to do your part, too. Most state federations will have to raise per capita dues."

This is the hidden catch everyone was waiting for. In most states where the Federation is active—Michigan, Minnesota, Illinois, New York and others—membership is concentrated in one or a few large locals, and state federation activity has a low priority with the leadership.

O'Meara persists. "You mean state federations will have to raise dues? If we do, we'll lose members and we'll be worse off than we were."

"Maybe some state federations will have to raise dues," I concede. "But some of you have substantial treasury balances which can be used, and you may be able to raise money in other ways, too. Anyway, teachers join a union when they think it can do something for them that they can't do alone or through the Association. They don't join just because it's cheap."

O'Meara is silenced but not convinced. I know that he has voiced the main concern of many of those present.

The rest of the day is spent explaining the details of the Co-Org plan and discussing the methodology of collective bargaining campaigns. I am relieved to find that Mundy is wholeheartedly supportive. I leave it to him to start negotiating with the various leaders in order to work out the specifics for Co-Org plans in their states.

As the meeting is breaking up, I spend a few minutes alone with Eliot Birnbaum.

"Well, what do you think now?" I ask. "We've come a long way from the times when I used to stay with you in Syracuse to save the price of a hotel room."

"You've come a long way," he responds testily. "As for me,
I don't know. I guess I'm still pretty much where I have always
been. In the old days we just went straight ahead and hoped
teachers would join us because we were right. Now we're talking about power, and power corrupts."

Eliot is right about one thing: the AFT is entering a new era.
Throughout its history it had relied on persuasian for carrying
out its program. But principle without power is futility; power
without principle is corruption.

I fervently hope that as it enters the new era the organization
can find the right balance between the two.

## L.A.

Winning campaigns in the big cities was crucial to the Co-Org
plan. The AFT could not depend on borrowing and IUD grants
indefinitely. At some point, the union would have to become
self-supporting. The quickest way to accomplish this was by
winning bargaining rights in the big cities where thousands of
new dues payers could be gained at one stroke. A few days after
meeting with the state federation officers, Mundy and I flew to
the West Coast to meet with leaders of the Los Angeles local.

The AFT had an uneven record in the southern California
metropolis. A local started in the 1930s had come under control
of suspected Communists. In 1949 the AFT had expelled the
local and recognized a new group as the union's standard
bearer. The switch in leadership only made matters worse. In
the 1950s the intrepid Henry Clark, who was just beginning his
career as organizer for the California Federation of Teachers,
captured the exclusive right for federation members to join the
new Kaiser health plan.

For a while the health plan stimulated rapid growth of the
Los Angeles local. But when the California Teachers Association also gained accessibility to the Kaiser plan, unionization
slowed drastically. It was not until the 1960s that the AFT began
to grow again in the city. Even then progress was slow.

Yet, Los Angeles was an inviting organizing target. It was
the third largest school system in the nation, and conditions in
the schools were deteriorating fast. Except for its climate and

glamor, Los Angeles was no different from any other large American city. I visited schools built for 1,500 pupils that were trying to take care of 2,500. I saw harried and frightened teachers, just as I had seen them in other large cities. In the desk drawers of assistant principals were dozens of guns and knives confiscated from students.

Mundy had checked out the Los Angeles local during the year before our joint visit. He had concluded the city was not a good prospect for collective bargaining. I wanted to see for myself.

When Mundy and I met with the local's executive board I knew why he was not enthusiastic about underwriting a campaign in Los Angeles. The leadership group reminded me of the prebargaining executive board of the New York Teachers Guild. The members had accepted the minimal role of powerless gadfly. Small wonder the union was not growing.

The root of the problem in Los Angeles was the leadership. Hank Zivetz, the president, was charismatic and aggressive, but for all his ability he was unwilling to risk defeat in a collective bargaining campaign. Mundy and I did our best to arouse enthusiasm among other members of the board, but they held back, waiting for Zivetz to take the lead. We wanted the union to jump into the campaign with a demand that the board of education schedule a representation election, as outlined in *Winning Collective Bargaining*. This initial move was to be backed by a strike threat. The national AFT would lend the local enough money to hire a dozen part-time organizers to help.

But Zivetz balked at putting the local in debt. He was also evasive about calling a strike. Mundy and I left the city with only a weak commitment. Zivetz had agreed to accept a loan of $2,000 a month for two years without a firm deadline for repayment. He issued a public announcement of the collective bargaining campaign, but I was the only person talking about the possibility of a strike.

The half-hearted Los Angeles collective bargaining campaign failed to ignite the spark of militancy among the teachers. I saw that starting a nationwide collective bargaining campaign would be harder than I had thought.

## QUEEN'S MOVE

Even before Cogen and I moved to the national headquarters in Chicago, the basic strategy for the AFT's national collective bargaining campaign had taken shape. Following the UFT's election victory, Harold Ash, one of the two organizers from the AFL-CIO Industrial Union Department, was sent to Philadelphia. Lucille Swaim, the other IUD staffer, was sent to Boston. These moves paid off.

In Philadelphia, where I had friends from my days as an AFT field representative, I had outlined what needed to be done to mount a credible campaign. When Ash came in he took with him a carton of flyers and other materials used in the UFT's campaign. In Boston, Swaim had much rougher going—mainly because of factionalism and conservatism among the leaders.

With the support of the UAW, I tried to stimulate a campaign in Detroit. The Federation had begun as a study group meeting in the public library during the early thirties. Arthur and Rennette Elder made their home a center for teachers union activity for Detroit and the entire state. I had worked with the Elders and their coterie during my Dearborn days. Through them I became friendly with other Detroit leaders, including Helen Bowers, who had become executive secretary of the local in the 1950s.

Michigan has long had a property-tax limitation for schools. It requires a voter referendum before an operating tax rate higher than 15 mills can be levied. Such overmillage must be reapproved every few years. Because school districts cannot operate within the 15 mill limit, teachers, parents and other proschool people are constantly at war with the real estate interests. In the spring of 1963, a millage vote in Detroit was defeated. The cutbacks in programs, larger classes and possible layoffs stimulated the union to launch a drive for bargaining rights.

My friendship with the original Detroit leaders opened the way for acceptance by Mary Ellen Riordan, who had recently become president. At my urging the union's demands for collective bargaining became more insistent. Many teachers began to wear buttons demanding "Name the DATE." There were suggestions that teachers might have to strike "just like New York."

Charles Cogen, who had not yet been elected national president, was brought in from New York to speak at a rally.

Mary Ellen Riordan presided over this mounting excitement with great aplomb. She had a progressive attitude toward unionism even though she was a reluctant striker. She relied heavily on Bowers and on Edward Simpkins, the executive vice-president of the local. Simpkins was less cautious about direct action.

By Christmas of 1963, it was clear that the board of education would not hold a collective bargaining election unless it was forced to do so. Without question, the situation called for a strike—or at least a strike threat—but a strike threat is futile if those on the other side do not think you mean it. To close the credibility gap, I drafted a strike vote procedure which involved several steps. It was designed to ease the Federation into a strike vote some thirty days after the process began. There were opportunities for settlement of each step along the way.

In the meantime, the Detroit Education Association (DEA) had been taking potshots at the union and hoping that the Detroit Federation of Teachers (DFT) would fumble. It called the union "unprofessional" and its leaders "agitators." Nationally the NEA was still pushing professional negotiations, its substitute for collective bargaining. The DEA followed the NEA line. The DEA also insisted that there was no need for an election because a majority of the city's teachers were members of the Association. This assertion was probably true, but the Federation was confident it could win in a secret vote free from administrative coercion, because even DEA members wanted the union's "toughness."

The final showdown began a week before the Easter recess in 1964. The DFT had set a strike date for the day schools were to reopen after the spring vacation break. The school board had taken refuge behind the legalism that collective bargaining for teachers was contrary to Michigan law.

The United Auto Workers, whose leaders had watched unobtrusively throughout the campaign, persuaded the state superintendent of public instruction to request an opinion from the state attorney general as to the legality of the Federation's demand. The attorney general, Frank Kelley, who was just beginning his long tenure in that office, declared teacher collective bargaining legally permissible.

With the legal obstacle removed, the DFT called a mass march on the board's meeting the week before the spring vacation was to begin. This was also two weeks before the strike date. Thousands of teachers jammed the school administration building.

The DFT executive board was jubilant when it met after the march on the board. There had never been a day like that in the history of the school system. At last teachers were standing up for their rights. But one excruciating decision remained for the union's leaders. As they met, Irving Bluestone, assistant to Walter Reuther, entered the meeting room with a message from the board of education. If the Federation called off the strike, a referendum would be held immediately after the spring vacation. If the teachers voted yes, the representation election would be held the following week.

The referendum idea was obviously borrowed from the New York procedure, but there was a catch. The Federation had to call off the strike without revealing the secret plan. Apparently the school board wanted to show teachers and the public that it was still running the school system. The union would have to go on faith for several days, even though many teachers would accuse their leaders of selling out. Simpkins and I did not want to go along with the board's scheme. We did not doubt the good faith of Bluestone and the board, but we also did not want to dampen the militancy of the teachers.

It was Helen Bowers who pointed out the advantages of the board's offer. She said the union had victory within its grasp, and it should not risk defeat by overreaching. The teachers would vote for collective bargaining in the referendum, just as they had in New York. Afterwards, the DFT would surely win the representation election. The details would become mere footnotes to the history of the event.

Francis Comfort and a close friend of Bowers from the Elders's inner circle, called acceptance of the board's secret offer "the queen's move." To win at chess, you play until you think you have your opponent trapped. Then the queen, most powerful piece on the board, is moved into position, and the game is over.

The Detroit Board of Education announced the referendum as promised. The Association watched helplessly as the teachers voted overwhelmingly for collective bargaining. The union was the decisive winner in the election which followed.


## ST. LOUIS

In the 1930s, the St. Louis local had scarcely three dozen members. The founders, a small band of Norman Thomas Socialists in the 1930s, had been reconciled from the start to minority status. As Socialists in mid-America they expected nothing better. Betty Finneran, elected president in the early 1960s, was the admiring daughter of a strongly unionist father. Using *Winning Collective Bargaining* as a manual, she and a few friends set out to make the Federation the bargaining agent for St. Louis teachers.

One surely would not have picked St. Louis as a likely place for a successful teachers union. The city is a southern town with strong aristocratic Germanic traditions. Its school system had been racially segregated until the Supreme Court outlawed segregation in 1954. Its board of education was tightly controlled by the city's old families. The local labor movement, with the possible exception of the Teamsters, was not strong.

Most teachers were members of the local association. Furthermore, the legislature had passed a law that, while allowing collective bargaining for most public employees, specifically excluded highway patrolmen, prison guards and teachers. Undaunted, nevertheless, Finneran and her friends distributed leaflets, spoke at school board meetings and attended meetings of the St. Louis central labor body. The union began to grow. In a few years, nearly a thousand of the forty-five hundred teachers had signed up.

Alarmed, the NEA gave its St. Louis affiliate funds to hire a full-time executive secretary. Finneran countered by asking the AFT to send in an organizer. When President Megel said the union had no one to send, Finneran turned to the UFT for help. I arranged for Robert Lieberman, one of the New York teacher activists hired as an organizer after the city bargaining election, to move to St. Louis.

Lieberman had never been west of Buffalo, but he acclimated quickly to his new location. He was received by Finneran and her cohorts as an organizing expert. He soon was using his flair for public relations to flood the press, radio and television with press releases about the Federation. The teacher war began to heat up in St. Louis.

Following the New York pattern, Lieberman concentrated on building a corps of school representatives who would stuff teachers' letterboxes with literature. He and some of the other activists were also going into schools at noontime to talk with teachers, as I and other organizers had done in New York. Suddenly a new rule was promulgated by the school superintendent: no material could be placed in a teacher's letterbox without advance permission from the teacher, and only one person from each organization would be permitted to enter schools.

The one-two punch by the administration had a chilling effect on the Federation's organizing drive. Lieberman came to Chicago to confer with me at my new post. We discussed the St. Louis organizing problem at length.

*Winning Collective Bargaining* had suggested that because teachers had been excluded from the Labor and Management Relations Act and the jurisdiction of the National Labor Relations Board (NLRB), the American Arbitration Association (AAA) could be used to conduct elections. However, the AAA can intervene only if all parties in the election agree. There was no possibility that the St. Louis Board of Education would go into collective bargaining voluntarily. Some way had to be found to force the board to consent to an election.

Lieberman and I decided to run an authorization card campaign as if teachers were under NLRB jurisdiction. We would ask teachers to sign cards authorizing the AFT to act as their bargaining agent. Then, we would ask some trusted third party to certify that the union had enough cards to demand an election. In this way the union's claim would be validated without having to reveal the names of the card signers to the board of education. To avoid suspicion of collusion or fraud, we decided that the third party to whom the cards would be given should be a committee of clergymen.

Lieberman returned to St. Louis full of enthusiasm. Within a few days he found a Catholic priest, a Lutheran minister and a rabbi who were willing to serve on the verification committee. In another few days he sent a mailing to all teachers: a piece of literature, a letter, and an authorization card printed on a prepaid postcard addressed to a post office box number. The card authorized the St. Louis Teachers Union to bargain for the card's signer.

Two weeks later, I heard from Lieberman again. He had found out from a member of the postal workers union that only eight hundred or so cards had been returned. Fourteen hundred cards were needed to reach the thirty percent total usually required by the NLRB. I suggested that he send out another mailing.

"Yeah, Dave," Lieberman answered, "I already thought of that, but the minister won't let me do it."

"Who?"

"The minister—the one I got for the verification committee."

"Why?"

"He says it would be like letting them vote twice."

"But they can't count more than one card for any teacher."

"I know. The rabbi and the priest are OK, but they can't convince the minister. The other two won't do anything unless he agrees."

In the days that followed, the St. Louis Teacher unionists conducted an intensive telephone campaign to get teachers to return the authorization cards, but it was no use. Some still had the cards and promised to mail them, but most said they had thrown the cards away. After two weeks of effort the card total had gone over 1,000, but it was still short of the 1,400 goal.

"What do we do now?" Lieberman wanted to know.

Sadly, I told him that we would have to admit defeat. The cards must be destroyed without counting them. "Once that number gets out," I said, "it will always haunt us. It is better to be vague and hope that everybody soon forgets about the whole thing."

Later, Lieberman told me that a bizarre "funeral" procession had descended the basement stairs at the Catholic chancery on Lindell Boulevard. The three members of the verification committee were in the lead. Then came Betty Finneran followed by Lieberman carrying a mail sack. They approached the hulking, old-fashioned coal-burning furnace. The priest held the

furnace door while Lieberman fished out the postcards and
flung them into the flames. The first St. Louis teachers' collective bargaining campaign was cremated. It was another five
years before St. Louis teachers would win collective bargaining
rights.


## PAWTUCKET

Among the out-of-town teachers who found their way into my
office at the UFT in New York was Gregory Coughlan from
Pawtucket, Rhode Island. Coughlan certainly did not look or
talk like a teacher rebel. He was in his fifties and very humble.
Yet, the lure of collective bargaining had brought him to New
York to find out more about the new movement.

Rhode Island had long been a hotbed of teacher unionism.
In fact, the first teacher strike in which I was ever involved was
in Providence in 1950 during my AFT organizer days. The
teachers were out for a week and won a good settlement. Even
before that there had been a strike in Pawtucket which had
lasted five weeks. The 1950 Pawtucket strike had ended with
a rudimentary contract, one of the first in the nation. The idea
was so far ahead of its time and Pawtucket was such a small,
out-of-the-way city that the teachers' accomplishment had little
impact elsewhere.

The Pawtucket AFT local had remained strong. In the 1950s
there had been another strike, but the outcome had not been
as felicitous as the first one. The school committee had gone
to court for an injunction. Under the threat of heavy fines the
strike had been called off. The union had then tried and failed
to win the right to strike in the courts, but the teachers had
been forced into sullen silence.

Gregory Coughlan lingered around UFT headquarters for
most of the day. I could see that he was assessing the appli-
cability of the new ideas to Pawtucket. Thus, it was not entirely
a surprise when in the fall of 1964, Cogen received a telegram
from Coughlan. Coughlan was now president of the union, and
it had voted a strike to begin the next day.

I urged Cogen to leave for Rhode Island at once. The bargaining movement was gaining momentum, and it was impor-

tant to show that the AFT supported its locals. The best way to show support was to have the national president marching on picket lines, speaking at strike rallies and issuing defiant press statements.

Cogen, however, was a modest militant. He rejected the role of roving cheerleader. James Mundy and I left immediately for the scene of the coming walkout.

Pawtucket is an old New England mill town, and the dingy, red brick factories are still standing. Most of its people are of Irish, Italian or Portuguese derivation. They are lower-middle-class, hard-working and home-loving. Everybody knows everybody else.

Mundy and I were picked up at the airport and whisked off to a rally. I said the things visiting union officials say on such occasions: "representing President Cogen"—"complete support"—"just demands"—"solidarity"—"stay united and we will win!" There were the usual cheers. Then a teacher stood up and walked to the front. He reminded the others of the previous strike—the one that had been suppressed in the courts during the mid-fifties. I groaned inwardly. It was not the time to talk of defeats.

But the speaker went on. Gradually I realized that he was not speaking against the strike. He was calling for support.

"I didn't go out last time," he said. "You all know that. But I am going out and staying out this time." There were more cheers, but he cut them off.

"If any of you is thinking of going in to work," he continued, "I just want you to know what it means. For seven years nobody said hello or good morning. Nobody spoke to me during all that time unless it was absolutely necessary. Until you've been through it you don't know what it means. This time I'm going out!" There was a moment of silence. He walked back to his seat as the teachers applauded wildly.

The strike went on for a week. As expected, the school committee went to court for an injunction, which was granted and served. A strikers' rally was called. The teachers were asked to meet in front of the city hall. When all had assembled, Gregory Coughlan stepped to the microphone. He first praised his colleagues for their courage. Then he placed his picket sign on the steps of the building and asked the others to do the same.

When the teachers had completed their sad march, deposited their signs and reassembled, Coughlan drew a piece of paper from his pocket and read carefully. "The strike is now officially over," he said. "We have complied with the judge's order. However, the dispute which caused this work stoppage has not been resolved, and until it is, I for one will not resume my teaching duties." A great shout went up, and Coughlan walked away with most of the teachers following behind him.

The stoppage continued without pickets; strike headquarters was moved across the state line to Massachusetts. But Rhode Island is an intimate and informal state. Its public officials are never as remote from the people as they are in many other states. After a few days Governor John Chaffee called in representatives of the school board and the union to meet with him in the historic old state house. Overcoming the resistance of the school board, Chaffee patiently worked through the points at issue. As each disagreement was resolved the governor carefully wrote the terms on a yellow pad. When at last his mediation was finished he had produced the first holograph—collective bargaining contract for teachers—and written by a state governor at that!

Everybody signed the yellow sheets, and the governor signed as witness. Then we all left. The school committee did not offer to shake hands with the teacher representatives. Neither did the teachers make such an offer. Memories are long in Rhode Island.

# Chapter 11

---

# BUILDING THE STRUCTURE

## ANATOMY OF A MASS MOVEMENT

There are hundreds of "tales from the teacher wars." Those told here were selected because they give a sense of how it was and because they tell of events which I know about personally.

There are seventeen thousand school districts in the United States, and at least a thousand felt the effects of the teacher rebellion directly—through strikes, near-strikes or hard-fought representation contests. Perhaps another two or three thousand districts experienced the effects of the movement in milder forms. However, because many of the districts which saw militant teacher activity were large, big-city systems, it is no exaggeration to say that a clear majority of the nation's teachers were involved.

The teacher rebellion was a nationwide upheaval carried on at the local level, district by district. There was no epic theme which created a movement from these struggles, as in the civil rights and antiwar movements, which took place during the same period. The goals of the embattled teachers were the usual worker goals—higher wages, better benefits and improved working conditions. Perhaps the ultimate goals were higher status and dignity. Thus, the teacher rebellion was like an echo of the great worker rebellion of the 1930s, delayed thirty years.

Nick Zonarich, the director of organization for the IUD, often came from Washington to New York City to sit in on UFT delegate assembly meetings in those early days. Zonarich had been forced to leave school to work in the coal mines and the steel mills. He had participated in many union battles when the CIO was gathering strength. He marveled at the fierce militancy of the teacher delegates. Invariably he would exclaim after a meeting, "God damn, Dave! These don't sound like college graduates. They sound like coal miners!" It was this sense of worker solidarity which gave the diffuse militant teacher movement its unity.

In spite of the long effort by the educational associations to convince teachers that they were professionals far removed from the need for unions and the necessity for collective bargaining, the increased stress in the schools during the postwar period forced teachers to acknowledge that they were workers. Throughout the 1960s and into the 1970s, the AFT was the organizing force behind the teacher rebellion, driving it forward and giving it coherence even when the movement spread far beyond the borders of the union. I consider myself fortunate to have been able to participate in it.


SETTLING IN

In September, 1964, when Charles Cogen and I began our administration of the AFT, the union's headquarters was located in a renovated brownstone in Chicago at the edge of the Near North Side entertainment district. President Megel had proudly acquired the building for the union a few years earlier.

Originally the house had been the home of a branch of Chicago's famous McCormick family. Its three stories still retained some of the original panelling and parquetry. There was even a small, sedately moving elevator. A previous occupant had been a sporting goods company, and some of the rooms were still covered with wallpaper featuring sporting themes.

The contrast between the modest office of the AFT and the headquarters of the NEA on Sixteenth Street in the nation's capital signified the basic problem confronting the AFT. The Federation not only had to battle against school boards and administrators, but it had to contend against an entrenched rival which far outnumbered it. The NEA possessed all the trappings of success. Although the collective bargaining war was being fought district by district over local issues, the prestige of the Association gave it an advantage which the Federation could not match. The union's central organization was inadequate. AFT organizing pamphlets were poorly written and unattractively printed. Its monthly publication, *The American Teacher*, was stodgy and filled with amateurish diatribes culled from local union newsletters, and pictures of award presentations and banquets, one looking like the other, were scattered through its pages. The union issued only occasional research studies, and these were often of questionable validity.

In addition to James Mundy, the director of organization, the professional staff consisted of Robert Porter, the national secretary (title later changed to secretary-treasurer); Pete Schnaufer, a presidential aide; and George Reuter, the research director, who was on long-term leave to look for another job. Out in the field there were five organizers. That was the entire staff.

It took more than two years to revise the Federation's image and to overhaul its headquarters operation. The first step was to replace the research director with someone capable of producing studies which would contribute to the union's reputation. In fairness, it must be said that the union's limited funds was the main obstacle to building a better staff.

Pete Schnaufer was shifted to research director, where he produced studies which helped build the union's reputation and opened up new areas for progressive activity. David Elsila, a professional editor and teacher from Michigan, was put in charge of the *American Teacher*, which became an upbeat, attractive paper. Patricia Strand, another professional journalist, became Elsila's assistant.

The Federation also began publishing a professional quarterly, *Changing Education*. I recruited a board of directors, which included well-known educational and public figures. I envisioned a provocative publication like the *Nation* in tone and format but restricted to educational matters. Unfortunately, *Changing Education* was not able to fulfill my hopes because of lack of funds, but even so, it helped round out the union's image.

The AFT's organizing effort remained under Mundy's direction, but new organizers were hired as quickly as funds permitted. In addition, John Schmid, a skilled organizer and troubleshooter, was made director of state organizations to improve the Federation's functioning at that level. Robert Lieberman, who had demonstrated his flare for publicity activities in St. Louis, became the AFT's public relations director.

When the changes in the national office were complete, the AFT had an extraordinarily effective headquarters and organizing team. The organization had a new vitality and progressive thrust. It had become a worthy competitor for the Association in spite of the union's diminutive size. I had not thought that the AFT would replace the NEA as the chief spokesman for the nation's teachers, but the union had gone a long way toward achieving "equal billing."

## AFT DEMOCRACY

During the overhaul of the Federation's staff, attention was also given to strengthening AFT democracy. I assumed that a democratic organization would be more attractive to teachers than a bureaucratic organization like the NEA.

The founders of the AFT had drawn up a constitution which reflected their liberal, democratic faith. The highest authority was the membership. Its will was expressed at the annual convention, or by referenda. Delegates to the convention were elected by each local according to a weighted membership formula designed to prevent larger locals from exerting undue influence.

Every two years the convention elected a president and a number of vice-presidents who comprised the executive council. The council was expected to carry out policy adopted by the convention or by referenda. It was to extemporize policy only when necessary. To reduce costs, the council met only a few times a year. An executive committee of the council met more frequently. The council also elected a secretary-treasurer, who was intended originally to be the operating head of the union. During the Megel administration, however, the secretary-treasurer was down-graded, and the president became the head of the union in fact as well as in name.

The simple, straightforward plan of the Federation had several internal flaws. Under the referendum procedure, extremely important if the union was to maintain its grass-roots vitality as it continued to grow, the ballots were mailed to the president of each local. The president was responsible for distributing them to the members and returning them to the national office.

There were many chances for error and manipulation in the referendum procedure. Packets of ballots often went astray in the mail. Sometimes local presidents did not bother to distribute the ballots, or if marked, to return them to the national office in time to be counted. In larger locals where mailing to members was costly, the presidents or other officers often marked the ballots without consulting with members. At my insistence, the council improved the referendum procedure by mailing a ballot to each member, with a secret, two-envelope return. At the time, the NEA did not have a national referendum procedure.

At Schnaufer's suggestion, I also persuaded the council to establish an internal review board to hear complaints by members about the functioning of any local, state or national officer or employee. Members who thought they had been unfairly treated could bring charges before the review board and get a fair hearing. If the board thought a complaint had merit, remedial action could be recommended. To insulate the board from possible influence by the union, its members were from outside the Federation. Its first five members were from religious, civil liberties and civil rights groups.

Another democratic change was in the budget procedure. Budgets had been classified documents to make sure that the NEA did not gain information which would be damaging. The budget was usually presented to the executive council at a meeting immediately following the convention, affording no chance for review by the delegates.

This secretive procedure was changed by submitting the proposed budget to the council well in advance of the convention. With the changes made by the council, the proposed budget was distributed to all convention delegates. The final budget was then approved by the postconvention meeting of the executive council as before.


## A FAILED REFORM

I tried to make the executive council itself more representative by having seven of the fifteen vice-presidents elected by regional voting instead of having them elected at-large by the convention every two years. As a result of the at-large system, all vice-presidents were often from the same caucus. There was no representation of minority views.

I proposed that seven of the vice-presidents be elected by the members in designated regions. The boundaries of the regions would be set by the American Arbitration Association to prevent gerrymandering.

The regional vice-president plan brought on my first collision with Shanker. The UFT by then comprised more than a fifth of the union's total membership. Its support was thus crucial in the at-large election. Under the regional plan, that support would still be crucial for election of eight of the fifteen vice-presidents, and for its regional vice-president. Thus, even if the remaining six regions chose to elect vice-presidents opposed to the UFT, the New York local would still have a three-fifths majority.

Shanker had become a vice-president in the 1966 sweep of the council positions by the Progressive Caucus. Before presenting the area vice-president plan to the council, I consulted with Shanker and got his agreement. At the council meeting, however, one of the vice-presidents suggested that the regions be comparable in area, rather than membership. When another vice-president supported this change, Shanker withdrew his backing, and the plan was defeated.

The close relationship between Shanker and me had cooled somewhat by that time, but the attempt to institute regional vice-presidents was the first time we took opposite sides on an issue.

# Chapter 12

## BECOMING PRESIDENT

### COGEN LEAVES

The AFT continued to grow during the 1960s. At the start of the decade the union's membership was sixty thousand. When Cogen and I went to Chicago four years later, it was a hundred thousand, largely due to growth in New York. Four years after that, the Federation's size approached a hundred and seventy-five thousand members. In eight years, the AFT's size had almost tripled. The Federation had become the bargaining agent in New York, Chicago, Philadelphia, Detroit, Boston, Kansas City, Cleveland, Washington, D.C., Newark, Toledo and many other cities.

The union had also gained prestige. AFT leaders were frequently called on to be speakers and panelists at educational conferences. Although our Chicago headquarters was away from the media centers in New York and Washington, the AFT's name was frequently mentioned in news stories about educational matters. Gaining "equal billing" with the NEA was close to reality.

Yet, Charles Cogen was not happy. He had never shown a zest for union politics. He was not a hail-fellow-well-met. His interest in the functioning of the national union was minimal, and he was increasingly reluctant to engage in new ventures.

Furthermore, Charles Cogen was a New Yorker. His family and friends were all in the East. In Chicago, he was only a visitor. He was largely indifferent to the bustling life of the midwestern city. He had never learned to drive. Consequently, every journey, inside Chicago or outside, had to be planned with meticulous care: hotels, meals, meetings and conferences.

Bored with the humdrum of office routine and endless meetings in an alien land, with little sustaining purpose, Charles Cogen dangled in space. He had been wrenched from his familiar New York City and flung into the universe of the national union.

Inevitably, Cogen's psyche rebelled. He began to have difficulty staying awake in the office and when presiding at meetings. Often one had to wait long minutes for an answer to a routine question while he struggled to bring his mind to bear on the problem at hand. He sought medical advice and was prescribed a drug to make him more alert, but it was an uphill struggle.

Midway in his second term, I asked Cogen if he intended to run again when the convention met the following summer. My question hit him with great force. No one who has achieved a position of honor and prominence lightly considers putting it aside. When Cogen's answer came it was a barely audible, "No."


MOVING UP

When I asked Cogen whether he was going to run for reelection to a third term I had not yet decided to run in his stead. I had been the behind-the-scenes operator for so long that I was hesitant about stepping out in front. My first thought was to look for another leader to replace Cogen so that I could continue in my customary role. I asked Mary Ellen Riordan, the president of the Detroit Federation of Teachers, to run.

Riordan would have been an excellent national president. She was an appealing leader with a confident political touch and a knack for public appearances. Whereas Cogen often appeared cautious and uncertain, Riordan exuded confidence and charm. Her midwestern background and her gender were also assets. The AFT needed a president with wide appeal. Two-thirds of the nation's teachers are women. I thought I could work with her in much the same way I had worked with Cogen, but Riordan flatly refused to be a candidate. She said there was still too much work to be done in Detroit, and she also wanted to be available to help her elderly mother.

I next talked to Robert Porter, the AFT secretary-treasurer. Porter was well-liked throughout the union, particularly in the Midwest. I admired his pragmatic good sense and his strong liberal commitment. I was quite sure I could work with him. I told him that if he wanted to run for president, I would back him, but that if he did not want to run I would run myself.

Porter's response was direct: he would not run and he would support me. Buoyed, I looked over the field for possible competitors. Only John Ryan, president of the Philadelphia Federation of Teachers, appeared to be a threat.

Ryan had led the Philadelphia local to a spectacular victory in a collective bargaining election in 1965. He was young, personable, highly intelligent and an excellent speaker. Even though I got along well with Ryan on a personal basis, however, I knew he was too conservative politically for me to be his assistant if he were to become president. I therefore proposed that he back me for two terms, after which he would have my support. I was gambling on being able to accomplish my main objectives in the four years which would be available. Ryan agreed.

And so, in August, 1968, I headed for the AFT convention in Cleveland, a candidate for elective union office for the first time since I had become president of the Dearborn Federation of Teachers.

## Part III

---

## MILITANCY MATURES

# Chapter 13

## UNITY PROBES

It is 11:30 at night in Cleveland's worn-out downtown district. From the rostrum in a large meeting room in the Sheraton Hotel I am looking out over several hundred Progressive Caucus delegates to the 1968 AFT convention. They are waiting for me to finish speaking so they can go to a party. I have been chosen by the caucus as its candidate for president of the union. I am about to give my acceptance speech.

Usually such speeches are mere curtsies, noncontroversial generalities designed not to alienate possible supporters. I have another purpose. I want to move the union onto a new course.

I begin by talking about the great changes the Federation could bring to education through collective bargaining: drastic reductions in class size; psychological and remedial programs for troubled children; experimental programs to utilize teacher creativity; higher salaries; better pensions; and other benefits. I refer to the More Effective Schools program I had helped develop when I worked in New York. It is a carefully designed plan for upgrading education for children in low socioeconomic areas.

I say that such sweeping changes could not be brought about unless much more money were allocated to the schools. I estimate that educational expenditures would have to be increased at least a third. Then I ask a rhetorical question. "Do you think that's pie in the sky?" I pause, then answer, "Well, I don't!"

*My audience thinks I am indulging in high-flown oratory, but they applaud anyway. I try to make them believe.*

"I mean it. We will need to increase most school budgets by at least a third, and we can do it, but not by local collective bargaining alone. There just isn't that kind of money lying around in most school districts, and there isn't enough taxing power to get it if there were. There isn't even enough money at the state level in most cases. What is needed is multi-level bargaining: local, state and national."

*Now the delegates are genuinely puzzled. Many of them do not yet have ordinary district-level bargaining. What do I mean, "multi-level bargaining?" I go on.*

"When the UAW bargains with General Motors, it doesn't just bargain at the plant level. It bargains with representatives of the corporation's board of directors. It bargains with Chevy, Oldsmobile, Fisher Body and so on. It also bargains over conditions at each plant. That's the way it should be for us, too. We should bargain with Congress and the national administration, with the state governments and at the school district level. Otherwise, it's like going after an elephant by shooting him in the leg."

*Now the delegates are thoroughly mystified. What am I talking about?*

"How are we going to do all that?" I demand. "Well, obviously you can't do it as long as teachers are divided into two warring organizations that are more concerned with fighting each other than they are in creating schools where teachers can teach and children can learn. Effective multi-level bargaining can only be achieved through teacher unity, by building a single, powerful organization to which all teachers can belong. The first step toward that objective is merging the AFT and the NEA. Therefore, while we continue to press for collective bargaining at the local level as the best means available now to win benefits and a share in policy making, we must remember that teacher unity is our larger goal."

*I pause for a moment for effect. I have been speaking in a passionate, intense tone, trying to pull my listeners along with me. Now I drop my voice. "If I am elected president of the AFT at this convention, my highest priority will be to bring about the merger of the American Federation of Teachers and the*

*National Education Association. I intend to appeal directly to the leaders of the NEA to meet with us to explore the possibility of merger. If they do not respond, I will appeal directly to the teachers of the nation in the hope that they will force their leaders to support unity."*

The response from the caucus delegates is overwhelming. I have shown them a new vision of the future. At that moment, the leadership of the AFT stands solidly behind the unity-through-merger strategy.

## PORTENTS

AFT conventions are hectic events, particularly in the even-numbered years, when the president and vice-presidents are elected. In addition to the daily morning and afternoon business sessions, there are countless committee meetings, caucus meetings, special events and parties which go on far into the night.

Because of the crowded agenda, candidates for AFT president are allowed only five minutes to address the convention. I used my time to deliver a condensed version of the speech I had given to the Progressive Caucus. Neither of my opposing candidates—Edward Bolstad, the executive director of the Minnesota Federation of Teachers, or Zeline Richard, a dynamic woman from Detroit—addressed the teacher issue, but the themes they talked about were portents of future happenings.

Bolstad, who was supported by the remnants of the National Caucus, stressed the need for greater cooperation between elected officials and staff—particularly the organizers. I took his remarks as an indication that some staff members were opposed to the new direction I was taking. Richard, on the other hand, stressed the need for community control of schools and opposition to the Vietnam War. She was the candidate of the left-leaning United Action Caucus.

The result of the election was no surprise to anyone. The superior forces of the Progressives delivered a majority—although small—over the combined vote for Bolstad and Richard. I knew that my victory was as much the product of politics as it was an endorsement of my AFT-NEA merger strategy, but at least I had put everyone on notice.

Yet, there were signs of trouble ahead. One sign was a heated floor debate over a resolution calling for community control of schools. It was favored by almost all the black delegates and by the left-wing caucus, but opposed by several big city delegations, especially the UFT. The community control issue had significance primarily in larger school districts with de facto segregated schools. Such schools are usually less effective than others. By giving the communities in which these schools are located control over important aspects of school functioning, community control advocates argue, student achievement would improve.

Although teachers recognized the importance of establishing community links, they were fearful of becoming scapegoats for the shortcomings of their schools. The first experiment in community control in a small area of New York had already resulted in hostility between community leaders and the UFT, and greater conflict seemed about to occur. The convention resolution, after intensive debate, was amended to avoid sanctioning outright "control" while calling for greater community involvement in school policy making.

Another bad omen was a struggle over raising the per capita dues paid to the national union by the locals. Even though it was clear that the national union needed more money to expand the nationwide collective bargaining campaign, Shanker strongly opposed the increase. The dues motion went to a roll call vote, an attenuated process. The senior delegate from each local gets the ballots from the election committee and distributes them among the local's delegates present at the convention, as equally as possible. The ballots are marked and given to the senior delegate who returns them to the committee.

I was one of the delegates from the United Federation of College Teachers (UFTC) from New York. The ranking delegate was Israel Kugler, a longtime friend. Kugler obtained the ballots from the election committee and divided them into equal shares for the delegates attending the convention. Because he did not see me in the room at the time, however, he marked my share—but he marked them as opposed to the dues increase even though I had been leading the floor fight for it.

According to the report by the election committee, the roll call had failed by one vote. But then I learned, from an AFT staff member who had overheard Kugler reporting to Shanker, that my ballots had been incorrectly marked. I immediately demanded that the UFCT delegation be polled. Cogen, presiding over his last AFT meeting, did not wish to offend Shanker, but he was eventually forced to accede to my point of order. The dues increase was passed.

The struggle over the per capita increase was important because it showed that Shanker's priorities clearly lay with the UFT, not with the national collective bargaining movement. It was a conflict which later was to intensify.

## GROWTH OF AN IDEA

I had not put forward the teacher unity concept impulsively. My first thoughts about combining the two teacher organizations were the result of an incident in 1952, at a banquet honoring Rebecca Simonson, who had been president of the Teachers Guild for the ten years before Cogen was elected. One of the speakers was Johanna Lindloff, a veteran leader of the elementary school teachers. Lindloff referred to the NEA in a complimentary way, and a few Guild zealots booed and hissed.

The redoubtable teacher-warrior rounded angrily on her hecklers. Shaking her finger, she warned that the AFT had a lot to learn from the Association just as the NEA could learn from the union.

In spite of my years of struggle against the Association, I had not developed the hatred for the NEA that many other union activists felt. I found myself agreeing with Johanna Lindloff. Although the NEA was obstructing teacher militancy, it was also benefiting teachers through its research, its advocacy of state and federal aid to education and its liberal attitude toward most educational policy issues.

A few years later, during the New York collective bargaining campaign, I taunted NEA speakers with whom I debated by asking the audience to suppose that each of us had a "doomsday button" which could make the other organization disappear. "I would not use my button," I would say, "because teachers benefit from many of the NEA's activities, but I would not trust my opponent not to use his."

At one point I tentatively proposed to Eric Rhodes, the person in charge of the NEA's New York City campaign, that a merger be worked out between the two local organizations. I pointed out that if the NEA-sponsored Teachers Bargaining Organization and the UFT merged, there would be no need for an election. The new, united organization would have no effective opposition.

My purpose was to get inside the NEA and to join with other militant groups to form a nationwide caucus that would become the dominant influence in the organization. Although the associations were the handmaidens of the administration in most school districts, some of them maintained a fierce militance. In Norwalk, Connecticut and Mamaroneck, New York, for instance, teachers had had work stoppages. Outbreaks of teacher rebellion had occurred in other association districts.

Under the tentative New York City merger proposal, the UFT local would have been affiliated with both national organizations. It would have become the biggest local affiliate of both the AFT and the NEA. Through collective bargaining, the deterioration of the New York City school system could be reversed, the concept of "professional negotiations" could be swept away and the bargaining movement could spread within the Association. If the NEA did not become a union under such an assault, the militant faction might split off to combine with the Federation to form a more effective national union.

I wrote the details of the merger plan and showed it to a few close friends and associates, including Shanker and Richard Parrish, the only black member of the UFT executive board. Shanker had no interest in building a national union; Parrish thought the scheme was too impractical.

I mulled over the New York City merger idea for several days but concluded that I could not get enough support for it. It would be sure to set off a divisive argument which might cost the UFT the coming representation election if the merger were not consummated. It would also be misunderstood in the AFT national office and in the other locals. Reluctantly, I called Eric Rhodes, the NEA staff chief, and told him that I could not arouse any interest in the plan. It would have to be dropped.

The tentative New York City merger plan was an extension of the CATU-Guild merger idea, which had led to the formation of the UFT. It was a decade before its time, and I suspect that if the UFT had given its approval, the NEA would have backed out. The leaders of the Association were even less ready for teacher unity than those in the AFT.


## OTHER UNITY EXPLORATIONS

Although organizing was my immediate concern during my early years at national AFT headquarters, I still kept an eye open for chances to advance the unity cause. When I learned that the 1965 NEA convention would be held in New York City, I tried to take advantage of that lucky coincidence.

My plan was embarrassingly unimaginative. The AFT should have set up a reception for the delegates or have arranged some press-worthy happening such as a picket line. Instead, I decided to hold an open meeting featuring a talk on teacher unity. I enlisted Myron Lieberman as speaker. He had become the coauthor of the most authoritative text on teacher collective bargaining. I called on George Altomare, who had become a vice-president of the UFT, to round up a crew of volunteers to distribute flyers to the delegates to the meeting.

The "meeting" was a complete failure. Altomare was unable to get the flyers distributed because no one was interested in national teacher unity. At the meeting itself, only a spy from the NEA showed up, and he only came to find out what was happening.

Undeterred by my lack of success, I tried again at the next NEA convention. With great difficulty I persuaded Cogen to recommend to the AFT executive council, which would be meeting the week before the NEA's conference, that a telegram be sent to the NEA proposing that the two organizations explore the idea of merger.

The AFT vice-presidents were flabbergasted when Cogen made the merger recommendation. They had been fighting the organizational war so long that they could not visualize its termination. They quickly found a way to defuse the unity scheme. Herrick Roth, a vice-president at the time, moved that the telegram be sent, but with the stipulation that any NEA-AFT merger be within the AFL-CIO. Council members approved the "unity" motion knowing that such a precondition would provide an "easy out" for the Association.

When the AFT telegram arrived at the NEA meeting, the president, Richard Batchelder, read it to the delegates and called for a vote on whether they wanted to "join the union." The response was a thunderous "No!" Ironically, Batchelder became a convert to the unity cause and played key roles in merger drives in California and Florida a few years later.

The abortive AFT merger proposal did put the unity idea in the public domain. Soon after, a more practical series of talks occurred which could have led to AFT-NEA merger. They took place under the auspices of the American Arbitration Association (AAA). The AAA was being called on to conduct representation elections in many school districts as the teacher collective bargaining movement began to spread across the nation. Much confusion had resulted because the rules for each election varied from one district to another. In order to standardize precedures, the AAA asked representatives of the AFT, the NEA and the National Association of School Boards (NASB) to establish a uniform format.

If the negotiations initiated by the AAA had succeeded, teacher collective bargaining rules would have been established and growth would have been accelerated. The interested organizations could have established the new process in a majority of the nation's school districts, and pressure for teacher unity would have increased greatly. But neither the school boards nor the Association was ready for such a leap into the future.

In the American Arbitration Association discussions I was the spokesman for the AFT. John Ligtenberg, the union's general counsel, and James Mundy were also members of the committee. The AFT positions asserted that teachers should have all the rights that were granted to employees in private industry under the National Labor Relations Act and the AAA should function in place of the NLRB.

The NEA was represented by its chief counsel Donald Wollet and two staff members. It was obvious that Wollet was sympathetic to the AFT position. But after meeting over the course of three months, he was forced to declare that "after long and earnest discussion, his client (the NEA) had decided that it could not continue the present discussions." Because the school board association representative had made it clear from the beginning that he was only an observer, the discussions collapsed.

Nevertheless, the arbitration association's initiative was not a total loss. Wollet's interest in the possibility of an AFT-NEA merger had been aroused; two years later, on his own initiative, he arranged a meeting with AFT representatives to talk about the merger idea. The meeting was held in the Drake Hotel in New York City. Again, I was the AFT spokesperson. The others present were Shanker, Rose Claffey, the AFT vice-president from Massachusetts, and Frederick Livingston, Wollet's senior partner.

The discussion proceeded amicably enough. The two lawyers assured the AFT representatives that a majority of the NEA board of trustees—a body which has since been discontinued—was in favor of merging with the AFT. I urged that merger discussions begin as soon as possible, but Wollet and Livingston were never able to follow through.

## THE INSTITUTE FOR TEACHER UNITY

In the spring of 1967, I conceived a new plan for promoting amalgamation of the AFT and the NEA. I called it "The Institute for Teacher Unity." It would be headed by a board that consisted of an executive director and trustees from the AFT and the NEA. The institute would seek members from both teacher organizations. Its purpose would be to develop interest in unity among teachers by issuing a newsletter, holding conferences, placing articles in various publications and public relations activities. To get the institute started, $25,000 to $50,000 would be needed. I hoped that this seed money might come from the IUD or the UAW as a loan or a grant.

The most important task in starting the Institute for Teacher Unity would be to find a suitable executive director. The director should be someone who was knowledgeable in the teacher organization field and who was also in favor of the merger idea. The obvious choice for this position was Myron Lieberman. Lieberman was recognized as the ranking expert on

collective bargaining, and he had also maintained friendly relations with many leaders on both sides of the organizational
fence.

While I was mulling over the best way to approach Lieberman, I learned that he would be passing through Chicago. I
arranged to have breakfast with him at a motel near O'Hare
Airport. I suggested that as a first step he arrange an off-the-
record meeting with NEA leaders. His reaction was so negative,
however, that I refrained from giving him the details of my plan.

A month after my aborted approach to Lieberman, I discussed the idea of the institute with Donald Pierce, an AFT
member from Miami who was also a member of the NEA and
a staff employee of the Dade County Teachers Association. This
meeting was also held at O'Hare. Pierce met with me between
planes on his way back from the NEA convention.

Pierce declared himself a strong supporter of the merger concept, but he was hesitant about giving up his staff job in Miami
for the uncertainty of the institute. The meeting was unproductive, as was a later one in Miami, but I kept in touch with
him. Pierce was far less suitable than Lieberman. He lacked
Lieberman's reputation. Still, if he could become the operating
head of the project, Lieberman might agree to lend his name to
it.

I met with Lieberman again a few weeks before the AFT convention in 1967. This time I laid out my institute plan in detail.
He listened carefully but he was critical and noncommittal. He
said that he wanted to think about it and that I should call him
in a couple of weeks. Again, Lieberman's negative attitude put
me off, and I shelved the Institute for Teacher Unity. Five years
later, however, I gave it another try.


THEORY AND PRACTICE

The theory of the AFT-NEA national merger strategy was based
on the Guild-CATU merger, which had led to formation of the
UFT in New York City. I was convinced that what had worked
in the city would work nationally. I thought that once the unity
goal had been set before them, the nation's teachers would demand that the two organizations work out an amalgamation.

Then, if the Association's controlling cadre of state executive secretaries, administrators and national officials did not respond to teacher demand, militant individuals and whole associations would break away—just as the Hochberg-Parente group had split off from the Secondary School Teachers Association in New York. I called the strategy "merge or split."

It was a challenging theory, but my assumptions did not exactly coincide with reality. New York City was not the nation. The anger of New York City teachers was directed at the New York City Board of Education, which they understood to be the cause of their difficulty and frustration. In the city teacher militancy had a single, clearly visible target, and collective bargaining was a uniquely appropriate remedy for teachers' problems. Nationally, however, educational authority was diffused among 17,000 local school boards, 50 state governments, the federal government and a score of special boards and commissions at all levels. In the nation as a whole, the connection between teacher needs and national teacher unity was not readily apparent.

Would an AFT-NEA merger bring higher salaries for teachers? As state and federal aid was increased over the long run, yes. But teachers were concerned about next year. Would a merger reduce class size and the number of classes a teacher would have to teach each day? Yes, but not immediately. Would merger solve the student discipline problem? More money would permit increasing the number of staff, and this would increase control over students, but the connection with teacher unity was tenuous.

My personal reasons for advocating teacher unity had little to do with the immediate, practical concerns of teachers. I believed that the entire educational system would have to be renovated and reconstructed. This could not be done without a coherent, generally agreed upon philosophy and much more money. Teachers could not be easily motivated by such utopian goals. I also believed that a united teacher organization was essential for building a liberal labor political force similar to those which functioned in most European countries. This objective had scarcely more appeal than my sweeping educational goals, and as I traveled around the country making unity speeches I was forced to rely on other arguments.

Local sources of revenue were running dry, I would point out. Money for schools would have to come from state and federal sources, which could only be increased through united action by teachers. I stressed the inequities in educational quality resulting from reliance on local support of education. Variations in wealth among states and localities were only partially corrected by state "equalization" formulas.

I talked about the duplication of effort involved in maintaining two teacher organizations and the cost of employing large organizing staffs whose main function was to fight each other. Teacher unity would eliminate such wasteful effort. The attention and energies of the united organization's staff could be directed toward helping teachers get good collective bargaining contracts.

The biggest obstacle to merger was the "credibility gap." Why should the big, prestigious Association want to join with the scruffy, little Federation? The source of the credibility gap was directly related to the difference in size between the organizations. This could only be changed by vigorous AFT organizing.

Soon after the AFT's first public announcement of its desire to merge with the NEA, Stanley Elam, editor of the *Phi Delta Kappan* magazine, asked me when I thought the merger would occur. His inquiry was facetious, but I replied seriously that I thought merger would occur when AFT membership passed the two hundred and fifty thousand mark.

When I became AFT president in 1968, AFT membership had just passed a hundred and fifty thousand.


MEMORY TAPE: THE COUNCIL OF ELDERS

*I am sitting in a chair in a waiting room outside one of the small ballrooms in the old Commodore Hotel in New York City. At one end of the room is a blue velvet wall beyond which the AFL-CIO executive council is meeting. I am scheduled to make a brief talk.*

*This morning I have flown to New York from Washington, where AFT headquarters has been relocated. My new assistant, Al Loewenthal, has a wide acquaintance in the labor move-*

ment. Most of his experience has been gained as a member and staff person in the International Union of Electrical Workers (IUEW). I had become acquainted with him when we were both teaching extension classes in labor education for Rutgers University in the 1950s. I had been attracted by his liberal philosophy and his wide knowledge of unionism. When he had applied for the position as my assistant, I had readily hired him. He has used his friendship with AFL-CIO officials to schedule today's appearance.

I think of my previous meetings in the Commodore—the prestrike meeting with George Meany in 1960 and many negotiating sessions during completion of the first New York contract a year and a half later. The once grand hotel was highly favored by union people. George Meany claimed that he had put in the original plumbing himself.

My appearance has the vague purpose of emphasizing that I have replaced Cogen as head of the union. Cogen was thought visionary and unreliable. It is hoped that I will be different. Ironically, probably that perception was based on actions which I had urged him to take.

One of the AFL-CIO staff people emerges from behind the velvet curtain and beckons me into the meeting. I look around this council of elders and recognize many of them: Meany, Lane Kirkland, David Dubinsky, Jacob Potofsky, Paul Hall from the Seafarers, Jerry Wurf from the American Federation of State, County and Municipal Employees (AFSCME), and others.

I am introduced to the council and I thank the members for inviting me to speak to them. I explain the unique organizing opportunity confronting the AFT. I point out that unlike the situation in other industries, most of the teachers are already in another organization, and the AFT's problem is to bring them into the labor movement. I describe my merger strategy and finish by holding out the promise of adding two million new members to the AFL-CIO.

After my brief talk I am accosted by Dubinsky.

"What is your membership?" he asks brusquely.

"A hundred and fifty thousand."

"And how many does this other organization have?"

"About a million."

*Dubinsky gives me a withering look and shambles off. I do not know whether he disapproves more of my presumption or of my folly.*

## CLEARANCE FROM KIRKLAND

As soon as I returned to the AFT national office following my election as president, I issued a public declaration asking the NEA to appoint a committee to meet with the AFT to explore the unity question. I called a press conference to answer questions.

Q: Why do you want to merge the two organizations?

A: Because America's schools are not good enough. Neither the NEA nor the AFT is able separately to bring about the improvements that are needed.

Q: What kind of improvements?

A: We need smaller classes, more remedial programs, better salaries and working conditions to attract better teachers, and many other things.

Q: Do you want to be president of the merged organization?

A: I would renounce that possibility right now if it would help bring about merger negotiations.

Q: What about AFL-CIO affiliation?

A: Teachers could gain many advantages by joining with organizations of other workers. We need that strength, but I would be willing to discuss how affiliation could be worked out without violating anyone's rights or feelings of conscience.

There were many more questions in a similar vein, and my answers were given wide media coverage. The NEA's official response was to the effect that as long as the AFT insisted on affiliation with organized labor there was no use talking about merger. I was convinced that the Association leaders were using the labor affiliation issue as a shield to avoid dealing with other issues. I knew that most NEA officials were not personally opposed to unions. In their legislative activity in Washington and in the state capitals they frequently worked with the labor movement. I knew that in some of the state associations there was strong antilabor sentiment, but I thought that resistance to AFT-NEA merger in most cases stemmed simply from reluctance to disturb the status quo. It was important to clear away the Association's cover so that there could be honest discussion of the merger issue.

In my first "president's column" for the *American Teacher*, the AFT newspaper, I outlined my ideas about teacher unity and gave a detailed explanation of just what AFL-CIO affiliation involved. I pointed out that it was inexpensive—twenty cents per member per month—and that teachers needed the support of friendly organizations. I stressed that AFL-CIO affiliation was voluntary. I pointed out that a union could disaffiliate any time it wanted to, and that some unions had done just that. I was trying to speak not only to the leaders of the Association, but to teachers at the grass-roots level, including Federation members.

Having launched the unity drive, I set up a meeting with Lane Kirkland, then AFL-CIO secretary-treasurer, to explain what I was trying to do. I took to the meeting Shanker; my assistant, Loewenthal; Secretary-Treasurer Robert Porter; and Carl Megel, still functioning as legislative representative.

I first emphasized the need for greater AFL-CIO understanding of the AFT's problem. My main purpose in meeting with Kirkland was to determine what the attitude of the labor federation would be if an AFT-NEA merger were worked out on the basis of partial AFL-CIO affiliation. Under my scheme, state and local affiliates would be permitted to choose whether to affiliate. Those choosing affiliation would be members of an "AFL-CIO Department." Per capita would be paid on the total membership of the organizations in the department.

The model for this hybrid creation was the Industrial Union Department. When the AFL and the CIO were merged in 1955, the IUD was established to give the former CIO unions a "home" within the merged organization. If a similar plan were followed in AFT-NEA amalgamation, many associations in addition to the AFT locals would eventually choose AFL-CIO affiliation. The result would be that AFL-CIO membership would be much larger than the current membership of the AFT. Having an AFL-CIO department within the merged organization also would put a stop to the flow of antiunion propaganda from the NEA. Given a climate favorable to labor affiliation and no difference in dues between affiliated and nonaffiliated locals, membership in the AFL-CIO department would increase until it included most of the members of the merged organization.

Kirkland, a man of swift intellect and judicious temperament, responded by saying that the AFL-CIO had to take the word of its affiliates about the number of members they had. He said that he knew of no instance where affiliates overpaid—a droll reference to unions' shortchanging the national federation on per capita payments. If a union said it had so many members, that was it. Kirkland said the plan was entirely feasible.

Then the secretary-treasurer added a surprising comment. He said he believed that it was so important that the two organizations get together that he would favor a merger *without* affiliation, if it would facilitate the negotiations.

We were dumbfounded. I hastily assured Kirkland that we had no thought of disaffiliating from the AFL-CIO, even temporarily, but that we were pleased by his understanding of our problem.

# Chapter 14

# TALKING UNITY

## PERSONAL DIPLOMACY

For several years after I became president of the union, I tried to establish friendly relations with NEA leaders so that I could talk frankly with them about teacher unity. These efforts did not produce immediate results, but in the process I learned a lot about the Association. I also acquired an appreciation of the very real difficulties that would have to be overcome before merger talks could be successful. One of the main problems was that power was so diffused within the Association that no person or small group could discuss the merger question with any authority.

NEA presidents at that time served single one-year terms. The delegates to the annual representative assembly chose a president-elect who waited in the wings to become president the following year. Every NEA president was, in effect, a lame duck.

When I became president of the AFT, Elizabeth Koontz was the NEA president. I tried repeatedly to arrange a luncheon conference with her, but she proved extremely elusive. Koontz did not return my phone calls, and when I ran into her at Washington social functions, she was polite but aloof.

Finally, I managed to meet Koontz for breakfast at the Statler-Hilton Hotel. The Statler-Hilton has two coffee shops, and I chose the wrong one, a busy, quick-service eatery which was the worst possible place to carry on a serious discussion. I soon realized, however, that the NEA president had only come for breakfast and not for discussing merger. My efforts to talk about teacher unity evoked no response. In forty-five minutes I was out on the sidewalk, exasperated by my failure.

Koontz resigned her presidency after a few months to become head of the Women's Bureau in the Department of Labor. George Fischer, the president-elect, moved into the top spot, and I reinstituted my luncheon campaign.

Fischer was a gregarious, midwestern Association pol. I was more successful with him than I had been with his predecessor. Even so, I found the new president hard to pin down in spite of his friendly manner. He agreed to set up an informal meeting between AFT representatives and the NEA executive committee, but for exploratory purposes only.

This meeting was held in a suite in the Jefferson Hotel on Sixteenth Street across from NEA headquarters. Attending with me were AFT Secretary-Treasurer Robert Porter and William Simons, president of the Washington Teachers Union and an AFT vice-president as well. The NEA was represented by its executive committee. Sam Lambert, the newly chosen executive secretary, was also present.

Drinks were served, and an hour was devoted to small talk before I proposed that exploratory talks on possible AFT-NEA amalgamation begin as soon as possible. I suggested that the talks be private but on the record.

Fischer, apparently speaking by prearrangement, responded by saying that the NEA was not ready to move that fast. The door to teacher unity which had been opened a crack was firmly slammed shut.

After the meeting, Simons, Porter and I stopped for coffee at a hamburger stand. We agreed that we "had a long row to hoe" before a merger could be worked out.


*MEMORY TAPE: A SOCIAL EVENING*

*I am standing in the dining area of my home in suburban Virginia. It is several months after the disappointing meeting with the NEA executive committee. In the light streaming from the windows I can see that it is still snowing. I look at the clock:*

seven o'clock. The phone rings. It is George Fischer, the NEA president.

"Is that you, George?"

"Yes. Say, listen. The streets are covered with snow. I'm calling to let you know that Maggie and I will be a little late. I hope that will be all right."

"Sure, George. No problem."

I had come to like Fischer. I was convinced that he would see the logic of the merger idea if I could explain the details to him—especially the AFL-CIO Department scheme.

An hour or so passes and the phone rings again.

"Dave?"

"Yes, George."

"Maybe we had better call this thing off. We have just crossed the bridge, and traffic is all tied up. It's still snowing hard."

I had tried so long to make contact with an NEA leader that I could not give up this opportunity because of a little snow.

"Use your own judgment," I say. "Everything is all ready, and we don't mind waiting."

There is a pause. "Well, OK. We'll do the best we can."

More time passes. I keep looking out the window at the snow. Bernice and I have been in Washington four years and we have seen nothing like this. We nibble some of the hors d'oeuvres and continue to sip our drinks.

It is ten o'clock. The radio is now saying that we may be experiencing the worst storm in Washington history. I shovel a path to the driveway. I am beginning to worry about the Fischers and I keep looking out toward the street. It is nearly eleven when a car stops in front. I throw on my coat and run out with a flashlight. It is the Fischers at last.

We do our best to make our guests welcome. George immediately gulps down a half-tumbler of bourbon. Maggie accepts a glass of sherry. I build up the fire in the fireplace. We talk excitedly about the storm.

Fischer and I spend the next two hours exchanging stories about our experiences in our respective organizations. Strangely, we have difficulty getting to discussion of the merger question.

At two o'clock in the morning, Maggie says that they should be heading back to Washington. I try to get them to stay all night, but they politely refuse.

"One for the road," I cry desperately. George accepts.

"We never did get down to cases on the merger," I say, my speech just a bit slurred.

Fischer concurs solemnly. He is swaying slightly. "Now, Dave," he says slowly, "just how serious are you about AFL-CIO affiliation?" He watches me narrowly, waiting for my reply.

"I'm serious," I answer, "but there are ways it can be handled."

He shakes his head. "No, Dave. As long as you insist on that, there is no use talking."

So, after all the effort of the night we are back on square one, but I say, "Let's get together again and talk about it. Some time when it isn't snowing!"

"Sure," he replies, but we never do.


## LOCAL UNITY

In my talking and writing about teacher unity I made it clear that I was talking about a nationwide amalgamation. I thought that merging at the local or state level before the national organizations had reached agreement would erode AFT strength by allowing the NEA to neutralize the trouble spots. Such mergers would result in a hodge-podge of conflicting arrangements which would complicate national negotiations later on.

In the spring of 1969, I received an urgent phone call from the leader of the AFT local in Flint, Michigan. He informed me that the local had merged with the Flint Education Association. The teachers were going on strike the following day. There would be a rally, and I and the president of the NEA were being asked to speak. Reluctantly I agreed to come to the Michigan city, where I gave a strong speech of support in spite of my misgivings about local mergers. First things first! I thought. After all, they were on strike.

The Flint merger scheme illustrated the problems inherent in the piecemeal approach to unity. The plan required all Flint teachers to join the Association—local, state and national—but for an extra $10 a year dues they could also be members of the Federation. The Association obviously had got the better of the deal, and a dangerous precedent had been set. More mergers like the one in Flint and the union would be out of business.

In the months following the Flint amalgamation, many local AFT and NEA organizations attempted to unite. This indicated that teacher unity had a widespread appeal, but local urges to unify inevitably ran into financial obstacles. A merger at the local level burdened the new united organization with paying dues for affiliation to the Association and the Federation at the state level and at the national level. This required that membership dues be higher than most teachers were willing to pay. In a nationwide merger, the organization would be unified at all levels, obviating the double dues requirement. Duplicative costs and expensive competitive organizing campaigns would also be eliminated. Perhaps dues could actually be lowered.

As a footnote to the Flint episode, I met the young executive secretary of the Michigan Education Association at the rally. His name was Terry Herndon. He went on to become executive secretary of the NEA a year or so later.

## PART WAY WITH UTLA

One night in the fall of 1969, I received a phone call from Roger Kuhn, a former AFT organizer who was working for the California Teachers Association, Southern Section. Kuhn had incredible news. He said that the Los Angeles Teachers Association was about to propose a merger with the AFT local. Did I have any suggestions?

My disappointing experience in Los Angeles four years before was fresh in my mind. The Federation had since spent nearly $100,000 there with only minimal results. But in spite of this discouraging history and my negative attitude toward local mergers in general, I was excited by Kuhn's call. A merger in Los Angeles would be a great boost for the unity movement.

More important was the undeniable fact that the Association was about to turn the tables on the Federation. The Federation would have to accept the Association's challenge. Refusal would expose the AFT to charges of lack of sincerity about teacher unity in general.

"Sounds good," I finally told Kuhn, trying to sound more enthusiastic than I felt, "but keep me informed."

A week later I received another excited call. This time the caller was Larry Sibelman, the president of the Los Angeles AFT local. Sibelman reported that he had received a letter from Robert Ransom, president of the Los Angeles Teachers Association, proposing a local merger. I did not want to deflate Sibelman by telling him about Kuhn's call, so I responded as though his information was fresh news. We discussed Ransom's letter and finally agreed that Sibelman should respond positively.

The organizational situation in Los Angeles had been almost as frustrating for the Association as it had been for the union. There had been two competing associations. Under Ransom's leadership they had merged and hired Don Baer, a talented organizer from Milwaukee, as executive secretary.

The unified and well-staffed Los Angeles Teachers Association had more than twenty thousand members. It outnumbered the AFT ten to one, but the Association had not been able to win benefits for teachers.

The Federation, under Sibelman's leadership, had begun to rally teachers. The previous June the AFT had called a moderately successful work stoppage. This action had convinced Ransom and Baer of the need for combining forces with the AFT.

The Los Angeles merger negotiations moved rapidly. Sibelman checked new developments with me several times a week. Within a month the proceedings had reached a crucial stage, and I felt it was time other AFT leaders were brought in. I invited Sibelman to New York for a conference. The meeting was held in Joe's Restaurant, a political hangout in downtown Brooklyn. Sibelman and I met with Shanker, Rose Claffey and Robert Porter.

For several hours we discussed every detail of the Los Angeles problem. The proposed plan called for allowing teachers who joined the organization after the merger to choose whether to be affiliated at the state and national levels with the AFT and the state federation or the NEA and the state association.

While this affiliation option avoided paying double per capita dues at the state and national levels, it established a competition which would only end when the Federation or the Association gained complete control—or when there was a national merger. Because the Association had many more members than the Federation, there would be considerable risk involved for the AFT until the odds were evened by organizing more AFT members.

Sibelman was eager to push ahead. The others, veterans of union politics, held back. They did not want to be blamed if the Los Angeles merger backfired later. Before the meeting ended, all agreed that the merger should be consummated with certain modifications.

I suggested that the merger agreement incorporate a strong program for salary increases, fringe benefits and improvements in school conditions. This program was to be backed by a declaration that the new organization would strike if necessary. As events worked out, a strike proved necessary, and after staying out for two weeks, a good settlement was won.

The Los Angeles merger was later given the blessing of the AFT executive council as a "promising experiment in teacher unity." Following the merger, AFT membership grew steadily. The Los Angeles merger gave new credibility to the teacher unity drive, but it also alarmed those in both organizations who were opposed to the unity concept.

As a side effect the Los Angeles amalgamation brought me in contact with Richard Batchelder, former president of the NEA, who was strongly supportive of the merger concept. He later became executive secretary of the Florida Education Association, where he continued to work for the unity cause.

# Chapter 15

## OCEAN HILL-BROWNSVILLE

MEMORY TAPE: TEN YEARS

*I enter the new state administration building in Raleigh, North Carolina. It is 1951 and I have come to Raleigh to explore the possibility of mounting a campaign for a state teacher tenure law. I want to talk with the state attorney-general about how to word the proposed law correctly.*

*I have been trying to organize teachers in North Carolina for nearly a year. Starting in Winston-Salem in response to an inquiry from a local teacher, I had organized small locals in four or five districts, but it had been rough going. The North Carolina Classroom Teachers Association is progressive enough to divert widespread interest in joining the union, but it was far from being a militant champion of teachers' rights.*

*My organizing efforts have also been handicapped by racial barriers. Many of the white teachers are too conscious of their elite position to join a union, and most blacks are afraid of losing their jobs as a result of joining. Nevertheless, I have insisted that all locals be integrated even though the only place in the state to hold a public integrated meeting is at Guilford College, a Quaker school near Greensboro.*

*I walk to the bank of elevators, observing en route a display of Civil War memorabilia: flags, bloodstained uniforms, swords and other artifacts from the Confederate forces.*

*The attorney-general's office is on the tenth floor. I enter the waiting room, give the receptionist my card, and to my surprise* am admitted almost immediately to the inner office. The state official stands and offers a hearty, politician's handshake.

I begin to explain my mission. Before I get very far we are interrupted by the intercom. The attorney-general from Virginia is calling. As I start to leave I am urged to sit down. For the next fifteen minutes I listen to an extraordinary conversation. The two officials discuss in detail a lawsuit involving racial segregation in the schools. Apparently the attorney-generals of many southern states are joining forces to defeat a suit to integrate public schools. The suit involves districts in several states and is backed by the NAACP.

The lawyers discuss their chances of winning in the circuit court. They agree that win or lose the case will go to the United States Supreme Court. They run down the list of the justices, trying to assess how each will vote. They are particularly worried about Justice Felix Frankfurter, considered influential in the Court. They are sure he will be against them, and they speculate about whether he will be able to swing a majority of the Court.

The conversation draws to a close with the North Carolinian conceding that they will probably lose the case, but that it will be ten years before anything would have to be done to comply with the Court's decision.

After a few good-ole-boy pleasantries, the attorney-general returns his phone to its cradle and gives me his attention. With great difficulty I ask my questions about teacher tenure. They no longer seem of great importance. I get the information I need and leave.

In the elevator on my way to the ground floor I am no longer thinking about tenure. My mind is filled with the conversation I have just heard. Ten more years of buying time with legal maneuvers. No, stealing time!

I leave the elevator and walk through the lobby past the cases of Civil War relics. A class of small black children enters the lobby on a tour. In a line, they are dressed in their best clothes, solemn. What will their teacher tell them about the blood-stained uniforms and the rusted weapons? What would she say if she had heard what I have just heard?

I smile ruefully and try to catch the teacher's eye, but her glance passes over me without response.

*Ten more years!*


MARCHING

Although the militant civil rights movement of the 1950s and 1960s and the teacher rebellion had only incidental contact, the impact of racial problems on the schools and teachers was far-reaching and pervasive. Few school districts below the Mason-Dixon Line complied promptly with the Supreme Court's dictum that separate schools for blacks are unequal to white-only schools, and that they should be integrated with all deliberate speed. The whole South adopted a policy of massive resistance in all public institutions, including the schools. Inevitably, the teacher organizations were drawn into the struggle.

The AFT's response to the Supreme Court's desegregation decision was far ahead of its time. Both teacher organizations maintained racially separate locals in the South. But in 1956 the union required all locals to admit to membership all teachers who applied, regardless of race. Although the NEA did not eliminate its segregated locals until ten years later, in fairness it must be pointed out that the Association was faced with a much more difficult organizational problem than the Federation. The AFT had scarcely a dozen locals in the South, but a third of the NEA's membership was in that area. Furthermore, many of the black affiliates feared that blacks, particularly those in administrative positions, would lose their jobs when the separate school systems were combined.

By the 1960s the civil rights struggle had become a widespread militant movement. The AFT had long had a higher proportion of liberals among its membership than the NEA had. Richard Parrish, at the time a prominent member of the UFT, had worked on the plaintiff's brief in the Supreme Court desegregation case. The union had also filed an *amicus* brief. "Freedom schools" for blacks in Mississippi and in Prince Edward County, Virginia, had been organized by the Federation to replace schools which had been shut down to avoid integration. In the great 1963 "March on Washington," four busloads of teachers came from New York, and many came from other areas.

The AFT's civil rights activities, undertaken without organizational motivation for the most part, helped win the support of black teachers, who constituted substantial voting blocks in many collective bargaining elections. In the Philadelphia election, for instance, black teachers comprised nearly a third of the teaching staff. An endorsement of the Federation by Dr. Martin Luther King, Jr. was an important factor contributing to the victory of the Philadelphia Federation of Teachers. The support of black teachers provided the winning margin in St. Louis, Kansas City, New Orleans and many other districts.

## INTEGRATION IN NEW YORK

I had been involved early in the effort to integrate the New York City school system. Soon after the Supreme Court's 1954 *Brown* decision, the board of education had established a large "blue ribbon" commission to prepare a plan for integrating the schools. Paralleling this official body was a smaller, more militant coalition of the city's civil rights and liberal organizations. I worked closely with the coalition.

Integrating the New York City school system proved to be an enormous undertaking which, after years of effort, had scarcely begun. It was doomed from the beginning, but in those days I shared with many the innocent hope that it could be done. I attended dozens of meetings, wrote scores of flyers and position papers and learned the new civil rights movement songs.

The official integration commission, after more than a year of effort, finally persuaded the board of education to adopt an open enrollment plan based on voluntary busing of pupils. Parents were free to put their children on the bus and send them to any school in the city where their attendance would contribute to integration.

Few parents took advantage of the voluntary school busing plan, however. Few parents, black or white, wanted to ship their children away from their home areas for the day for the sake of what was viewed as a social experiment. If there had been careful planning and extensive community involvement, so that large numbers of students would have participated, vol-

untary integration might have worked in some areas. On the
perfunctory basis on which it was offered, however, it did not
stand a chance.

To encourage voluntary transfers of children and teachers,
and to upgrade teaching and learning conditions, in 1962 the
UFT developed its "More Effective Schools" plan. An outstanding union committee met many Saturday mornings to work out
the details. The plan called for increased staffing and educational services in low socioeconomic areas. With great effort
the UFT convinced the school board to initiate the MES plan
in a few schools, but even though the MES schools were successful, the city refused to extend the plan to enough schools
to have much impact on the total problem.

One by one, other plans for voluntary integration—"pairing"
black and white schools, redrawing school attendance district
lines to include more of one race or another, building schools
in areas which were integrated, closing schools in all-black
areas—were tried and discarded. Many liberals who supported
the voluntary and piecemeal integration efforts withheld their
support from the more drastic plans which would be necessary
to make real progress. The city's civil rights movement, never
strongly united, had been weakened by internal disputes and
by appointment of leaders to governmental and other positions
which removed them from the struggle. The assassination of
Dr. King left the integration movement without a universally
accepted leader. Into this policy and leadership void stepped
a most unlikely champion: the Ford Foundation.

## THE BIRTH OF COMMUNITY CONTROL

By coincidence, I was present in a midtown hotel room in September of 1967 when Albert Shanker met with McGeorge
Bundy, president of the Ford Foundation, and Mario Fantini,
a young, innovative educational sociologist in charge of the
Ford Foundation's decentralization project. The two foundation officials were trying to persuade Shanker to support an
experiment in "community control." The experiment would be
carried on in a demonstration project to be set up in a slum

area of Brooklyn encompassing two neighborhoods known as Ocean Hill and Brownsville.

The foundation had been looking for a new, progressive way to spend the flow of money which in those days poured in from its investment portfolio. Since its headquarters was in New York, what better place to spend this accumulating pile than at home? And what better place to begin than the all-pervasive school system.

Over the years there had been many plans to reorganize the New York City public school system. Even plans that got beyond the report stage were never fully implemented. Many of these studies had recommended administrative decentralization, but they had not recommended the shift of real decision-making power downward to grass-roots community representatives.

It took a book to begin the transfer of power from the central board to neighborhood boards. The book was *Reconnection for Learning*, the report of a committee on school reform appointed by Mayor John V. Lindsay soon after his election in 1965. The chairman of the mayor's committee was McGeorge Bundy, formerly the United States Secretary of State. After leaving government, Bundy moved on to head the giant foundation, which underwrote the costs of research and publishing for the committee.

While previous studies had looked at the school system from the top down, as one would examine a multi-purpose corporation, *Reconnection* began with a consideration of how children could be encouraged to learn. It reasoned that if parents had more control over the way schools were run, parents would take more responsibility for their children's educational achievement. The schools would also become more relevant to the needs of the city's children, and blacks and other minorities would gain more power in the city's social structure.

## THE STRUGGLE FOR COMMUNITY CONTROL

Shanker and the UFT, after extensive discussion of the community control proposal, reluctantly agreed to support the Ocean Hill-Brownsville project. Two union representatives

were among the seventeen members on the project's governing
board. Before long it became clear that the other members of
the board regarded the UFT representatives as "the enemy."
This attitude by the community control advocates was bewil-
dering to most teachers. It seemed grossly unfair because the
teachers had fought city hall and the school authorities for years
to gain school improvements, and yet now they were considered part of the city's oppressive power structure.

After trying unsuccessfully to improve their relationship
with the other members of the Ocean Hill-Brownsville board,
the union representatives resigned. With the formal relationship between the UFT and the governing board severed, a showdown became inevitable. In May of 1968, nineteen teachers and
minor supervisors were removed by the demonstration district
superintendent from their positions and told to report to the
central headquarters of the school system. They were said to
be "uncooperative" or to have a "bad attitude." Within a day,
some of those dismissed were allowed to return to their jobs.
Those recalled were black; those who were not recalled were
white. Increasingly, the struggle for community control was
polarized into a black-white racial clash.

A hidden but powerful issue in the community control struggle was the strong attack by the procommunity forces on the
city's competitive examination system for filling teaching and
supervisory positions in the schools. Reflecting immigration
trends, first teachers of Irish, then Italian and finally Jewish
background were appointed to the instructional staff through
operation of the examination system in the 1920s, 1930s and
1940s. In spite of their increasing numbers following World
War II, however, blacks and Puerto Ricans did not benefit. One
of the objects of the community control movement, therefore,
was to change or eliminate the examination system so that
school staffs could become more representative of the racial
composition of the areas in which the schools were located.

The attack on the examination system was seen by some as
an attempt to go back to the spoils system, while for others it
raised the spectre of centuries of discrimination against Jews.
More concretely, it was a threat to literally thousands of job or
promotion seekers who had already passed examinations and
were on lists waiting for appointment, or who were working

their way through the attenuated procedure in order to get on a list. It was mainly because of the threat to the examination system that the Council of Supervisory Associations backed the UFT throughout the Ocean Hill-Brownsville episode.

I became involved in the community control struggle in the spring of 1968, when Shanker discussed the teacher dismissals with me. I was deeply concerned because of the effect the conflict was having on AFT national interests. It had long been part of teacher union doctrine to establish a teacher-community alliance in order to force the politicians and other power brokers to grant more money for education. The Ocean Hill-Brownsville fight would preclude UFT cooperation with supporters of the community control side and might set up negative reverberations not only in New York but in other cities, too.

Entering the dispute, I found that it had become so embittered that the UFT was faced with only two alternatives: allow UFT members to be summarily removed from the jobs, not only in the Ocean Hill-Brownsville project, but in any subsequent community control districts; or call a strike in the demonstration district in the hope that the governing board would reinstate the teachers pending the outcome of hearings and arbitration. For a union, the first alternative was unthinkable, and so the limited work stoppage was called.


## THE LONG STRIKE

Most of the teachers in the demonstration district supported the strike, which continued throughout the closing month of the 1967–68 school year. The superintendent of schools appointed a respected retired judge to hold hearings, but the Ocean Hill-Brownsville governing board refused to recognize the superintendent's action. It maintained that it had the right to manage the affairs of the district, regardless of what the union contract said.

In early July the judge ruled that the transfers had not been justified. The governing board maintained that since it had not agreed to the arbitration procedure, it was not bound by the result. The citywide board of education and the superintendent of schools, not visibly displeased to see the union in such a trying situation, did nothing to alleviate the problem. In July, the board held a hearing which was dominated by hundreds of school children who stamped their feet and clapped in unison. I found it a frightening and disheartening experience, almost like training for fascism.

In my remarks to the school board I demanded that the board resolve the Ocean Hill-Brownsville conflict by its own action or by some form of third-party intervention. But the board allowed the community board to hire a hundred and fifty teachers to replace those who had been on strike at the close of the previous school year. Now it was not just a dozen teachers who had been transferred without notice; it was one hundred and fifty teachers who were being fired outright.

The union and the central board stiffened their positions, and public alarm began to mount. As long as the dispute involved only a thousand or so black and Puerto Rican children and one hundred and fifty teachers in a slum in Brooklyn, city and school authorities would do nothing to resolve the conflict. To the union, it appeared that the only way to get action was to extend the strike to the entire city. A citywide strike was therefore set to begin on the opening day of school in September.

The day before the deadline, Mayor Lindsay called a meeting of the two sides. A small army of participants in the struggle—the UFT executive committee, the Ocean Hill-Brownsville governing board, the central board of education and many school and city officials—occupied city hall for most of the day.

I worked to find a formula for averting the approaching battle. After hours of intricate diplomacy, a shaky compromise was reached. Then the chairman of the governing board, in answering questions put to him by a crowd of reporters as he was leaving city hall, seemed to contradict what had been agreed to just a few minutes earlier. A UFT member who heard the impromptu press conference rushed back to the meeting room to tell Shanker what had happened. Shanker was incensed. In a rage he stalked out to meet with the press. He heatedly denounced the governing board chairman and left city hall. The Ocean Hill-Brownsville strike was on.

The Ocean Hill-Brownsville struggle will haunt the participants as long as they live. On one side were the UFT and the teachers, supported by school supervisors and their organizations, most of the city's labor movement and a good share of the city's Jewish population. On the other side were the Lindsay Administration, the Ford Foundation, the Civil Liberties Union, every known leftist in the city and almost all of the city's black leaders. City and school officials could have prevented the strike but they did not. Even after the strike had begun, there were several truces which offered additional chances for settlement. In each case the truce was broken and hostilities were resumed.

Mayor Lindsay could have insisted that the governing board abide by the simple rules of due process, but he did not. Although New York City is strongly Democratic, Lindsay, a Republican, had been elected while the Democrats were fighting among themselves. Lindsay knew he would have to find a winning constituency if he were to be reelected in 1969. He wanted to build a coalition of blacks, Puerto Ricans, liberals and Republicans. The governing board and its allies had become the gatekeepers to Lindsay's political future, and he could not risk alienating them.

The strike polarized the city ethnically and racially. Both sides fanned the flames of prejudice. Crude homemade handbills containing anti-Semitic references were distributed on picket lines. Two such flyers were cut-and-pasted together in UFT headquarters to make up a particularly scurrilous anti-Semitic leaflet. A half million copies were run off in the UFT's print shop. They were distributed at subway entrances and shopping centers by UFT staffers and volunteers. The leaflet united the city's Jewish population behind the UFT. Shanker denied any prior knowledge of the flyer operation.

The Ocean Hill-Brownsville strike dragged on for 13 weeks. The dismissed teachers were restored to their jobs. The thousands of teachers who struck to support them were allowed to make up lost time and they suffered no loss of pay. Six months later the UFT and the city signed the famous "Christmas tree" contract, which provided spectacular increases in salaries, fringe benefits and working conditions for a three-year period. When he finished reporting the terms to the delegate assembly, Shanker said, "Some of you wondered why it was necessary to stay out so long last fall when there seemed to be no salary or other economic issue involved." He paused for dramatic effect, and then concluded, "Now you know."

Shanker's implication that the Ocean Hill-Brownsville strike had been only a power struggle between the union and the blue-blooded mayor was certainly not the way those who had participated in that agonizing conflict saw it.


## THE AFTERMATH

The effects of the Ocean Hill-Brownsville strike were profound. The advocates of community control had intended the demonstration district to be the beginning of an expanding movement which would change racial relationships throughout the nation. The UFT strike weakened the movement in New York and sent up warning signals which alerted opponents of the concept nationwide.

Following the strike, bills were introduced into the legislature to divide the huge city school system into 32 autonomous school districts. Under the plan, each community district would have the right to elect its own school board, determine the details of its own budget, hire and fire its own teachers and supervisors and establish its own policies. Although the community districts did not have taxing power, they were to be treated as separate districts for state aid purposes, which would greatly increase the amount of available funds in the poorer areas of the city and probably decrease funds in other areas.

As a result of intense lobbying by the UFT, the proposed legislation was changed to provide for central hiring of teachers and uniform taxing and budgeting throughout the city. The elected community boards were retained, but within a few years the UFT had developed a powerful political machine which made the union the controlling force in most community elections.

The Ocean Hill-Brownsville struggle consolidated Shanker's control of the UFT, which in turn led to his control of the national union. It also made him a local, and to some extent national, political figure. Day after day during the strike, he had appeared on television and in the press, defending the teachers and the union against the attacks of interviewers. He drove home his points in direct, unmistakable terms. There was no one else who even approached his following among teacher union members.

Those few teachers and liberal leaders who sided with the community control forces were forever damned in the eyes of Shanker and the UFT. A few of them had tried to reopen some of the schools during the strike. Some had taught a makeshift class or two, but they were far from being antiunion hirelings of management. They did not deserve the epithets directed at them by teachers. Torn between their commitments to unionism and the civil rights movement, they had sided with the governing board from a sincere desire to help blacks and other minorities gain a measure of justice and dignity. But to the UFT, they forever became "scabs, strikebreakers and Communists."

One of the victims was Bella Abzug. Abzug had participated in an effort to reopen the High School of Music and Art during the strike. Shanker and the UFT subsequently tried to defeat her in Congressional elections. If she had been content to stay in the House of Representatives, she would probably still be there. However, she ran for mayor in 1973 and for the senate in 1976. The opposition of Shanker and the UFT contributed to her defeat in each case. The victors in these contests were Abraham D. Beame, for mayor, and Daniel Patrick Moynihan, for senator. Mayor Beame supported budget cuts which caused class size increases. Senator Moynihan became a champion of tax credits for private school tuition, a device opposed by both the AFT and the NEA.

Following settlement of the Ocean Hill-Brownsville strike, I suggested to Shanker and other UFT leaders that they try to mend their relations with black and Puerto Rican community leaders. I suggested that Richard Parrish, the longtime executive board member and civil rights activist, be made "vice-president for community relations." During the strike Parrish had formed a black caucus of teachers at Shanker's suggestion. Instead of giving total support to the UFT, as Shanker had expected, the caucus issued a statement supporting the community control concept in general terms and urged the union to work for speedy settlement of the strike. Parrish was subsequently expelled from the Unity Caucus mainly for his failure to control his group.

The Ocean Hill-Brownsville strike also had a strong adverse effect on the teacher unity movement. The Association's black leaders, citing the UFT's opposition to community control as antiblack, strongly opposed merger talks. Also, the top NEA officials hoped the strike would have a negative effect on AFT organizing and decided to wait and see what would happen.

The strike, while enhancing Shanker's power, was also a watershed in his public career. Never again would the former Socialist be able to get back on the high road of progressivism.

As for the children, in whose name the battle of Ocean Hill-Brownsville had been fought, they were left much as before, mired in the hopelessness of their ghettoes.

# Chapter 16

## THE UFT MACHINE

### THE UNITY CAUCUS

In my days as general factotum of the union in New York I was devoted to making the apparatus of union government work democratically. The officers, none of whom were paid by the union, met every Wednesday after school. Twice a month the executive board, consisting originally of thirty-five members, but enlarged to fifty-five when the UFT was formed, met in the evening. The delegate assembly met every month. There were membership meetings at least four times a year.

Then there were the committee meetings. Committees are the essence of democracy. They are needed to produce group decisions, but it is not easy to make them function. I worked hard to build "The Elementary School Committee," "The High School Committee," "The Sick Leave Committee," "The Teacher Examinations Committee" and a host of others. Some worked well, and others always were being reorganized. Committees get people involved, however, and the more involvement of members there is, the stronger the union is.

After I left New York for the national headquarters in Chicago, I began to hear disquieting complaints that the UFT committees were falling into disuse. I asked Shanker if he could not involve more members in the functioning of the union. He replied that it was better to let staff handle most matters. The members would be better served; that was what they paid their dues for. Very few members ever attended committee meetings anyway. Furthermore, he said, letting staff handle problems formerly handled by committees let members know whom to hold responsible. If they didn't like the way the union was being run they could get a new president.

Yet, unions can become political machines, and that is what happened to the UFT. Although most of the basic committees continued to exist on paper, their function declined as time passed. The number of staff persons increased steadily. The UFT functioned more like an insurance company than as part of a movement. More staff meant increased dues, which were made acceptable by the flow of benefits delivered by the union.

The staff members were chosen by Shanker, with the nominal concurrence of the officers, all of whom were members of the Unity Caucus—hardly an internal checks-and-balances system. The officers and a large proportion of the caucus and the executive board became employees of the union, full- or part-time. Their employment depended on the favor of Shanker.

Many union functionaries were given "free" time from their responsibilities in the school system. Chapter chairpersons were given an extra free period a day to take care of union business under the terms of the union contract. Chairpersons of each of the thirty-two community subdistricts were given even more time off. All such functionaries were granted expense allowances from the union. Union offices were established in each of the boroughs of the city and staffed by full-time union representatives. Political action was coordinated through these field headquarters.

When the machine achieved its full development in the early 1970s, it included at least 2,000 persons who were full- or part-time employees of the union or who received valuable perquisites under the collective bargaining contract. Most of the members of this elite group held elective offices at the school, district, borough or citywide level, and all of the delegates to state and national conventions came from the same group. Behind the official structure and giving it discipline was the Unity Caucus.

Caucuses have long been a part of Federation functioning. When the UFT was formed, the Old Guilders feared that union positions might fall into the hands of "irresponsible" newcomers. Shanker capitalized on this fear to build the Unity Caucus, which elected him to the UFT presidency in 1964 and has sustained him since. It is a closed caucus; one must be voted in. Its decisions must be followed by the members in every detail. Several members have been expelled because they opposed the Vietnam War or were not supportive enough of the union's opposition to community control.

Behind the caucus was that ubiquitous tool of modern autocracy, the computer. In the early 1960s the UFT negotiated a welfare fund. Fund policy was determined by a joint board of union and school board appointees, but the fund was administered by the UFT. The fund's computer is housed at UFT headquarters. Information about every teacher in the system is readily available to Shanker and his agents.

Two changes in election rules were made during Shanker's second presidential term. The UFT structure had been planned to reflect the special interests of teachers, specific to their functions in the school system. Vice-presidents were elected for elementary schools, junior high schools, high schools, vocational high schools and auxiliary services. Portions of the executive board were chosen in the same way.

These provisions were adopted at the insistence of the CATU group which merged with the Teachers Guild to form the UFT. The CATU members all taught in the high schools. They feared they would be overwhelmed by teachers from other divisions of the school system. In order to separate these special interest elections from at-large elections of other officers and executive board members, the special constituency elections were held in the odd years. The at-large elections were held in the even years.

On grounds that holding an election every year was inefficient and costly, Shanker persuaded the executive board and the delegate assembly to change the constitution so that the special interest officials and the at-large officials were elected in the even years. This change emphasized the importance of caucus voting; it opened the way for another change: slate voting. Under the slate-voting rule, a member can with one "X," vote for thirteen officers, some fifty executive board members and several hundred delegates to state and national conventions. It is winner take all. There is no apportioning of delegates according to the share of the total vote received by their faction.

## WIND, RAIN AND FIRE

The chaotic 1969 AFT convention in New Orleans was my first convention as president of the Federation. A hurricane raged during most of the convention week. One night the convention had to be evacuated because a disturbed teenager set a fire on a top floor. The evacuees included Congressman Carl Perkins, chairman of the House Committee on Education, to whom the union had given an award. He and fifteen hundred delegates huddled in dark doorways and other shelters from the wind and rain until the hotel could be reentered. Several times during the convention the proceedings were recessed so that the delegates could picket two bars across the street which discriminated against blacks.

The 1969 convention also marked my first open break with Shanker. The New Yorkers attended the convention in force. The UFT had never sent all the delegates to which it was entitled because of the expense involved. In New Orleans, New Yorkers comprised a fifth of the delegates.

Prior to the convention, the executive council had approved a proposed constitutional amendment providing for direct election of the AFT president by referendum vote. I had consulted David Edelstein, an expert in union democracy. We had devised a plan which called for nomination by petition and election by mailed secret ballot. There were also provisions for allowing candidates to send campaign material to the members and there were other democratic safeguards.

My primary purpose in advocating direct election of the president was to establish a participatory process which would contrast with the "arranged" elections of NEA presidents. Permitting the president to appeal directly to the members would also make the membership a court of last resort in case of a dispute between the president and political powers in the union.

At the executive council meeting just prior to the convention, Shanker moved reconsideration of the amendment that allowed direct election of the president, on grounds that the vice-presidents had not known what they were voting for when they agreed to submit the amendment to the convention. It appeared that Shanker had talked with the vice-presidents privately before making his motion. Reconsideration carried, and the council withdrew its support. The direct election amendment went down to defeat with the help of a phalanx of New York votes.

The defeat of the amendment was not my only setback in New Orleans. I had also proposed a motion opposing the Vietnam War. From my viewpoint, the war issue was dividing the liberal movement at a time when unity was essential.

The AFT executive council voted to back the antiwar resolution, just as it had voted to support the direct election of the president. John Ryan, from Philadelphia, worked successfully throughout the five-day meeting to defeat the resolution. Again, the New York delegation voted solidly.

And so it went throughout the week. I supported a resolution submitted by a local of university teachers. It called for support of college students who wished to engage in collective bargaining with their college administrations. Shanker ridiculed the idea, saying that the *New York Times* would accuse the AFT of encouraging campus radicalism. Although other speakers spoke in favor of the resolution, it was swamped by the wave of New York votes.

The Black Caucus, which had been particularly militant throughout the convention, tried to win acceptance of two resolutions on community control of schools and racial integration of the labor movement. Its efforts were also defeated with UFT votes.

When the convention ended, I sat in my hotel suite with my wife and a few friends. Suddenly, Shanker stalked into the room followed by his secretary and an aide. He was walking in what was intended as a humorous imitation of the Groucho Marx crouch.

"We have come to take over," he intoned dramatically.

The remark was intended as a joke, but I did not appreciate it.

"Here, too?" I replied grimly.

# Chapter 17

## TROUBLE

### THE CHALLENGE

Only a few union leaders ever embark on campaigns to bring about basic changes in their industries or in society. Their objective is survival. They keep an eye on the shifting political currents within their organizations and search for the lowest common political denominator. They follow a defensive strategy and wait until they or their unions are attacked before going into action. Thus, most union leaders move from crisis to crisis and election to election until they retire. Once a union leader is entrenched he is rarely deposed.

When I became president of the AFT I knew that I was living dangerously. I was trying to lead the teacher unity movement and work for progressive change in American education and society in general. I once remarked to John Schmid, my close friend and associate in the union, that when I had more than fifty-one percent support for anything, it was time to start worrying because it was likely that I was compromising too much.

Many AFT members were opposed to merging with the NEA. Many were not enthusiastic about my liberal stands on civil rights, educational policy, the labor movement and social issues. But I had not become AFT president just to be president.

Although I had known that I would run into trouble sooner or later, I had not expected it to come at my very first convention as president. Neither had I expected it to come so quickly from Albert Shanker. Our relationship had remained cordial through many difficult times, but the sudden realization of how our courses had diverged was a shock. After our initial exchange, Shanker tried to smooth the situation over. From his standpoint the convention had been a triumph. He was not conscious of how far he had moved from the liberal cause which we had jointly espoused a short time before.

I tried to explain how I felt. "We just do not want the same things," I had begun, but I had been too overcome with emotion to say more.

A week later, when I had returned to my office in Washington, I wrote to the chairperson of the Progressive Caucus. I was resigning from the caucus because it was "no longer progressive, nor was it a caucus." In a few brief sentences I listed some of the progressive stands the caucus had taken in the past. I pointed out how these positions had been reversed at the convention with the active support of prominent caucus members.

I sent copies of my resignation letter to all Progressive Caucus executive council members. I had no idea what my next move would be, but I knew I could not fit in with the new shift to the right.


MEMORY TAPE: REUTHER AT BAY

*Twenty or more men are crowded into a room in the Hay-Adams Hotel in Washington across the street from AFL-CIO headquarters. They are genteelly dressed, but most of them have removed their jackets and loosened their ties. I am acquainted with all but a few. They are the leaders of the unions of the old CIO. It is spring, 1968.*

*Walter Reuther enters, followed by his brother Victor. Walter moves around the room, shaking hands, patting shoulders and exchanging casual remarks. After a few minutes he takes a position at one side of the room and looks around, waiting for attention. There are many who are missing. Some of them have called friends in the AFL-CIO building across the street to find out if it would be held against them if they attended this gathering.*

*"Some of you asked that I meet with you," Reuther begins. "I appreciate that. For a year now we in the UAW have been going it pretty much alone. We have made no secret of our*

dissatisfaction with what has happened to the labor movement in the 13 years since the merger. We are going to do what we have to do but we do not want to be accused of wrecking the movement."

Unfortunately, "wrecking the movement" is just what many of those in the room think the red-headed labor leader is doing. Nobody speaks, and Reuther continues.

"Unless there is some change in the situation, which I do not foresee, the UAW executive board will recommend to our convention that we disaffiliate from the AFL-CIO when we meet this summer, but what each of you does is up to you." He pauses and looks at each of us in turn.

I had been sent a copy of Reuther's first manifesto to George Meany many months before. It was in the form of a lengthy letter to sympathizers and all UAW functionaries. Reuther's declaration had enumerated the grievances of the Progressives in the labor movement: the lack of an effective organizing campaign; the failure to dramatize the truly liberal AFL-CIO social program; the organization's jingoistic support of the cold war and the war in Vietnam; the hostile attitude of the labor federation leaders toward the more militant groups in the civil rights movement; the lack of pressure on old-line AFL unions to admit more minorities into membership; and the aging, nearly all-white leadership of the Federation.

I had agreed with all of Reuther's charges, but I had thought that Reuther and the UAW should have pressed their case within the AFL-CIO before taking the drastic step of disaffiliation. I knew that the AFT could not afford to alienate itself from the mainstream of the labor movement. The struggling locals needed the support of their AFL-CIO central labor bodies and state organizations just as the UFT had needed that support when it was starting out. I tried to persuade Cogen, who was finishing his last months as AFT president, to send an open letter to Reuther supporting Reuther's criticism but urging him to stay within the AFL-CIO and fight.

Cogen had balked. "What good would it do?" he had demanded. "Reuther wouldn't pay any attention to us." "I know it," I had answered, "but there are many people in the AFL-CIO who agree with him even though they do not like the idea of disaffiliation. We ought to associate ourselves with them.

And if we speak out, maybe others will too." Cogen had been
adamant, and I had been forced to retreat.

Reuther leads the men in the hotel room through the familiar
litany of AFL-CIO failures and shortcomings. Then he begins
to talk of Meany's leadership.

"George Meany once told me," he declaims, "that when it
comes to the labor movement, 'jurisdiction' is everything. Well,
let me tell you that I helped form the AFL-CIO because I thought
a united labor movement could lead this country to a better
way of life. The trouble with Meany is that he thinks he's still
a business agent for the plumbers union."

Now Reuther has reached his peroration. Not usually given
to scatological terms, his speech becomes all the more dramatic. "For the labor movement," he says, "I would eat shit
for breakfast. I would eat shit for lunch and I would eat shit
for supper. I would even eat shit in Macy's window. But I'll be
god-damned if I will eat shit for George Meany."

The meeting is over.


A DECLARATION OF INDEPENDENCE

The 1969 AFL-CIO convention was my first as AFT president.
I viewed it as a test of my determination to establish the AFT
as an independent liberal organization. I supported the AFL-
CIO as an institution, but I wanted it to follow a more progressive policy, similar to the non-Communist labor movements in other countries. I was realistic enough to know that
the AFT would not be a major formulator of the labor federation's policy, but I was also idealistic enough to want the union
to have an impact.

In 1966 a council of unions for professional and technical
workers was formed by the AFT. It included representatives of
the musicians, airline pilots, insurance agents, radio engineers,
electrical engineers, actors and others. The AFL-CIO's opinion
of the advisability of the council was not asked, but some of
the associated unions wanted it to become an AFL-CIO department.

After two years of sporadic meetings, the council decided to
try to get the blessing of George Meany. Meany regarded the

council with suspicion, perhaps justifiably from his point of view. Nevertheless, a meeting was arranged. It was decided that department status could wait, but the organization's official name would be, "Council of AFL-CIO Unions for Professional Employees" (CUP).

As the CUP representatives were leaving Meany's office, Lane Kirkland, then Meany's assistant, asked Cogen if he "had to be president" of the council. Charlie hesitated but then said no. Jerry Wurf, president of the American Federation of State, County, and Municipal Employees, became the first official president of CUP. A person working in Kirkland's office was chosen to be executive secretary.

There were two items of interest on the 1969 AFL-CIO convention agenda. One was the expulsion of the Chemical Workers Union (CWU). The other was the election of several new vice-presidents to the executive council.

I decided to oppose the ousting of the CWU. I believed in labor unity, and unity could not be achieved by expelling the CWU. It was the kind of sectarian action that had limited the movement in the past. Also, the CWU's crime did not seem offensive. It had accepted organizing assistance from a new co-alition called the Alliance for Labor Action (ALA). The ALA was an unlikely partnership composed of the Teamsters, ex-pelled from the AFL-CIO in 1959 for corruption, and the UAW, which had disaffiliated in protest against Meany's policies. The leaders of the ALA wanted to show the AFL-CIO how to or-ganize; hence its grant to the Chemical Workers. The AFL-CIO called this "dual unionism."

When the CWU item was called, I reminded the convention that dual unionism was more prevalent within the AFL-CIO than outside it. Many AFL-CIO unions were spending huge sums to try to win bargaining units away from other AFL-CIO unions. The Chemical Workers could hardly be blamed for using money from the ALA if they could not get any from the AFL-CIO. I urged the AFL-CIO to follow a policy of labor unity, not "an eye for an eye and a tooth for a tooth."

My remarks were supported by the president of the Typo-graphical Union and several other speakers. I was answered by Lane Kirkland, who said the AFL-CIO could not accept the transgressions of the CWU with "sweet forbearance." Paul Hall, president of the Seafarers Union, accused the Chemical Workers' leaders of "selling out the AFL-CIO for thirty pieces of silver."

The Chemical Workers Union was expelled by an overwhelming vote. My opposition was viewed by those at AFL-CIO headquarters as evidence of a lack of political regularity, a quality more highly prized than commitment to building a progressive, united labor movement. My action prompted some in the AFL-CIO hierarchy to look for a more "reliable" AFT standard bearer.

On the night before the executive council positions were to be filled, the ten-member AFT delegation met in Carl Megel's hotel room. Megel raised the question of winning one of the seats for the AFT. I had considered trying to place Cogen on the council at one time, but I realized that this could not be done without reaching an understanding with the Meany administration.

I explained to the other delegates that I did not want the AFT to be preempted by the conservative forces in the labor movement and that it was better for the AFT not to become entangled in AFL-CIO politics.

There was a pause. Megel, distorting my meaning, said, "Well, Dave, if you don't want to go on the council, how about putting somebody else on?" Then, turning to Shanker, he asked, "How about you, Al?"

"OK with me," Shanker quickly answered.

I was trapped. There was no further discussion. Shanker was our nominee.

# Chapter 18

## SKIN OF MY TEETH

RAPPROCHEMENT

Following the Atlantic City AFL-CIO convention in the fall of 1969, I took stock of my situation. I would have to decide whether to run for reelection when the AFT convention met the following August. During my first year in office I had severed my connection with my caucus, strained my relationship with the AFL-CIO and lost the support of my strongest ally. On the other hand, I had made significant progress toward the goal of teacher unity. If I could be elected for another term, I thought that goal could be realized. I could leave the presidency with a sense of accomplishment.

To resolve my dilemma, I listed conditions under which I would run again. In effect, these were demands to be made on Shanker, the executive council, the Progressive Caucus and the convention. They were specific. They included earmarking 25 cents a month per member for a national strike fund; reversal of several of the obnoxious stands on civil rights and student activism adopted at the New Orleans Convention; and adoption of a council rule that unless a vice-president served notice of intent to oppose on the convention floor, a position taken by the council, the vice-president was bound to support the council's position. I also wanted a formal declaration of support for the teacher unity policy from the executive council and the convention.

In effect, my list of conditions was a platform on which I would run for reelection. When the list was complete, I phoned

Shanker and asked for a meeting to see if we could iron out our differences. The arrangements were made with some difficulty, but we finally met in a Chinese restaurant on upper Broadway, two blocks from the apartment complex where we had lived when we were helping to build the UFT.

It was a curious meeting. I told him my conditions, checking them off mentally against the list I carried in my pocket. Shanker offered almost no substantive objections. Still, this was no sentimental reunion of old comrades-in-arms. His manner was detached and preoccupied, but when we parted, we shook hands. I had his verbal agreement on all the essential points.

The executive council met in Pittsburgh early in 1970. I alerted two or three friendly vice-presidents to what was coming up. Then, one by one, I presented the recommendations I had worked out with Shanker two months before. Each was adopted without dissent. At the end of the council meeting I announced that I was rejoining the Progressive Caucus and that I hoped to have its endorsement when I ran for reelection the following August.

## INTERNAL TENSION

Charles Cogen and I came to the AFT in 1964. Six years later, when I ran for my second term as president, membership in the union had doubled. This increase made possible greatly increased organizing activity, which required a rapid expansion of staff. I was not enthusiastic about such a buildup. Too much staff inhibits grass-roots involvement.

As Max Weber pointed out many years ago, all organizations, including unions, churches, political parties, corporations and governments must deal with the problem of bureaucracy. Bureaucrats almost inevitably come to attach more importance to the bureaucracy than to its purposes. Sometimes, however, a staff may try to take over an organization, establishing itself as a controlling force independent of elected officials and membership. Some of the most bitter struggles in the labor movement have stemmed from such staff revolts.

By 1970 there were three staff unions for AFT employees. The clericals were members of the Office and Professional Employees International Union, AFL-CIO (OPEIU). The research, editorial and other professional workers at the national office belonged to a unit of the Washington-Baltimore Newspaper Guild. The organizers belonged to an independent union called the Committee for National Representatives (CNR).

AFT organizing during the 1960s was as exciting as CIO organizing had been during the 1930s. It was "us against them," and the union won often enough to keep spirits high. The organizers came to regard themselves as hybrids of Robin Hood and Superman. With good salaries, credit cards and footloose life-styles they shuttled from crisis to crisis, becoming instant heroes of the teacher proletariat.

The organizers were highly skeptical of my unity strategy. Some of them were openly antagonistic. In promoting merger between the AFT and the NEA I seemed to be surrendering to the Association. Also, a merger would make a large part of their work unnecessary, and the "good times" would be gone.

I tried to counteract the antagonism of the organizers by holding frequent staff meetings with long question periods. I sent special reading materials to them. I scrupulously maintained proper relations with James Mundy, the organizing director. I reiterated the assurance that in the event of a merger, all staff people would be retained.

My efforts to come to terms with the organizers were largely unsuccessful. To them, teacher unity was a menace.

A few months before the 1970 AFT convention, I began to hear rumors that Kenneth Miesen, a charismatic young organizer, would run against me. A few weeks before the opening of the convention he became a candidate in earnest. Miesen was an ambitious and able organizer, but he had no commitment to social reform. Furthermore, the union contract had a section which forbade organizers from advocating the election of any candidate for local, state or national AFT office. They were also forbidden to contribute money or services to the campaign of any such candidate.

I did not consider Miesen a threat until after the votes were counted. I sent out no literature. I did not court key local leaders, as any sensible union politician would have. With the support of the Progressive Caucus, which included most of the larger locals, I did not see how I could lose. As a result I was almost defeated.

The organizers dug out every possible vote. Miesen had no platform worth considering. His campaign was based on apprehension about merger and the personal loyalty the organizers had accumulated over the years. My narrow winning margin turned out to be due to my opposition to the Vietnam War expressed in the current convention and the previous one. Miesen took no stand and lost the support of the liberals.

This was the last "free" AFT election. Voting was by secret ballot, in accordance with the procedure used for a roll call vote. Shanker, however, believed that some delegates were "talking one way and voting another." Before the 1972 election he succeeded in changing the procedure so that every delegate's vote was public.

Following the defeat of the organizers' mutiny, Mundy resigned as director of organization. I appointed John Schmid in his place. Miesen resigned as a national representative and took a job working for the Minneapolis local. Subsequently, he gave up organizing and became an insurance representative.

The outcome of the election meant that my efforts to establish teacher unity would continue. In fact, the merger strategy was specifically endorsed by convention resolution.

# Part IV

## A RACE AGAINST TIME

# Chapter 19

## NEA UNDER SIEGE

*MEMORY TAPE: TIT FOR TAT*

From time immemorial the school superintendents of the nation have gathered each spring at Atlantic City for the meeting of the American Association of School Administrators (AASA). They come to exchange gossip, have a few drinks out of sight of the folks back home, look for new jobs, confer with each other and listen to presentations of new ideas which may or may not be applicable to their own school systems. Usually, more than seven thousand of them make this trek, and expenses are paid by their local school boards. There are also in attendance thousands of company representatives selling educational materials guaranteed to make kids learn—textbook publishers, purveyors of electronic forced-learning gadgets and salesmen of other kinds of equipment. This army of affluent education officials and their camp followers jams the hotels and parades four and five abreast on the boardwalk. Most of the convention events are carried on closed-circuit television throughout the city.

This is my first AASA convention. I have been invited to speak at a session on collective bargaining. I had driven to Atlantic City the night before and had mingled with the educators. Now I listen as the chairman, a superintendent from Ohio, reads off the background facts which comprise my introduction. I walk to the lectern.

I give my standard collective bargaining speech, throwing in a new quip or two as they occur to me. I compare the typical

school district structure to that of a medium-sized manufacturing company, and I equate the superintendent of schools
with the executive vice-president. I point out that in the private
sector, collective bargaining is the law of the land, and that
progressive managements have learned to live with it.

"Education," I say, "is just a little late in coming to it,
but most school systems will soon be bargaining with their
teachers."

"There is nothing to worry about," I add. "You shouldn't be
ashamed of being a boss. We are still a long way from the cooperative commonwealth, but we're working on it."

I conclude with a pitch for teacher unity. I try to convince
them that they will be better off if the teachers have a stronger
organization. A united teacher organization can squeeze more
money for education from the state legislatures and the federal
government. There is polite applause. I certainly have not cap-
tivated them, but then nobody had expected me to. My role is
more like "Exhibit A." Now comes the question period.

The first questioner asks whether superintendents should
bargain for school management personally.

"Not if they're smart," I answer. "Stay out of the meat
grinder, and leave the bargaining to the experts."

The next question requires a longer answer. "Mr. Selden, if
teachers and administrators are enemies, as you imply, what
can be done to bring them closer together?"

"I'm afraid you're not going to like my answer," I begin. "I
can think of three things. First, all administrators should teach
a class, one a day, perhaps, or a full load every third year." A
few of the superintendents applaud, but most sit silently.

"Second, the power to evaluate teachers should be placed
in a neutral body outside the school system. As things now
stand, the teacher rating power is used by most administrators
to keep teachers in line. More often than not, it isn't the bad
teacher who gets rated low; it is the one who does not conform
to what the superintendent thinks is proper."

There is no applause. Feet shuffle nervously.

I press on. "The third thing which could be done to lessen
the tension between administrators and teachers," I say, "is to
reduce the salary gap. The status difference is too great. It cre-
ates resentment and makes a relationship based on collegiality

impossible." I pause, and then conclude, "And I hope that could be done by raising the salaries of teachers, rather than holding down the salaries of administrators."

This time there are a few boos.

"Time for one more question," the chairperson says quickly.

A superintendent in the back of the room stands up. "Mr. Selden," he begins. "You have had a lot to say about what we should do." There is a tinge of sarcasm in his voice. "Now I want to know when you are going to get your own house in order. What are you going to do about getting rid of the incompetent teachers and deadwood in your own ranks?"

I pause before replying. There are many responses which flow through my mind. I could say that when teachers have the responsibility for hiring their colleagues they would be willing to take the responsibility of deciding who gets fired or who gets tenure. Or I could point out that no one likes to fail, least of all a teacher. What is needed are better school conditions and more help for teachers so that more of them can succeed.

But I don't say any of these reasonable things. The questioner, unfortunately, has exasperated me. "Well," I finally drawl, "maybe we could make superintendents of some of them."


## NEA CIRCLES THE WAGONS

Throughout the 1960s the National Education Association found itself under a mounting two-pronged attack, on the one hand from the new educational establishment which emerged during the Kennedy and Johnson administrations, and from its own members on the other. The Association, as it had developed over the years, had taken on a form closely paralleling the education enterprise. Education was decentralized and so was the NEA. In fact, the Association was more a coalition of state associations and other educational organizations such as the American Association of School Administrators and other groups organized according to function and status within the schools.

Below the Mason-Dixon Line most educational institutions were still segregated, in spite of the Supreme Court's dictum in *Brown v. Board of Education*; likewise, the NEA and its state affiliates. The Association had separate organizations for black and white teachers at both the national and the state levels.

Instead of appointing an Association stalwart as his new commissioner of education, as most incoming presidents had, President Kennedy brought the maverick dean of the Harvard Graduate School of Education to Washington. This was Francis Keppel, who had never taught school, had never been an administrator and did not even have a Ph.D. He was a refreshing change from his predecessors, but for the NEA he was a constant problem. "Change" became the watchword in education. The schools must be integrated, curriculum must be made "relevant" and teaching methods must be modernized. Any obstacle, including the NEA, must be pushed aside or bowled over.

At the same time, the growing challenge from the AFT, flaunting its new-found banner, "Collective Bargaining!" was making Association members increasingly dissatisfied with their organization's mode of operation. Efforts to substitute "professional negotiations" for bargaining met with little success, even though the Association had devised a system of "sanctions"—penalties against recalcitrant school boards—to strengthen its negotiating posture. On paper, "professional negotiations" and "sanctions" seemed excellent methods for winning benefits for teachers, but in practice they were no substitute for the more direct appeal of collective bargaining. Gradually, local associations began to adopt the union method.

THE UNITED PROFESSION

The Association structure was highly decentralized. Unlike the AFT, where one membership covered all levels of the organization, there were separate memberships for the local, state and national associations. In many cases teachers were pressured to join their local and state organizations by superintendents and principals. Such coercion was less frequently applied to build NEA membership, however, and consequently, membership in the national Association was much less than the total of all the state memberships. In 1960 for instance, the total state

association membership was 1.8 million, while NEA membership by teachers was about half that number.

To increase national membership and consolidate their
forces, NEA leaders, under the slogan "United Profession,"
campaigned to make NEA membership compulsory for all state
association members. Initially, the state associations objected.
They feared their members might balk at paying higher dues
and withdraw from the state associations. To reassure state
leaders, the NEA had to guarantee the state associations against
income loss. Separate negotiations had to be carried out with
each state. It took ten years to make the "United Profession"
universal, but when the process was complete, the Association
had been greatly strengthened.

One effect of the "United Profession" campaign was that it
obscured the true relative membership positions of the AFT
and the NEA. Much of the growth of the NEA during the 1960s
was a result of united profession agreements. AFT growth, however, reflected a change in allegiance by the new members, most
of whom were switching from the Association to the Federation.

At the same time that the "United Profession" campaign was
being carried out, the NEA was eliminating another source of
disunity by integrating its state organizations in the South. This
was a difficult task. If the prointegration forces pushed too hard,
some of the white state organizations and some of the black
state organizations would become independent.

The black state associations were members of a nationwide
organization, the American Education Association (AEA).
There were vested interests in the AEA and the white and black
state associations which resisted changes in the status quo. The
AEA and the black state associations were dominated by administrators who feared losing their jobs when school systems
and organizations were integrated. Amalgamation also threatened staff jobs in the black and the white organizations.

By one means or another, however, the black and white associations were gradually amalgamated. The demands for integration by liberal association members were too insistent, and
the cost in votes in collective bargaining elections was too high
to continue to maintain the segregated organizations. In 1970
the AEA was disbanded. Three years later the NEA constitution

was amended to give guarantees of proportional representation of minorities on official bodies. In each case, difficult negotiations were required, but finally the task was completed.

## A STATEWIDE REBELLION

One of my chief criticisms of the NEA and its affiliates had long been that they would not use their power on behalf of society in general, not to mention teachers and children. While the AFT struggled to build locals at the district level to raise salaries and improve school conditions, the state associations could have provided the needed strength if they had been more militant. In 1968 however, the Florida Education Association (FEA) came close to realizing its potential.

There had been many statewide actions by teachers associations over the years. Some had even resulted in walkouts, but they were more like demonstrations than strikes. Most of them only lasted a day or two, and they were supported and probably instigated by administrators, since they were directed at state authorities rather than local power structures.

One of these near strikes by teachers occurred in the unlikely state of Utah, in March, 1963. Following a ten-year struggle for better conditions and salaries comparable to those in surrounding states, a special convention of the Utah Education Association (UEA) voted to urge teachers not to sign their contracts for the following year unless the governor called a special session of the legislature to consider education needs.

The Utah crisis was settled without a work stoppage. A face-saving formula for both sides resulted in substantial improvements.

In Florida there had also been a protracted wrangle between the state government and the teachers, which had resulted in the "radicalization" of the Florida Education Association. Just before the beginning of the 1967–68 school year, more than thirty thousand teachers met in the Tangerine Bowl in Orlando. They voted to "resign" at the beginning of the year's second semester in February if the governor and the legislature had not provided additional funds by that time.

The teachers used the term "resign" to avoid the consequences of conducting an illegal strike. However, if a work stoppage is unsuccessful, the workers lose, regardless of what it's called. The only way to win a work stoppage is to win it—and be ready to walk out again if the strike settlement is not adhered to.

The Florida governor, Claude Kirk, was the first Republican governor in ninety-six years. The legislature was solidly Democratic. The Florida Education Association demanded a detailed program of educational reforms, including salary increases. A few weeks before the resignation deadline, the state authorities adopted a tax relief and benefit package which gave the teachers substantial raises but left school conditions unchanged. The FEA voted not to accept the package, and the strike was on.

The Florida teachers' strike degenerated into class warfare very quickly. The chambers of commerce and local business leaders reviled the teachers and recruited strikebreakers. Some companies paid their employees to go into schools and teach. After a few weeks the strikers began to lose heart. Their leaders tried to hold the strike together, but by the middle of March it was clear that the teachers had lost, and the strike began to crumble. County teachers associations began to negotiate separate settlements. Some of these settlements were achieved by sacrificing the jobs of the more militant strikers.

## WHY DID THE FLORIDA STRIKE FAIL?

Why did the teachers lose in Florida? This question must be asked because it has an important bearing on the course of the teacher rebellion. If the Florida strike had succeeded there would have been similar actions in other states. In the organizational struggle between the AFT and the NEA, the momentum would have shifted to the NEA because the associations were dominant in most states.

Looking back, it is clear that the FEA should have hailed the actions of the legislature and the governor as a great victory and lived to fight another day. There would have been no walkout with its exhilarating effect, it is true, but the teachers would have known that the threat of a strike had forced the state to act. Not all strikes or strike threats end in clearcut victories. Such half victories are often accepted by experienced organizers, and they are usually remembered as triumphs by the participants.

Why did the FEA go ahead with the strike? There were two reasons, one "moral" and the other political. The moral position of the Association had been established in the years preceding the strike. Children were not getting the education to which they were entitled. Classes were too large, remedial services were lacking, textbooks were outmoded and facilities were poor. Attracting and holding educators of high quality required higher salaries. Given these needs, teachers could not settle for a minimal package of property tax relief and pay raises.

The political motivation for calling the strike was more complicated. There were scores of heroic leaders in the Florida strike. Two of the most prominent had their own agendas, however. One was Cecil Hannan, the NEA assistant executive secretary for professional development, an aggressive career staffer. His temperament and organizational philosophy contrasted sharply with the moderate views of his superior, Sam Lambert, who had been chosen national executive director only a year before the Florida crisis.

The other behind-the-scenes operator was Pat Tornillo, executive secretary of the Dade County Teachers Association (DCTA). Tornillo, a volatile, wise-cracking former New Yorker, was a veteran teacher organization functionary.

Only Hannan and Tornillo know whether they started the Florida adventure with the idea of taking control of the NEA in order to turn it into an effective, militant teacher organization. In the heady 1960s anything was possible, and in the early weeks of the strike it certainly looked that way.

Hannan arrived in Florida in late June, 1967. He was billed as the NEA's chief expert on "sanctions." He toured the state delivering militant speeches, and he wound up at the Tangerine Bowl rally in Orlando bearing a $50,000 check as evidence of the NEA's support of its Florida affiliate.

If the Florida strike had been successful the immediate effect might have been dramatic. Apparently, Hannan's and Tornillo's scheme was to make the DCTA president, Janet Dean, president of the NEA. Dean was charismatic. She appeared frequently on national television during the walkout. Coming into the NEA convention in June, three months after leading a successful statewide strike, she would have been a formidable candidate.

By the time the NEA delegates convened in Philadelphia, however, the Florida teachers had lost their battle. Dean ran a poor fifth in a field of five. The key factor in her defeat was the opposition of a large part of the NEA hierarchy. They had been badly frightened by the Florida upheaval, and they wanted a "safe" president.

## UNISERV

The Florida strike had cost the Association more than a million dollars, and the FEA had been so weakened that the AFT was able to establish strong beachheads in several counties. Furthermore, the Federation was continuing to gain in other areas of the nation. At the same convention that Janet Dean and the Floridians were repulsed, Uniserv was adopted.

The Uniserv plan follows the bureaucratic rule that *if you have a problem, hire somebody to take care of it.* For half a century the Association had been controlled by a coalition of school administrators and staff members. The coalition was shattered by rising teacher militancy and the exodus of the superintendents and principals from the Association. The organization's traditional infrastructure was replaced by professional organizers. Uniserv guaranteed local associations a staff person for every twelve hundred members. Annual dues to the national Association were raised to $25 from $15 to pay the salary and expenses of a thousand new field representatives.

It took several years for the Uniserv plan to be fully implemented, but it became a powerful force binding the highly decentralized Association together. It also became a wall against teacher unity. Just as the field organizers in the AFT had rejected the peace which unity would bring, so did their counterparts on the other side of the organizational struggle.

## MEMORY TAPE: FORT COLLINS

I board a limousine at the Denver airport with several other teachers bound for the special NEA constitutional convention on governance. It is being held at Colorado State University in Fort Collins, seventy miles to the north. The other passengers seem to be well acquainted with each other. They are carrying on a lively conversation. I am able to ride obscurely as I listen.

It is the summer of 1971. The demand for reform within the Association has been recognized at last by its leaders. From around the nation, some five hundred local leaders selected by computer are participating in a two-week brainstorming session. The recommendations of the conference will be sent to the appropriate official bodies of the NEA and, perhaps, to a membership referendum. I have learned this much from the material I have been sent, but because I am the guest of one of the factions and not an official delegate, I am unprepared for what I find when I get to the meetingplace.

I check into my room and walk over to the modern and functional conference center. I find out that not only have the delegates been selected by computer, but the entire conference has been computer-designed to provide maximum partcipation. There are very few staff members in view.

I am taken aside by a few leaders of the progressive group which is responsible for my invitation to the meeting. They thank me for coming, but they are worried. One of them warns me that "the meeting is mined."

"Mined?"

"Right. One wrong step and that's it."

"You mean that some people don't like the idea of the AFT president attending an official NEA meeting?"

"You better believe it! But more than that, they are dead set against the merger. Our group is all for it, but if we say so it will be used against us, and we won't get the changes in the NEA structure we are after."

They explain that the Fort Collins meeting could produce a new constitution for the Association which would give grassroots members much more power. I begin to get caught up in the extraordinary nature of this meeting. "You mean that if you

get a new constitution it will be a step toward teacher unity?"
I ask.

"Exactly. And if you say that here you will kill our chances
of pushing the new constitution through."

I realize that this is indeed an explosive situation.

In the afternoon I speak briefly to two of the dozen or more
task forces. Some of the delegates try to get me to say that the
NEA constitutional reforms are needed to make it easier to
merge with the AFT, but I avoid the issue.

In the evening there is a large, milling party at which I am
a guest of honor. I meet Pat Tornillo for the first time. He is
wearing a sombrero, pretending he is a Mexican. I talk with
him about the Florida strike, and I find him likable. I maintain
a polite attitude, saying little. I know that arguments will get
me nowhere. I must be content with winning friends without
influencing people.

The next morning, I am given an hour to speak to a general
meeting. I am not an official part of the program, and attendance is voluntary. Nevertheless, two or three hundred people
are there. I give my standard teacher unity speech. I am careful
to say at the end that I know that AFT-NEA merger is not an
issue at the conference, but that I could not pass up the opportunity to speak to them directly about it.

Applause is not overwhelming, but I have given them something to think about.

I am taken back to Denver by my friend George Fischer, the
former president of the NEA. A friend of Fischer's drives, but
Fischer and I do most of the talking during the hour-long journey. Several years later the driver introduces himself to me—
again, for of course we were introduced at the time. I am much
embarrassed. The "driver" was James Harris, who became NEA
president in 1973.


## A FOOTNOTE

The end result of the Fort Collins conference? The high hopes
of the NEA Progressives were not realized. A new constitution
was sent to referendum vote. In order to win, it had to receive
the approval of a majority of the state associations, and a ma-

jority of the total vote. Many of the state executive secretaries and other more conservative leaders of the Association opposed the new constitution. It failed both of the referendum hurdles.

Even though the threat of teacher militancy and progressivism had been contained, many of the most important reforms were later adopted, albeit piecemeal.The spirit of Fort Collins was truly remarkable, and the efforts of those responsible were not in vain.

# Chapter 20

# AN OPENING IN NEW YORK

## A CHANGE IN UNITY STRATEGY

Reelection at the 1970 AFT convention revived my hobbled presidency. Although Shanker was fashioning alliances with the conservative leaders of the Philadelphia and Chicago locals, I felt my policies had been vindicated. The resolutions adopted by the convention, unlike those passed in New Orleans the year before, were liberal and progressive. A moral victory had even been won on the Vietnam War issue.

The AFT was experiencing a period of remarkable growth. Membership had passed the two hundred thousand mark and was still rising. With the organizers' revolt put down and Mundy removed from his position as director of organizers, the union's organizing effort had been placed under the direction of John Schmid. Unlike Mundy, Schmid was a strong supporter of the unity strategy.

However, Helen Bain, the new NEA president who had succeeded George Fischer, was opposed to unionism in general and to the AFT in particular. Blocked from unity talks at the national level, I explored mergers at the local and state levels in spite of my opposition to a piecemeal approach. I justified my policy switch by reverting to my idea of establishing a beachhead within the Association which could be the beginning of a progressive, prounity caucus.

In the spring of 1971, I was a speaker at the annual meeting of the New York State Secondary School Principals Association at the Concord Hotel in the Catskills. Afterward, I had lunch with Frank White, executive secretary of the New York State Teachers Association. Before coming to New York, White had been assistant to the executive director of the Massachusetts Teachers Association (MTA). He was generally prounion, and he had favored developing a unity plan in Massachusetts. William Hebert, the MTA executive secretary, had insisted on consulting the NEA, and the negotiations had been sidetracked.

White said he was still in favor of an AFT-NEA merger, but he had become more cautious in his approach. We discussed some of the obstacles that would have to be overcome. I was unable to get a commitment from him to begin formal discussions. Unknown to us, an NEA staff person assigned to New York was developing a plan of his own. He was Ned Hopkins, a creative organizer and public relations expert who had participated in the Los Angeles merger the year before and had become a convert to the unity cause. To Hopkins, it seemed foolish for teachers to continue to divide their strength. New York teachers had come under heavy attack in the 1971 legislative session. The tenure law had been weakened by extending the three-year probationary period to five years, the retirement system had been threatened, and the Taylor Act— New York's public employee bargaining law—had been amended to curtail the range of matters which were bargainable. Hopkins called Larry Sibelman in Los Angeles and asked him to sound out Shanker on his attitude toward a statewide merger in New York. When he got an affirmative answer, Hopkins set to work in earnest.

With Frank White already favorably inclined toward AFT-NEA merger, Hopkins convinced the state association president of the necessity for teacher unity. White drafted a letter to the local association presidents, urging that they cooperate in bringing about a statewide amalgamation. Unfortunately, White's letter, which was to have been the basis for a beginning-of-school news release in September, was mailed out in June. Hopkins had arranged a secret meeting with Shanker and White, but Shanker regarded the premature publicity as a serious breach of faith. He accused Hopkins of trying to embarrass him for the sake of a momentary public relations advantage and withdrew from further talks.

When I called Shanker to discuss the breakdown of merger negotiations, I found that he was unsure how to proceed. He was not enthusiastic about merging with an organization that had twice as many members as the UFT. I found that he had been playing the merger game in the hope of provoking a split in NYSTA, just as the Teachers Guild had split the old High School Teachers Association.

I urged Shanker to pursue the merger negotiations seriously and to establish a moratorium on public statements by both sides. He reluctantly agreed, and in the fall another meeting was held. Shanker was accompanied by Lucille Swaim, a former IUD staffer who had by then joined the UFT staff. After the meeting, Shanker asked Swaim whether she thought the NYSTA representatives were serious about merger. She assured the UFT president that the NYSTA officials were indeed serious, and that a statewide merger was within his grasp.

## NEW YORK MERGER TALKS BEGIN

The two New York teacher organizations were a "natural" fit. The strengths of one complemented the other's weaknesses. A third of the state's teachers taught in New York City, which was represented by the UFT. Most of the upstate teachers belonged to NYSTA. While the Federation was closely allied with the Democratic party, the Association had strong connections to the Republicans.

In October, 1971, Shanker, conforming to AFT policy, asked formal permission from the Federation's executive council to begin merger talks. Although I had often declared my opposition to local and state mergers, I realized that the UFT could become a Trojan horse within the Association.

I told the executive council that a New York state merger would be different from mergers in scattered cities and smaller states, just as collective bargaining in New York City had an effect different from bargaining agreements elsewhere. I told the vice-presidents that the merged New York organization would roll around inside the NEA "like a bowling ball in a room full of teacups." It could use its strength to form alliances with other state organizations to advance the unity cause.

I also said that I had no personal interest in the merger, and that once the New York merger had been consummated no one would know or care who was president of the AFT. For all intents and purposes, New York would be the Federation. Nevertheless, I urged the council to give its approval.

Although several of the council members had openly declared their opposition to the merger concept, and others were secretly opposed, they voted in favor of the New York merger. They explained away their votes on the basis of their belief in local autonomy. It is just possible, too, that they saw the New York merger as unstoppable, and so they wanted to get out of the way to avoid being run over.

Getting the New York merger talks going again proved to be difficult. The new NEA president, Catharine Barrett, was from Syracuse. She had strong support throughout the state association, particularly in the large cities of western New York. She was adamantly opposed to amalgamation with the big-city union and she did not like Shanker personally. Furthermore, NYSTA was undergoing a leadership crisis. President Kafka was a lame duck, and Executive Secretary Frank White had begun a slide from power which would culminate in his resignation a few months later.

In November the NYSTA House of Delegates chose Tom Hobart as the new president. Hobart, a young, liberal political activist from Buffalo, opened his term by holding a news conference in New York City, and declaring that NYSTA was about to launch a "$5 million organizing campaign to 'regain' representation rights in New York City." The statement ignored the fact that NYSTA had never represented teachers in the city.

Shanker responded to Hobart's unexpected attack by calling for the resumption of merger negotiations. Hopkins then began a series of covert discussions with the UFT leader. Shanker had the tiger by the tail, but two major issues would have to be resolved before the New York statewide merger could be completed. These were AFL-CIO affiliation and the distribution of power within the new organization.

Shanker favored a variation of the Los Angeles optional affiliation scheme. Members of each merging group would retain their national affiliations, but members joining after the merger would be affiliated with the AFT and NEA. When Shanker discovered that Hobart and the other NYSTA leaders had no hangups about affiliating with organized labor, it was quickly decided that the new organization would maintain NEA and AFT affiliation, including the AFL-CIO for all members from the outset. This plan would be made financially feasible by rebates and subsidies from both national organizations.

The issue of distribution of power was not so easily resolved.

## NYSUT

In March, 1972, Frank White resigned his position as executive secretary of NYSTA. Hobart and Hopkins were in complete command. By May, the plans for the merger had been ratified by both state organizations, even though NEA President Catharine Barrett had waged a last ditch fight in NYSTA against the merger. The new organization is called "NYSUT," the New York State United Teachers. Although NYSUT could not immediately become a part of the AFT or the NEA because of technical problems, Shanker and Hobart and a small entourage from the UFT and NYSTA attended the NEA convention in Atlantic City.

The impending New York merger had greatly alarmed NEA leaders, and they felt that the time had come to shut off any further amalgamations. The NEA executive committee sponsored "New Business Item #20" which, while allowing any local or state mergers which had been consummated already or were under negotiation, prohibited any further mergers between any affiliate of the NEA with any organization affiliated with the AFL-CIO.

To lay a basis for passage of New Business Item #20, in his annual address to the convention, Sam Lambert, the NEA executive director, warned local and state associations to steer clear of labor affiliation because unions were conservative, racist and corrupt. It was a new tack for the Association. Previous executive directors had behaved more like school superintendents than radical activists. In fact, Lambert, while a decent and moral man, was certainly no social militant.

Tom Hobart, still president of NYSTA, asked for time for Shanker to respond to Lambert. When that request was denied, ostensibly for scheduling reasons, arrangements were made for Shanker to appear at an unofficial meeting the next day.

Shanker ably defended the New York state merger. He showed how the threats against tenure and the pension system had given a special urgency to the need for teacher unity. He called for defeat of New Business Item #20 even though NYSUT would be unaffected by it. He explained that the Association should not tie its hands in dealing with similar crises, which were sure to arise in other states.

The NEA Black Caucus, however, took a stand against merger, and Shanker was booed after his talk. New Business Item #20 passed the convention easily, although the unity forces were able to muster a third of the votes. I did not consider it a fatal blow to the unity cause. The pending mergers in New York and New Orleans and in several counties in Florida could still go ahead, and merger discussions at the national level were not foreclosed.

# Chapter 21

# THE BREAK

## THE 1972 DEMOCRATIC CONVENTION

In August of 1972, the AFT sponsored a hospitality suite at the national Democratic convention in Miami. I was not a delegate, but I thought I might lure some of the many teacher delegates to the suite so that I could talk with them about teacher unity. I had flyers printed to advertise the suite, and I trudged from hotel to hotel to distribute them.

I had detested Richard Nixon since his unscrupulous campaign against Helen Gahagan Douglas twenty years before. During the 1972 primary elections I supported Senator Edmund Muskie, but when Muskie was knocked out of the running, I supported Senator George McGovern.

The AFL-CIO neoconservatives backed Senator Henry Jackson, who was never really in the running. At the nominating session of the convention, I. W. Abel, president of the Steelworkers, had delivered a blistering attack on McGovern and his supporters. But long before the convention, I had received an indication of Meany's low opinion of the South Dakota senator.

I had gone to see Meany about some now-forgotten matter, and for once the labor chief was in no hurry to conclude our conference. I was puzzled by this unwonted cordiality, but upon leaving I discovered the reason. There, waiting patiently in the outer office was George McGovern.

I once asked McGovern if he thought Meany's opposition stemmed entirely from their differences over the Vietnam War. McGovern said he didn't know. His voting record on legislation was better than Henry Jackson's, except for the war from labor's standpoint.

Considering the failure of the Jackson campaign, I doubt that Meany ever intended to endorse anyone in 1972. Like most successful politicians, Meany never strayed too far from his base, the New York City building-trades unions. In May, before the nominating convention, Governor Nelson Rockefeller had invited the leaders of the New York City labor movement to a picnic at Pocantico Hills, the Rockefeller estate.

It had been a drunken, singing revel. There could be no question about which political party the New York labor leaders were supporting this time. Neither was there any doubt who would cock a canny ear to his old friends in the city.


## EDUCATORS FOR McGOVERN

Although Meany and the AFL-CIO executive council remained neutral throughout the election of 1972, thirty-three AFL-CIO unions and several independents, including the UAW, supported the Democratic ticket of McGovern and Shriver. A month after the team had been nominated, the AFT convention met in St. Paul, Minnesota. I invited Senator McGovern to address the delegates with a view to winning their endorsement, the first by the Federation.

I was under no illusion that McGovern could be elected. With employment and the stock market both up, it was unlikely that the voters would deny Nixon a second term. Nevertheless, the more votes McGovern received the stronger the liberal-labor-rights coalition would be. The AFL-CIO neutrality weakened the coalition and had the effect of supporting Nixon. I wanted to help counteract this lapse.

Soon after McGovern was nominated, Shanker wrote in his weekly column in space bought by the union in the *New York Times* that he saw little to choose between Nixon and Mc-Govern, because both were weak in the area of foreign policy, particularly in regard to support for Israel. When I pointed out to him that McGovern supported the right of teachers to strike, while Nixon was opposed, Shanker retorted that McGovern would say anything to get elected.

To soften Shanker's opposition, I arranged a breakfast meeting in my AFT convention suite. In addition to McGovern, I invited the six members of the AFT executive committee, Senator Walter Mondale, Minnesota Governor Wendel Anderson and two or three others. The seating placed the candidate between Shanker and me, and I told Shanker this would be his chance to ask any questions he might have.

Instead of asking questions, Shanker concentrated on his scrambled eggs. I tried to stimulate conversation, but apparently Shanker was not interested in anything McGovern might say. I finally asked, "Al, don't you have any questions for the senator?"

Shanker thought a moment and then said, "How do you stand on quotas?" A tricky question; the answer could alienate blacks if answered with a flat no. It could alienate others, particularly Jews, if answered affirmatively. But McGovern handled the thrust easily, saying he favored affirmative action and numerical goals, but not quotas.

McGovern's speech to the convention was a masterpiece. It aroused several standing ovations and prolonged applause. At the conclusion I called on a pro-McGovern delegate to move to endorse the Democrat. The motion was forthcoming, but before I could ask the delegates to rise, one of the New Yorkers raised a point of order. A series of parliamentary delays instituted by the New Yorkers followed. By the time these were untangled, the momentum for an acclamation vote had passed.

The maneuvers of the New Yorkers, including a roll call vote, postponed the endorsement action for several hours. The electric moment was lost, but when the vote was counted, the convention had given overwhelming support to the McGovern-Shriver ticket.

With the official endorsement in hand, I joined the McGovern campaign. In addition to speaking at meetings and writing pieces for various publications, I advanced the teacher unity cause. I invited Don Morrison, the immediate past president of the NEA, to join me in forming "Educators for McGovern-Shriver." We sent a jointly signed letter to the AFT membership and to several thousand selected NEA leaders. We asked for contributions. A return envelope and a bumper sticker were enclosed. The contributions covered the cost of printing and mailing and left a tidy sum for the campaign. Three hundred thousand bumper stickers were distributed. Significantly, as a result of "Educators for McGovern-Shriver," Morrison and I developed a strong friendship.


## THE FIRST VICE-PRESIDENT

In the meantime, I was under increasing pressure from Shanker. Since the 1969 AFL-CIO convention he had been working to become a vice-president of the labor federation. He had been told by his confidantes at AFL-CIO headquarters, however, that as long as he was only one of twenty vice-presidents, he could not be chosen in preference to the president and secretary-treasurer.

At a meeting of the AFT executive committee in the fall of 1972, Shanker proposed that the secretary-treasurer, Robert Porter, resign so that he could take Porter's place. Porter would be given another title, and Shanker could then be made an AFL-CIO vice-president.

I could not accept Shanker's scheme. I stated my arguments against "making a deal" with the Meany forces. It would mean giving up any attempt to liberalize the labor movement. Furthermore, if anyone were to be nominated for the AFL-CIO executive council it should be the AFT president. Although the committee approved Shanker's proposal, I announced I would appeal to the executive council.

The AFT council met a week after the executive committee. The AFL-CIO vice-presidency nomination was the main item on the agenda. Shanker had nine of the twenty-one votes going into the meeting. Five vice-presidents were from New York. Four more belonged to Shanker's "shadow caucus."

The bitterness of the 1972 presidential campaign, caused by the failure of the Meany forces to back McGovern, was fresh in my mind. I said that the AFT could best serve the interests of teachers, American society and the labor movement by not allowing itself to be co-opted by the conservative AFL-CIO leadership. I said that the recent election had demonstrated that unity of the liberal movement in America was all-important.

Therefore, the AFT should align itself with the liberals in the labor movement and in society in general.

Some of the vice-presidents who were not already committed nodded their heads in agreement. Sizing up the attitudes of these and other council members, Shanker suddenly changed his position. He said that it would not be necessary for him to become secretary-treasurer. Instead, he said he wished to be designated as "first vice-president." He maintained that the council had that authority even though no such position was listed in the AFT constitution.

The vote was taken, and the Shanker forces won, eleven to nine. Shanker asked that the vote be made unanimous in order to impress the AFL-CIO, and the vice-presidents who had supported my position dutifully changed their votes. I asked that my vote be recorded in the negative.

# Chapter 22

## RESIGNATION AND RESURRECTION

### TIME TO TAKE A STAND

There was no immediate visible result of the designation of Shanker as "first vice-president." Even in labor circles, as news of what had happened got around, it was assumed that all that was involved was a power shift. Only I knew that a profound change in the nature and political direction of the Federation would take place unless something could be done to stop it.

For nearly a decade I had guided the union in an independently liberal direction. The AFT had been in the forefront of the civil rights movement. It had supported the Great Society programs. I had restrained the Federation from reacting against progressive educational changes such as the use of paraprofessionals and the development of state and national programs for assessing progress in education.

I had remained hopeful, too, that the labor movement would become more progressive. I had supported efforts to make it more liberal politically and more attractive to young people who had been repelled by AFL-CIO support of the Vietnam War. Shanker's ascendency was moving the union away from the liberal policies I had worked to establish and placing it on the side of conservatism and reaction.

In February of 1973, the *New York Times* featured a report of the Shanker-Selden dispute. Within a week or so, other papers ran similar stories. The NEA's internal newsletter, *Today*, said the choice of Shanker as a candidate for an AFL-CIO vice-presidency indicated that the Federation would be adamant about labor affiliation as a precondition for entering merger talks.

A few weeks after the *Times* story, I happened to meet Bernard Bard, a reporter for the *New York Post*. He asked about the *Times* report. It was time for me to take a stand. The closer Shanker moved to the AFL-CIO, the more difficult it would be to stop the union's retreat. I had to alert AFT members about what was happening.

I gave Bard the complete story: Shanker's shift to the right; his adherence to the Meany line; his "neutrality" in the 1972 election despite the AFT's endorsement of McGovern; his continuing support of the Vietnam War; his backing of machine Democrats over liberals like Bella Abzug and Allard Lowenstein; his support for an AFL-CIO charter for school administrators while teachers throughout the nation were trying to free themselves from administrator control; and his resistance to a reasonable solution for the community control problem.

After Bard's story was published there was no turning back. I knew I had little chance to win, but I was relieved that the struggle was out in the open.

## MEMORY TAPE: A DAY IN MONTREAL

*It is two-thirty in the morning in March, 1973. I have been skidding over snow-covered roads in a taxi, on my way from the Montreal airport to a hotel in the city. I'm to be a speaker in the morning at the first merged convention of the New York State United Teachers (NYSUT).*

*As I enter the hotel lobby I see Velma Hill, a UFT functionary, trudging wearily toward an elevator.*

*"What are you doing up at this hour?" I ask.*

*"Trying to get to bed. We've been meeting all night, but we finally got it together."*

*I say good night and continue walking toward the registration desk. It is not until the next day that I realize the full significance of Hill's remark.*

In the morning, as I stroll through the throng of delegates outside the convention meeting room, I greet many old friends. Some are distributing flyers, handouts from caucuses. There appear to be three groups. One flyer bears the familiar letterhead, "Unity Caucus." Now I know why Hill was up so late last night. The Unity Caucus has gone statewide.

I encounter my old friend, Paul Rubin. He has a sheaf of flyers headed "Grass Roots Caucus."

"How's it going, Paul," I greet him.

"Hi, Dave. What do you mean, 'how's it going!' Big Al has his act together. Did you read the Unity stuff?"

I tell Paul that I skimmed it. He continues, "They say they had two-thirds of the delegates in there last night."

The convention session is being called to order. I leave Paul and make my way to the platform. I am thinking about a conversation I had with Shanker before the New York merger. He expressed concern about being able to control a statewide organization. It would have nearly 500 locals and 200,000 members. Now he has worked it out.

I have carefully tailored my speech to be firm without leaving an opening for an attack. I receive generous applause and I head for the door.

## THE RESIGNATION

Although I had crossed my Rubicon, I was unsure of my next step. In conjunction with an AFT legislative conference in Washington, I called an executive council meeting to take care of routine business. In a taxi from the Capitol to the meeting, Mary Ellen Riordan told me that the vice-presidents had been conferring about the "leadership crisis." She said a majority thought I should resign.

I had surmised that something of the sort might happen, but I had not decided what to do about it. When the council had assembled I called a recess "so I could confer with the executive committee." I was beginning to develop a plan.

The committee met in Riordan's room. When I called the meeting to order, Riordan repeated what she had told me on the way to the council meeting. I replied that I was prepared to resign, but the convention had elected me, and the convention should decide whether I should continue my term, not the council. Therefore, my resignation would be announced June 1, to be effective August 1. The convention, which would meet two weeks later, would fill the vacancy. I would be a candidate. By throwing the decision into the convention, I would have a chance to make the issues clear.

As I explained my resignation plan to the committee, Shanker frowned. Finally he said, "No, Dave, that wouldn't work. You'll have to resign now."

I replied that I couldn't do that, and in a few minutes the meeting was over. There would be no resignation, at least not for the time being.

## THE UNITY INSTITUTE REVISITED

While my political battle with Shanker continued its hectic course, I continued to pursue the teacher unity will-o'-the-wisp. In the midst of the 1972 convention I had met with a delegation from the National Council of Urban Education Associations (NCUEA), an NEA subgroup established in the early 1960s to ward off the AFT. The NEA had assumed that collective bargaining was a big-city phenomenon which could be counteracted by giving more attention to the problems of city teachers.

The NCUEA had soon developed a political life of its own. It had become increasingly militant and dissatisfied with its parent organization. However, the NCUEA was only a council of affiliates. Even if it were to defy the NEA rule against joining with any organization belonging to the AFL-CIO, there would be little practical effect unless the affiliates followed the council's lead. I had therefore arranged to have the AFT executive council meet in San Diego at the same time the NCUEA was holding its annual meeting there.

My efforts to establish a close working relationship with the NCUEA caused NEA operatives to raise opposition within the urban council. The friends of the AFT found themselves isolated.

While NCUEA and the AFT council were in San Diego, however, Shanker met with Lauri Wynn, the leader of the NEA

Black Caucus. Wynn held liberal views on most social issues, but she was adamantly opposed to AFT-NEA merger, mainly because of Shanker's record in the Ocean Hill-Brownsville conflict. The NEA Black Caucus remained an important stumbling block in the way of organizational merger.

The Wynn-Shanker meeting was arranged by Ned Hopkins. Throughout the three-hour private debate Wynn's position remained unshaken, and instead of producing a lessening of the stand of the NEA Black Caucus it tended to strengthen it.

When it became clear that the NCUEA would not be able to enter into a merger agreement with the AFT, I reverted to a variation of my institute for teacher unity scheme. If the institute were established as an independent entity, both the NCUEA and the AFT could then become members, and the effect would be almost the same as an outright merger. Formally, there would be no violation of the NEA's policy.

As when I first explored the institute idea, the main problem was finding someone with standing in the teacher organization field who had no connection with either the AFT or the NEA, and who would make a good executive secretary. After several weeks of search, I turned to Roy Lindstad, a former representative of the Association in Minneapolis. Lindstad professed to be a unity advocate. I checked him out with the AFT leaders in Minnesota, and although their evaluation was negative, I decided to go ahead anyway. I did not place as much credence in their opinion as I should have because the Minnesotans were generally opposed to the unity strategy.

# Chapter 23

## UNITY AT HAND

MEMORY TAPE: THE PORTLAND COLISEUM

The huge Coliseum in Portland, Oregon, where the 1973 Representative Assembly of the National Education Association is meeting, is brightly lit. More than seven thousand delegates are listening to a presentation by a speaker. In the eerie gloom behind the speakers' platform, a strange tableau is being enacted. Four figures are locked in a group handclasp as two others look on.

The handclaspers are Helen Wise, about to be installed as NEA president; Terry Herndon, recently chosen NEA executive secretary; Albert Shanker, designated as first vice-president of the American Federation of Teachers; and me, the AFT president. The onlookers are Larry Sibelman, an AFT vice-president from Los Angeles, and John Schmid, AFT assistant to the president in charge of organizing.

A year before, the teacher unity movement had received a powerful boost when the NEA and AFT branches in New York State had merged. A few weeks before this convention, Donald Morrison, the NEA past president, and I had reached an understanding on the AFL-CIO affiliation issue. The NEA executive committee had recommended to the convention that AFT-NEA merger talks begin.

Earlier in the day, there had been rumors that the NEA leaders were going to insist on preconditions before the talks would *begin. But when motions to this effect were made by delegates opposed to the merger, the NEA leaders had beaten them down.*

*And now, here we are—the principal leaders of the two teacher organizations, solemnly pledging to try to work out our differences in order to establish that one big union for all teachers.*

*It is the culmination of fifteen years of effort. Unity is in sight.*

## PRELUDE TO PORTLAND

Two months before the 1973 NEA convention in Portland, Oregon, I arranged a conference with Shanker to discuss strategy for the coming Association meeting. It was only two or three weeks after the "resignation meeting." John Schmid and I went to New York for the discussion.

This was the first year that the merged New York organization would be going to the NEA meeting. I hoped that NYSUT would use its great strength to promote the unity cause in other states. Unfortunately, however, two New Yorkers had become candidates for office within the Association, which would make it difficult to work out bargains with other delegations.

Shanker was evasive about his plans for the NEA meeting. He said that he left such matters to Hobart, the NYSUT president. His lack of interest was so obvious that for the first time I began to wonder if he were still in favor of an AFT-NEA merger.

Since Shanker would not take the initiative in advancing the unity drive, I arranged a meeting with Fred Hipp, the veteran executive secretary of the New Jersey Education Association (NJEA). Again I phoned Shanker. I asked him to accompany me, but he sent a representative from NYSUT. We spent all afternoon discussing the merger problem with Hipp and an NJEA field representative. We got nowhere.

Two weeks before the NEA convention the situation could hardly have looked bleaker. The New York merger, which had appeared to be a step toward national unity, seemed to be turning inward. The Association's counteraction against further local and state mergers, coupled with the rallying effect of the

Uniserv plan, had strengthened the antiunity forces. Furthermore, I knew that my days at the helm of the Federation were numbered. There was no way I could round up enough votes to offset the weight of the huge New York bloc. For the last year of my term I knew that I would be a lame duck president.

Suddenly, the situation turned completely around. The change began with a phone call from Don Morrison, the past president of the NEA, with whom I had formed Educators for McGovern-Shriver. Morrison wanted to meet with me. He said the NEA executive committee was holding its final meeting before the convention. It was his last as a committee member. He wanted to introduce a motion that the NEA open merger negotiations with the AFT!

We talked about various issues which might be raised by antiunion NEA leaders to forestall the opening of the talks. Morrison was particularly interested in how the AFL-CIO issue could be handled. He agreed that for some of the committee members, labor affiliation was only a subterfuge to avoid talking about merger, but for others it was real. Some way would have to be found to counteract their fear.

I warned Morrison that I did not have the support of the AFT executive committee, and that I could not guarantee acceptance of my ideas. I explained my option idea to Morrison. It would allow any present NEA member to choose not to have any portion of his dues to the new organization be used for AFL-CIO affiliation. I also said that perhaps after an initial period of affiliation of three or four years there might be a referendum on the question if enough members indicated they wanted such a vote by signing a petition. I said there were also a number of variations of these two ideas which could be discussed.

Morrison declared himself satisfied. Actually, neither the "opt-out" nor the referendum was new. Both had been described in my president's column in the *American Teacher*, which Morrison had read. The day after our meeting I received word from Morrison that the NEA executive committee had voted to recommend to the NEA board of directors and to the convention that merger talks begin. He said the committee's action was based on his report of his conversation with me, and that the committee had been favorably impressed with both the opt-out and the referendum ideas.

## AT PORTLAND

In order to prepare the AFT officers for the opening of merger talks, I called the executive committee to a meeting in Portland the day before the Association's delegate meeting opened. Mary Ellen Riordan was absent, but the others attended: Shanker; Rose Claffey; Nat LaCour, from New Orleans; Frank Sullivan, from Philadelphia. I gave them a complete report of my conversation with Morrison. I discussed the opt-out and the referendum, and opened the meeting for discussion. There were a few questions, but no objections. I said the next step was action by the NEA convention.

None of the several NEA candidates for president was willing to make a public declaration in favor of teacher unity. The one candidate who gave private assurances that he favored AFT-NEA merger gave a speech to the convention in which he attacked George Meany and Albert Shanker.

There was also a much more serious attack on Shanker which had a far-reaching negative effect on the unity cause. Prior to the business part of the week-long meeting, there were two days of "issues conferences" during which prominent educators and public figures gave speeches on controversial topics. One of the speakers at the 1973 convention was Jonathan Kozol, who classified himself as a "Marxist educator." Kozol devoted the major part of his speech to an attack on Shanker's actions in the Ocean Hill-Brownsville strike.

Shanker demanded and received fifteen minutes for a reply. He pulled out the oratorical stops and delivered a ranting, slashing attack on Kozol and Communists. He cited his actions against racial discrimination. Many of the delegates, unaccustomed to the rough and tumble New York style of public speaking, were repelled and frightened by Shanker's tirade.

Lauri Wynn, the Black Caucus leader, also spoke. Her mild and reasonable manner was in striking contrast to Shanker's performance.

## GOOD FAITH

The NEA board of directors acts somewhat like an upper house in the Association's scheme of governance. It is composed of state representatives, including the state executive secretaries. It is considered a conservative body. Somewhat to the surprise of veteran NEA watchers, the board of directors gave its approval to the merger recommendations. In spite of this good faith action, some of the New Yorkers charged that the NEA intended to kill the merger resolution by attaching a precondition which would prohibit AFL-CIO affiliation. When I heard this charge made in a meeting of the prounity forces, I decided to go directly to the NEA leaders to find out where they stood.

I made my way around the coliseum with Larry Sibelman and John Schmid to the back of the stage. I was able to pass a note to Terry Herndon, the newly elected NEA executive director. Soon, we were joined by Herndon and Helen Wise, the president-elect. Herndon and Wise quickly assured me that they were still committed to the merger talks without preconditions.

Satisfied, I was about to return to the unity meeting, when a new idea occurred to me. I asked Sibelman and Schmid to find Shanker and ask him to join us. While they were on their quest I explained to Herndon and Wise that I wanted Shanker to share the assurance I had just received. They understood immediately. A few minutes later, with Shanker present, they repeated their commitments.


## THE AFT CONVENTION

The 1973 AFT convention was held in Washington, D.C., in early August. I was acutely conscious of my tenuous hold on the AFT presidency, but I was sustained by the knowledge that merger discussions would soon begin.

In my annual address I again talked about my view of the proper relationship between the AFT and the AFL-CIO. I said that I had supported AFL-CIO policy most of the time, but that the AFL-CIO was not always right. It had been wrong about the Vietnam War and the 1972 presidential election. I reminded the delegates that the AFT convention had taken contrary views on these questions. This did not mean, however, that we would think of leaving the AFL-CIO. I favored labor unity, just as I favored teacher unity, but dissent should not be mistaken for disloyalty.

I also used my presidential prerogatives to stack the lineup of outside speakers appearing at the convention. Knowing that media coverage of the convention would skip the details and concentrate on the newsworthy people, I sought to project through the choice of speakers the liberal image I had maintained for the Federation. Among the guests were Cesar Chavez, president of the Farmworkers, and Atlanta Congressman Andrew Young. I also invited Al Barkan, director of COPE, to leaven the mixture.

At only one point during the convention was there a threat to the coming merger negotiations. Ronald O'Brian, president of the Connecticut Federation of Teachers and a strong opponent of AFT-NEA merger, introduced a motion which would have ruled out my opt-out scheme and made AFL-CIO affiliation a nonnegotiable precondition of the merger talks. I pointed out that any merger agreement would be submitted to the membership for referendum vote and that the plan would have to be judged in its totality. If the AFT were to place preconditions on the negotiations, it would be a breach of faith, and there would probably be no negotiations.

O'Brian then appealed to Shanker for support. Although I had strong misgivings about the New York leader's commitment to teacher unity, by this time, he rejected O'Brian's appeal. The motion was defeated.

The convention adjourned with no damage done to the unity cause. I was looking forward eagerly to the beginning of the merger negotiations.


## MERGER NEGOTIATIONS BEGIN

Following the Federation convention in early August, I tried to establish contact with someone in authority in the NEA in order to schedule the first negotiating session. Finally, the date of October 3 was set.

I also called a meeting of the AFT executive committee to discuss strategy and explore possible solutions for the problems which were certain to come up. The committee showed no eagerness to grapple with these problems, however. The merger question was relegated to the bottom of a long agenda of routine items. When it was reached, no one had any suggestions for facilitating the coming discussions.

The basic assumption of the merger strategy was that teachers had an urgent need for unity. Once they came to believe it could be achieved, they would insist that their leaders put aside rivalries and personal striving to achieve solidarity. The AFT, therefore, having finally brought the Association to the negotiating table, should have continued to push for unity until the negotiations had been successfully concluded. Instead, the AFT was proving a reluctant suitor.

The AFT merger negotiating committee consisted of the six members of the executive committee plus Secretary-Treasurer Porter, and my two assistants, John Schmid and Al Loewenthal. The NEA's team was headed by NEA President Helen Wise and Executive Director Terry Herndon. Other members included Robert Chanin, the NEA's general counsel and assistant executive director, and various other officers and staff members.

I opened the talks by pointing out that there was no conflict of interest in the talks. Both sides were trying to create a new, merged organization which could accomplish more than either could accomplish by itself. Neither organization should automatically take a negative attitude toward the other's proposals. I pledged that the AFT would give serious consideration to any idea advanced by the Association.

If the AFT had entered the negotiations properly prepared I would have been able to follow my introductory remarks by presenting a reasonable plan for bringing the two groups together. Instead, the Federation lamely looked to the NEA to lead. Completing the role reversal, the NEA presented a detailed and coherent statement of its position. The AFT called a caucus.

The Association's statement called for no affiliation with the AFL-CIO, guarantees of minority representation on official bodies and secret ballot voting on roll call votes at conventions. The statement also called for mediation and fact-finding if no agreement had been reached by February 1, 1974. It ended by outlining procedures for adoption of merger recommendations, a further indication of good faith.

In the AFT caucus it was immediately apparent that the long-standing hostility toward the NEA had not abated. The AFT representatives were scornful of the NEA's statement, and they spent an hour searching it for hidden traps. The situation clearly called for counterproposals, but since the Federation could not agree on any I was forced to send word to the NEA that the AFT would respond in writing later. It was a disheartening conclusion to such a long-awaited event.

## INTERLUDE IN MIAMI

A week following the opening of merger talks, the AFT officers and staff went to Miami for the 1973 AFL-CIO convention. Coincident with the convention were many meetings and conferences of related bodies, including the AFT executive council, the negotiating committee and various special groups. At this convention, Shanker was scheduled to be chosen an AFL-CIO vice-president.

One of the related meetings at the labor convention was the meeting of the Council of AFL-CIO Unions for Professional Employees (CUP). I had been elected president of CUP two years before. Lane Kirkland gave the keynote speech. During the obligatory cocktail party afterward, many of the leaders of other unions came by to say hello and exchange gossip. It was not until the next day that I learned what had been happening during the party.

While everybody was having a good time, Shanker and his lieutenants had been circulating a "pledge-of-support sheet" among the AFT vice-presidents. The pledge was to support Shanker for AFT president at the 1974 AFT convention, nearly a year in the future. All the vice-presidents except Riordan signed, and several months later, she too declared her allegiance to the New Yorker.

It was a crushing blow. That the vice-presidents had acceded to Shanker's solicitation was not too surprising. Half the members of the AFT were now in New York. His election was certain. Why sacrifice oneself for a lost cause? But what was Shanker's reason for moving now? Was it sheer vindictiveness, or was he still trying to take over the union a year ahead of time?

The following day I had another clash with Shanker. I had asked Congressman Andrew Young for a recommendation to fill a vacancy in the AFT civil rights director position. He recommended a person he had worked with in the Southern Christian Leadership Conference. I had nominated her for confirmation by the executive committee, but Shanker nominated Louis Hurt, an AFT vice-president from Kansas City. Hurt was selected, even though he had never shown much interest in civil rights.

An even more serious setback occurred when the merger negotiating committee met. I had prepared a draft statement in reply to the NEA's opening position paper. The draft statement discussed my opt-out proposal in general terms, and suggestions were made for resolving other issues. Shanker objected to mention of the compromise proposal. "Why give it away?" he asked. The others agreed with him. The statement which finally went to the NEA had no offer of compromise on any point.

In retrospect, AFT-NEA merger was lost in Miami, long before the resumption of negotiations with the NEA.

## LOOKING FOR HELP

Before leaving Miami I spent an hour with Jerry Wurf, president of AFSCME. Two years earlier he had formed the Coalition of American Public Employees (CAPE), with which the NEA was affiliated. While AFSCME's alliance with the NEA had not been in the best interests of the AFT, I thought Wurf might use his friendship with the NEA leaders to advance the teacher merger cause. The AFSCME president, however, claimed he had no influence with the NEA leaders.

As soon as I returned to Washington I explored other ways to advance the negotiations. I called Bill Dodds, head of the UAW's Washington political operation, to ask him for assistance in carrying out a special project. NEA leaders claimed that teachers were not interested in merging with the AFT, particularly if merger meant affiliation with the AFL-CIO. I believed just the opposite was true. A national teacher referendum would verify my judgment, I thought, but that would require the cooperation of the NEA, and that was not likely to be forthcoming. I therefore wanted to hire Lou Harris to conduct a nationwide survey on the question. I called Harris, who was intrigued by the idea. He thought the job could be done for about $50,000.

Fifty thousand dollars would not have been a large sum for the AFT to devote to such a project at the time, but considering the weak commitment of the union's executive committee to the unity cause, I doubted that I could get its approval for the expenditure. Furthermore, a poll commissioned by the AFT would be suspect in the eyes of the NEA leaders. I thought that the UAW could provide the funds and "launder" them by having another organization, perhaps one in civil rights, be the official sponsor.

Dodds was sympathetic but he said that he was well-acquainted with some of the Association leaders, and that he would like to try his hand at mediation before putting my poll idea into effect. I preferred going directly to the poll, but I held off while Dodds tried to work out a merger formula.

I also tried to use the National Coalition for Teacher Unity to induce the NEA to put the opt-out plan on the table. The NCTU had become institutionalized, with Roy Lindstad, the executive secretary, installed in an office in Washington. Lindstad had contacts within the NEA which I thought might help.

Neither Dodds nor Lindstad reported any progress by the time the second negotiating session occurred.

## Part V

# THE REBELLION TAMED

# Chapter 24

# PEARL HARBOR DAY

## THE SECOND SESSION

The second merger negotiating session was held October 30. The AFT's response to the NEA's position paper was delivered to the Association only a few days before the meeting. Without authorized counterproposals to the Association's three main substantive points, I turned to discussion of procedural and structural problems in the hope that the merger would acquire an aura of inevitability. Scattered through the AFT statement were many hints which could be picked up if anyone on the other side was trying to move toward merger.

For instance, after citing the AFT's 1972 convention resolution which seemed to place strict requirements for AFL-CIO affiliation on any merged organization, the paper stated, ". . . restrictions are placed on mergers at the local and state level, but much more flexibility is allowed at the national level." Attention was then called to action by both the AFT and the NEA conventions rejecting attempts to harden their respective positions on labor affiliation. Even though I had been foreclosed from presenting the opt-out proposal, I conveyed the idea that the Federation was open to compromise.

In discussing the structure of the proposed organization, I tried to strike a balance between the "states' rights" plan of the Association and the simpler, local autonomy plan of the AFT. To counter the tendency of the Association toward staff control, final authority was placed unequivocally in the hands of the elected officers.

215

The quota question and the secret ballot issue were also touched on. Under a section entitled "Principles of Merger," the AFT statement proposed: "The annual meeting should consist of delegates elected by secret ballot from local organizations in accordance with federal law (Landrum-Griffin Act). Also in accordance with federal law, no discrimination may be shown in admission to membership or eligibility to serve as a delegate or officer, on the basis of race, ethnic identification, sex, religion, or political belief."

The AFT had complied with the Landrum-Griffin Act as soon as it had been passed, but the NEA had refused to comply, and the issue was then in the courts.

The AFT response to the NEA's opening statement was weak. The strictures imposed by the negotiating committee prevented me from answering the three key issues the Association had listed. The AFT offered no assurance that members of ethnic and racial minorities would be included in the mainstream of the merged organization. No solution was offered for the problem of secret versus public voting on important issues at conventions. Neither the opt-out nor any other face-saving plan was offered on the AFL-CIO affiliation issue. Only rebuttals to the NEA positions were listed. This argumentative mode could only result in a continuing stand-off.

At the second negotiating meeting, the NEA representatives seemed far less eager than at the first session. Their enthusiasm for teacher unity seemed to have lost its urgency. Their attitude seemed to be, "If you want merger, make it worth our while. Otherwise, forget it!"

But the AFT offered nothing, and the second negotiating session was entirely unproductive.


*MEMORY TAPE: MEETING THE PRESS IN*
*ST. LOUIS*

*I am in St. Louis, a week or so after the second merger negotiating session. The St. Louis Teachers Union—after ten years of defeat and disappointment—has won for teachers the right to vote for a bargaining agent. I am holding a press conference* as a part of the public relations activity involved in the campaign.

Reporters from television, radio and the newspapers are crowded into a small room. My old friend Robert Lieberman, who is handling public relations for the local, introduces me.

I launch into an introductory statement about the virtues of collective bargaining for teachers. It is routine, and although the newspaper reporters are scribbling, the television cameras are not rolling.

One of the television reporters signals to his cameraperson and lobs the usual strike question to me. "Will you call St. Louis teachers out on strike if you win the election?"

I laugh. "I can't call anybody out on strike. If teachers decide to strike, the decision will be made by a democratic vote. But if the St. Louis school board bargains in good faith, it should not be necessary to strike."

The reporter has another "zinger." "Will St. Louis taxpayers have to come up with a tax increase?"

"No, not necessarily. There may be extra funds in the budget somewhere. Besides, school money comes from state and federal sources as well as local taxation."

Another reporter gets my attention. "Last week Dr. Wise, the president of the NEA, was here and she said that as long as the AFT insisted on AFL-CIO affiliation there could be no merger between your organization and hers. Do you have any comment?"

The NEA president's response to the merger inquiry had apparently been the routine response which NEA spokespersons had been using for years. My answer is also standard. "The AFL-CIO problem can be solved in many ways," I say. "For instance there can be a 'trial affiliation' for a few years. After the teachers have seen how it works there could be a referendum on the question."

The first television reporter now wants another shot at me. "Are you in favor of forced busing?"

The question has nothing to do with the subject of the press conference, and I reply flippantly. "No," I say, well aware of the consternation among the AFT members present. Then I add, "I prefer subways." The press conference breaks up in a short burst of laughter.

## THE SURPRISE ATTACK

Through the month of November I had a feeling of mounting tension. Two negotiating sessions had been held with little progress toward teacher unity. I knew that the opportunity for merger was slipping away. Yet, the negotiations seemed to be stuck.

In the middle of the month I returned to St. Louis for two meetings: the annual convention of the Missouri Federation of Teachers and a conference of the AFT organizing staff. Shanker was also a speaker at these meetings, and we sat next to each other at the head tables for several hours without exchanging more than a few words.

At the organizers' conclave I reported on the merger negotiations in detail. I also discussed the opt-out and the trial affiliation ideas, and other formulas for resolving the affiliation issue. I knew that most of the organizers were still opposed to the merger strategy as they had been all along.

I had been back at my desk in Washington only a few days when I received a telegram from Shanker moving that a special meeting of the executive council be held. The purpose of the meeting was not specified. I called Sibelman for clues as to what was happening. He told me that Shanker was going to ask the executive council to demand my resignation on the grounds that I had betrayed the negotiations.

I was astounded. Betrayed the negotiations? After the years I had devoted to bringing them about? Furthermore, Shanker's attack violated standards of democratic procedure and due process. No charges had been given, and the verdict would be rendered by a jury already pledged to support the accuser.

I sent a telegram to Shanker asking the purpose of the special council meeting. I added that if he would be presenting charges against me, what were they? I also consulted Joe Rauh, the civil rights and civil liberties lawyer, who was a friend. After studying the AFT constitution and related documents, he confirmed my opinion that the council could not force me to resign. He also advised that the constitution provided no method for recall.

Reinforced, I faced the ordeal of the special executive council meeting. Appropriately, the meeting had been set for December 7: Pearl Harbor Day.


## THE KANGAROO COURT

Sibelman called me two days before the December 7 special executive council meeting. He urged me to resign so that Shanker could become president. Shanker had told him that he would never support an AFT-NEA merger while I was president. If I stepped down, merger might be negotiated. This was a new consideration. Even though Shanker's enthusiasm for merger had obviously cooled, I still found it hard to believe that he would actually scuttle the unity talks.

When the vice-presidents assembled, I pointed out that *Robert's Rules of Order* states that the purpose of a special meeting must be set forth in the meeting call, and that business must be limited to that subject. Therefore, the meeting could only go on under protest. I would decide later whether to press the point.

The council members had met secretly the night before to discuss their strategy. For nearly three hours they hammered away. They charged me with publicly proposing a limited affiliation with the AFL-CIO as a way to facilitate AFT-NEA merger even though the negotiating committee had specifically rejected the presentation of such an idea.

A letter from Roy Lindstad was also read. Lindstad wrote that I had asked him to propose the opt-out idea secretly to the NEA. In addition, Louis Hurt, the civil rights director, testified that I had slandered Bayard Rustin, the executive director of the A. Philip Randolph Institute.

I had almost single-handedly brought about the merger talks. To say that I had sabotaged them was ridiculous. I pointed out that the opt-out and the trial affiliation ideas and many other formulas for getting around the labor affiliation stumbling block had been talked about for years. They had been described in the *American Teacher* more than a year ago.

More important, I had talked directly with former NEA president Don Morrison about these schemes, and it was on this basis that the NEA had agreed to negotiate. I had reported my conversation in detail to the AFT executive committee at its meeting before the NEA convention in Portland. No objection had been raised.

I admitted that there might be some truth to what Lindstad and Hurt had said, but that their reports were inaccurate and distorted.

At one point Shanker said, "Dave, why did you do it?"

I replied that I did not think that he was working for merger, an accusation which he did not deny.

There was no way I could win in the kangaroo court of the executive council. The members had already pledged their support to Shanker for president. The sooner I left office, the sooner this could be accomplished. The council passed a motion asking for my resignation. I said I would give their request careful consideration and called for a motion to adjourn.

A vice-president suggested a half hour recess while I made up my mind. I said I would need at least a week to decide, and again called for a motion to adjourn. Someone "so moved." I declared the meeting over.

Why had Shanker changed his mind about teacher unity? I believe it was because he had become convinced, after his confrontations with the Association at the 1972 and 1973 conventions, that he could never rise to the top of the merged organization. In a merged organization a new politics would prevail. The half million AFT members would be mixed with the million and a half NEA members. It would be difficult even to maintain the former AFT members as a national caucus. At the state level, only in New York and two or three other states would the former Federation members have a majority.

# Chapter 25

## END OF THE DREAM

### THE NEGOTIATIONS FAIL

The teacher unity negotiations between the leaders of the AFT and the NEA really came to an end on December 7, 1973, although there were two more meetings of the negotiating committees. On that cold, drizzly morning in New York, Albert Shanker, supported by the other members of the union's executive council, brought about a reversal of the long-standing AFT teacher unity policy. I had been the driving force behind the unity movement. By discrediting me, or at least alienating me from other AFT leaders, Shanker was able to halt the Federation's thrust toward merger with the NEA.

There is no way to ascertain Shanker's motive for his action. Perhaps he never really believed that teachers could become the progressive force I envisioned. Perhaps he believed that I had some sinister personal reason for favoring merger with the NEA, even though my years of effort toward that end could hardly leave my sincerity in doubt. Or perhaps Shanker's ambitions for advancement in the AFL-CIO, ambitions which might be forestalled if he were forced to rebuild his political machine in the larger universe of the merged organization, underlay his action. Whatever the reason, there can be no doubt that Shanker's attack on me disrupted the negotiations.

The third AFT-NEA merger negotiating session occurred only a week after the Pearl Harbor Day attack. Although I had decided against resigning before the end of the council meeting, so far as anybody knew I was still trying to make up my mind.

In order to further test Shanker's commitment to teacher unity,
I decided to absent myself from the third meeting with the NEA.
This would place Shanker in charge of the union's team. If he
moved aggressively to advance the negotiations, I would have
to reevaluate my position; if not, my assessment of the situation
would be confirmed.

The discussion with the NEA dealt only with generalities—
whether administrators should be admitted to membership, the
relation of state and local organizations to the national organization, the relation of elected officers to staff and the ratification process. No new proposals were made by either side.

Before adjournment the two sides agreed to meet again on
February 27, 1974.

I scheduled the executive council to meet an hour before the
fourth negotiating session. By that time I had not only announced I would not resign, but I was engaged in an admittedly
quixotic reelection campaign. I had formed, with William Simons, president of the Washington (DC) Teachers Union,
Teachers Cause, to arouse grass-roots support. In addition to
his local position, Simons was also head of the AFT Black Caucus.

I opened the executive council meeting by proposing three
compromises to be presented to the NEA. The first was the opt-
out idea. Any member of the merged organization who was not
a member of an organization affiliated with the AFL-CIO at the
time of merger would be permitted to stipulate, within thirty
days, that none of his dues would go to the labor federation.
There was heated discussion with Shanker and the other New
Yorkers opposed to the proposal, but finally, however, it was
passed.

My second compromise suggestion was that the question of
representation of racial and ethnic minorities be referred to a
committee composed of one person from the AFT, one from
the NEA, one chosen by the Anti-Defamation League, one chosen by the NAACP and a fifth chosen by the American Arbitration Association. Shanker objected to considering this plan
until the NEA had made its position clear on the opt-out proposal. It was therefore held in abeyance, but I nevertheless presented my third idea. The question of secret votes on important

questions at conventions would be decided by membership referendum a year after the merger.

When the meeting with the NEA got underway, I presented the long withheld opt-out proposal. It was too late. The NEA had come to the meeting determined to conclude the negotiations. Although I suggested the use of a mediator, the NEA refused. The negotiations were over. Teacher unity was a cause whose time had not yet come.

## UNITY SHREDDED

The final six months of my third term as AFT president were the most excruciating six months of my life. Through Teachers Cause, Simons and I tried to rally support, but the response was spotty. Teachers felt no urgency about building a united organization. They were accustomed to having local issues resolved through local action. Building a unified organization at the state and national levels seemed to have only a tenuous relation to their problems. Neither could they see how pursuing broad objectives of union democracy and educational and social reform would help them in their classrooms.

Shanker attacked our supporters as "scabs, strikebreakers and Communists." Many old friends succumbed to the pressure. The election turned into a rout. I received barely ten percent of the vote of the delegates at the convention.

Once I was gone from the AFT scene, Shanker and his associates set about making me an "unperson." References to me in AFT publications were systematically excised. The democratic reforms in AFT functioning which I had introduced were reversed, and the vestiges of teacher unity were obliterated. The dismembering of the New York merger was the final step.

Shanker had never been comfortable in the NEA. By 1975 it was clear that the New Yorkers would soon be leaving.

From the beginning of the New York merger, NYSUT publications had maintained a drumfire of criticism of the NEA while criticism of the AFT and AFL-CIO was suppressed. Following the breakup of the national merger talks, the Association launched a strong counterattack by sending special mailings to the New York members, but these merely intensified the conflict.

NYSUT made the NEA's requirement for proportional representation of minorities the chief target of its attack on the Association. When an NYSUT attempt to remove the minorities protection from the NEA constitution failed at the 1975 convention, it was clear that NYSUT would secede. By early 1976, the separation was accomplished.

In truth, no real attempt was made by the Association to hold the New Yorkers once their intent had become clear. After their brief flirtation with teacher unity in the merger negotiations, NEA leaders turned their attention inward. Although they regretted losing 150,000 duespayers, they were not unhappy about being rid of a source of political disruption.

And so the cause of teacher unity became a sham. From time to time leaders of each organization continued to issue ritualistic calls for unity, but no one on either side took these hollow pronouncements seriously.

# Chapter 26

## REBELLION, REVOLUTION AND REFORM

MEMORY TAPE: DEFINING TERMS

The literature storeroom at AFT headquarters when I arrived there in 1964 was part of what had been the butler's pantry in the days when the building was a millionaire's mansion. It was a narrow, windowless cellar fitted with floor-to-ceiling shelving on which were piled copies of the union's promotional leaflets and pamphlets. Even though the room was well-painted and spotless, a tribute to Fred Jameson, the janitor, the atmosphere was like a mausoleum.

I sift through the publications as Jameson calls my attention to various examples, some of them dating back many years. The janitor is a stout, dignified man in his fifties. He is a union enthusiast, an allegiance learned in his native Scotland.

"Before I came here there was no order at all," he says; "none at all. Everything was strewn around every which way. Now you can find whatever you want."

I note a pile of Winning Collective Bargaining booklets, the how-to-do-it handbook I had written. There are also boxes of the study of the effects of merit rating on teachers, yellowing reprints from the American Teacher and other publications.

"This is our 'best seller,'" Jameson says as he hands me an orange-colored pamphlet titled Questions and Answers About the American Federation of Teachers. I open it. The first question asks, "What is the American Federation of Teachers?" Answer: "The AFT is a national union of teachers, affiliated with the AFL-CIO." The next question asked when the union was founded. The answer stated simply, "1916." I slip Questions and Answers into my pocket and browse through other items in the motley accumulation.

"Some of these have been here for a long time," I observe dryly.

Jameson grins. "We ought to winnow out some of this stuff," he says.

"I'll work on it," I reply. "Bring one of each of these up to my office when you get around to it." I turn and make my way back through the building to my second-floor cubicle. I sit at my desk. What is the AFT? After a half dozen false starts I type, "The AFT is a national union of teachers with a three-fold purpose. First, it works to improve teachers' salaries, working conditions and other benefits. Second, it seeks to improve the quality of education, and third, working in cooperation with the rest of the labor movement, it is a force for social reform."

The statement is more hope than fact, but it is the first time I have tried to formulate the core of my understanding of teacher unionism.


## THE INDUSTRIALIZATION OF EDUCATION

The history of American public education is largely a record of the struggle between those who have wanted to expand educational services and those who have wanted to restrict them. It has been a principle of American public policy since the nation's earliest years that public schools, free to all, are essential to the functioning of American democracy. The ancillary questions of who should be educated, how well, at what cost and at whose expense have remained open. Answers to these questions tend to depend on self-interest and on one's definition of and enthusiasm for democracy.

Teachers and other educational workers and parents usually favor educational expansion, while business and real estate interests, which have to pay a large part of the cost of such expansion, are usually resistant. But if one is committed to the improvement of American society, one must certainly be an advocate of educational expansion.

It must be noted that there are also those who try to have it both ways. They say they would support more education "of the right kind," but they are critical of most of the things the schools are doing, which means they really oppose educational improvement.

Although there have been periods of retreat over the past two centuries, the general trend of American education has been expansionist. Before World War I, an eighth-grade education was all most people needed. High school was considered unnecessary for those who did not intend to go to college. Large numbers of young people—the children of farmers and blue-collar workers, mostly, and of blacks and recent immigrants especially—received minimal schooling. By the end of World War II, it was assumed that everyone should complete high school although nearly half of the school-age population was not achieving that goal.

The remarkable expansion of American education during the first half of this century greatly increased its cost. This generated increased pressure for more efficient educational methods. As Raymond Callahan pointed out in his seminal study, the *Cult of Efficiency in Education* (Chicago University Press, 1962), there were many attempts to adapt the new mass production manufacturing methods to schools. Although most of these schemes were short-lived, the forces which gave rise to them are still very much evident. Educational policy is still heavily influenced by economic factors. Students are taught in groups, rather than as individuals. They move along the curriculum at uniform rates like products on an assembly line. The larger the group, the lower the unit cost. Teaching has been standardized so that almost any college graduate can do it. This also reduces costs because it is unnecessary to employ teachers who are more than ordinarily innovative, energetic and capable of exercising mature judgment.

Even though the more literal transpositions of factory systems are no longer used in the schools, American education is still organized on an industrial model. Conformity and acceptance of authority by students and teachers are more highly valued than spontaneity and creativity.

At its roots the teacher rebellion was a struggle for status. Most teachers are the children of working-class parents. They begin their careers with strong feelings of pride and hope. Their diplomas signify that they have risen above their class of origin. They believe that they have gained respect and dignity, that they are professionals only a notch below doctors and lawyers. Then they are confronted with the reality that they are only workers in the education industry. They suffer the pangs of unrequited expectations.

The feeling that teachers were losing status was intensified as conditions in the schools declined during the 1950s and 1960s, particularly in the big cities. The spark of collective bargaining fell into ready tinder. Furthermore, the militancy and union activism necessary for effective collective bargaining were emotionally satisfying as well as economically rewarding. For teachers, collective bargaining became the engine of the teacher rebellion.

Rebellions which bring about deep and lasting changes in social structure are classified as revolutions. In that sense, the teacher rebellion did not quite make it. In spite of all the picketlines, rallies and strikes, the teacher rebellion left no deep impression on the structure of American society. Neither did it bring about deep and lasting changes in the way children are taught. However, it did bring about an irreversible change in the relationship between teachers and school administrators and school boards. The adoption of collective bargaining cut through the hypocritical cant of false professionalism which had obscured the paternalism and authoritarianism permeating the relationship between teachers and school management.

The American educational enterprise expanded during the 1950s, 1960s and early 1970s under the pressure of rising enrollments, teacher militancy and the newly acknowledged needs of blacks and others deprived of effective education. At the same time, the percentage of the gross national product devoted to public elementary and secondary education rose spectacularly. In 1950 that percentage stood at 3.3. Ten years later, it was 5.0. In 1970 it had risen to 7.3.

Historically, school districts have depended on local property taxes as their main source of revenue. The unprecedented expansion of education during the postwar period required marked increases in state funds. In 1965 the federal government passed the Elementary and Secondary Education Act and began to share responsibility for school support. The shift in the sources of support for education brought new challenges for the teacher organizations, challenges neither was able to answer adequately.

In the early 1970s, the annual increases in school enrollment, which had forced the provision of new funds, began to fall off. By mid-decade the number of students in public schools began to decline. As Gerald R. Gill wrote in *Meanness Mania* (Howard University Press, 1980), the progressive mood which had generated support for the Great Society programs of the Johnson administration—including increased aid to education—gave way to Nixonian "benign neglect" and increased hostility toward social programs.

By the mid-seventies, the big cities, power centers of the teacher rebellion, were beset by rising unemployment, mounting inflation, near-epidemic crime, growing racial hostility, and political reaction. The schools, repositories of hope, came under increasingly heavy attack from the right and the left.

The problems had become too great to solve at the local bargaining table.


## BACK TO NEW YORK

The first major school district to crack under the changed circumstances of the late 1970s was New York City, the place where the teacher rebellion began.

Since the 1960s, New York had been accumulating an ever-larger operating deficit, even though deficits were outlawed by the city's charter. But budgets, after all, are only estimates of revenues and expenditures. As long as nobody pointed a finger, the growing shortage was simply passed along from one budget year to the next by exaggerating anticipated revenues and under-estimating expenditures. Because the city always borrowed against these paper figures, the true state of affairs was not readily apparent. City financial leaders, who must have had their suspicions, did not cry out because they were raking in huge profits. The banks stored the city's cash without paying normal interest and brokered the sale of the notes which covered the borrowing. Even *Standard and Poor's* and *Moody's* regularly gave the city high credit ratings.

In the spring of 1975, *The New York Times* published a "secret report" that was supposedly made for the financial community. It indicated that the city had an excessive amount of "paper" outstanding. Most New Yorkers, conditioned by earlier cries of wolf, received this news calmly, but the *Times* vehemently accused the city of living beyond its means. It demanded reforms in the form of layoffs and cuts in services.

In the meantime, Mayor Abraham D. Beame was having trouble obtaining state approval for his 1975 version of the city's annual package of new state aid and taxing authority. The trouble stemmed from the fact that the State Senate was Republican and Governor Hugh Carey and the State Assembly were Democratic. Without senate approval, enabling legislation could not be passed. The city's government was being held hostage by a coalition of the *Times*, the financial interests and the Republicans.

Confronted by this lack of cooperation, Mayor Beame, supported by Governor Carey, issued a *pro forma* call for help to the Ford administration in Washington. William Simon, secretary of the treasury, deftly lobbed this fiscal serve of the Democratic duo back into their own court by insisting that the city make an honest effort to avoid bankruptcy before whining to Washington. Simon listed various remedial actions New York should take. These included charging tuition at the city university and cutting professors' salaries by five percent, charging tolls on the interborough bridges, forcing city employees to contribute to their pensions, limiting police vacation time to thirty days a year and raising subway fares. President Ford commented that the New York City crisis was strictly a state and local affair.

When I was the UFT's chief strategist, I tried to persuade the city to seek authority to levy a surtax on the state income tax. This would have provided a more equitable and flexible source of support than the grab bag of sales and nuisance taxes, fees and gambling money on which the city relied. This idea was rejected in favor of an increase in the sales tax, a regressive stop-gap solution. If the city had gained the right to levy the surtax, the 1975 financial crisis could have been avoided.

In June Governor Carey found it expedient to agree to the creation of a new supervisory agency for the city, the Municipal Assistance Corporation—"Big Mac." Big Mac was the creation of Felix Rohatyn, an expert in corporate mergers from the financial house of Lazard Freres.

It was into these storm-tossed budgetary and political waters that the UFT negotiators plunged and tried to win a contract to succeed the expiring three-year agreement. The union bravely approached the board of education with its usual list of two hundred and fifty demands. It included a 25 percent cost-of-living raise to compensate for losses over the past three years. The UFT backed up its action with a reiteration of its no-contract, no-work policy.

The board responded with demands of its own. It called for elimination of two and a half hours a week of free time which the union had won for teachers in the "difficult" schools. It declared its intention to eliminate many after-school programs, a source of added income for thousands of teachers. It also proposed reducing the board's contribution to the teachers' retirement system, cancellation of sabbatical leaves, forcing teacher layoffs and eliminating thousands of teaching positions.

Earlier in the summer, the mayor had imposed a freeze on the salaries of city employees. Even though the school system was considered to be autonomous, and the school budget contained funds for a five-percent salary increase, the board declared that it would comply with the mayor's wage freeze. In addition, Big Mac, now firmly in the saddle, required the board to eliminate five thousand teaching and other positions.

The UFT side-stepped. It asked that the frozen funds budgeted for salary increases be used to rehire as many of the laid-off school employees as possible. While the school board considered this idea, the *Times* called for even more layoffs.

Late in the summer, it was agreed by Big Mac and other concerned parties that the city's total debt was $12 billion, give or take $100 million. It would require $3.3 billion in ready money to get the city into stable operating condition. The rest of the deficit would be "funded." Felix Rohatyn, whose authority had grown as the weeks of crisis continued, recommended that the needed amount be raised through the sale of Big Mac bonds and that the state and federal governments act as guarantors. While most of this new issue would be bought by the banks—at interest rates more than double what the city had paid only three months before—Rohatyn insisted that a substantial amount be purchased by the city employee pension funds as a hedge against too aggressive bargaining in the future.

One by one the city employee unions swallowed the Rohatyn medicine, but the teachers could not be so easily subdued. A day before the UFT's no-contract, no-work policy was to take effect, a huge rally was held outside board of education headquarters in Brooklyn. The rally ended with more than 25,000 teachers surging across Brooklyn Bridge to surround city hall on the Manhattan side.

In the end the UFT was forced to capitulate. Although the settlement was hailed as a great union victory, it was a standoff at best. Some of the laid-off school employees were rehired, but thousands of positions were eliminated from the school budget. Conditions in the schools worsened notwithstanding the provisions of the contract. Worst of all, the board succeeded in "taking back" from the teachers two free periods a week in the "difficult" schools as an emergency measure, but it did so by shortening the school day for pupils. This Solomonic compromise became a source of public outrage against the union and the board. There was no general salary increase, and even the longevity raises the union succeeded in negotiating for veteran teachers were held in abeyance pending improvement in the city's financial condition.

On the weekend before the city was granted surcease from its financial troubles, an interesting luncheon took place at Pocantico Hills, the Rockefeller estate in Westchester County. The guests included Warren Anderson, Republican leader of the State Senate; Arthur Burns, Chairman of the Federal Reserve Board; and William Simon, U.S. Secretary of the Treasury. The host was David Rockefeller. Three days later, Governor Carey signed a measure which had suddenly cleared both houses of the legislature. It provided $2.3 billion in aid and additional taxing power for the city. New York was saved.

The New York City financial crisis demonstrated dramatically that local teacher collective bargaining has its limitations,

even in a great city where the teachers are well-organized, dis-
ciplined and militant. It was a demonstration that was to be
repeated in other cities: Chicago, Kansas City, St. Louis, Philadelphia, Boston, Cleveland and scores of lesser school districts.

## THE LIMITS OF POLITICAL ACTION

Undoubtedly, the law of diminishing returns applies in education. A point could be reached where spending more money
on schools would be unproductive, but few if any school districts have ever approached that point. The quality of education
depends upon staffing ratios, supplies and equipment, remedial and other supplemental services, and most of all, on the
quality of the teaching and supervisory staff.

While local collective bargaining is crucial to maintaining a
trustworthy relationship between teachers and school officials,
it cannot produce enough funds to maximize the quality of education except in very wealthy localities. Most local school
boards do not have enough taxing power. Thus, the quality of
American education has come to depend on state and federal
aid. Statewide and national collective bargaining—in conjunction with district bargaining—is the most effective way to increase state and federal support. Both teacher organizations
have turned increasingly to lobbying.

The AFT and the NEA were involved in state and national
legislative activity long before the teacher rebellion, although
the approaches of the two organizations differed. The Association tried to build an independent proeducation coalition
made up of teachers, school administrators, parents and public-
spirited citizens. The AFT proceeded from the assumption that
teachers and other workers have an interest in good public
schools which makes them natural allies. As a result, the Federation has operated as a part of the larger legislative program
of the labor movement. This difference in approaches produced
interesting results.

As the American system of public education expanded after
World War II, the AFT and the NEA increased their lobbying
activities. In 1966 the Elementary and Secondary Education Act

(ESEA) was adopted. For the first time, large amounts of federal aid were authorized for the support of public education, but there were still annual battles over the amounts appropriated by Congress. These struggles led to formation of the Full Funding Committee, which included representatives of the AFT, the NEA, the AFL-CIO and many other interested organizations. The Full Funding Committee could have led to cooperation in other fields as well. Neither the AFT nor the NEA took advantage of this opening.

Lobbying efforts must be backed by effective political action if they are to be productive. The AFT could call on the AFL-CIO Committee on Political Education (COPE) for political support, and as AFT membership grew the union increased its participation in the COPE program.

The NEA did not have a ready-made mechanism for stepping up its political activity, so it formed the National Education Association Political Action Committee (NEAPAC). But whereas the AFT relied chiefly on its network of school representatives and peer pressure to generate COPE funds, the NEA adopted a largely staff structure, supported by a dues checkoff to support NEAPAC.

The NEAPAC checkoff produced a side effect which eliminated a major point of difference between the Federation and the Association. The NEA had insisted that it was a "professional" organization, not a union like the AFT. Soon after the NEAPAC dues checkoff began, an NEA member, backed by a right-wing, business-oriented organization, sued the Association. The member charged the NEAPAC checkoff was not legal because it was not voluntary, as required by federal labor laws. The NEA claimed that the labor laws did not apply to it because it was not a union. The Supreme Court agreed with the member. The NEA was officially a union. The NEAPAC checkoff was then made voluntary, within the meaning of the law, and large amounts of money continued to be raised for political activity.

Before the creation of NEAPAC, the Association had dabbled in national partisan politics when it backed "Educators for McGovern-Shriver." "Educators" was purely a letterhead organization, but it distributed 350,000 bumper stickers and contributed approximately $30,000 to the campaign.

In 1976, however, the NEA plunged into national politics all the way. For decades the Association had advocated creation of a cabinet-level department of education. Armed with NEAPAC funds, the NEA became a strong supporter of Jimmy Carter during his long and successful primary campaign. Early in July, with the nomination assured, Carter appeared at the NEA convention and pledged to support the department proposal. Three years later, over the stubborn opposition of the AFT, incidentally, Jimmy Carter made good on his promise.

The success of the NEA's venture into partisan politics during the Carter administration seemed to confirm the soundness of the NEA's independent approach. In 1980 NEAPAC again went all out for Carter. But this time even a unified teacher organization could not have stemmed the conservative tide on which Ronald Reagan rode to victory.

The lesson to be learned from the NEA's political experience is that teachers cannot go it alone. If the schools are to prosper, they must have the support of substantial elements of American society. The AFT's experience during this same period also supports this conclusion, but with an additional twist. Although the AFT gained strength by its membership in COPE, the effectiveness of that coalition was crippled by the AFL-CIO's support of the war in Southeast Asia. Because of it the young were alienated and the Democratic liberal-labor-rights alliance was undermined, opening the way for the triumphs of Richard Nixon and Ronald Reagan.

Most teachers know that they cannot look to conservatives for support for education. When teachers and their leaders desert the liberal cause they desert the schools.

## BACKLASH

As a result of their rebellion, teachers had become unionized, even though they were not united in a single organization. The differences between their organizations had narrowed to insignificance.

As the militant teacher movement matured, demonstrations, picketing and strikes lost their shock value. School officials, the public and the courts began to take teacher militancy for granted. Conferences, clinics and coaching courses sprang up to teach school management representatives how to bargain. Counter-union training facilities became a thriving business. Erstwhile teacher representatives "jumped the fence" to feed on the greener grass on the management side.

The efforts of school management representatives produced negotiating strategy and tactics as standardized as the strategy and tactics of teacher organizations had become. Administrators learned not to cave in at the sight of the first picket line. They also learned "Bulware-ism"—the stonewalling technique devised by the former president of General Electric Corporation. At a certain time in negotiations a "fair," but minimal, offer is made by management and clung to in the hope that weaker members of the union will try to force their leaders to settle.

Even more significant, demands for "give-backs"—relinquishing gains won in previous negotiations—became a standard part of management strategy. When teachers were on the march in the early days of the rebellion, the idea that they could be forced to surrender benefits they had already won seemed ridiculous. When the backlash gained momentum, however, not even long-held rights and benefits were secure. In Philadelphia, for instance, in the fall of 1981, the union was forced, after a 50-day strike, to give up a ten percent raise which was already in its contract.

Like the teacher rebellion, the backlash by school boards and voters was largely a product of the times. The 1960s was a period when, for all the confusion and disruption, progressive forces were on the march, reforming and liberating American society. In the 1970s the nation seemed to be falling apart. The Watergate scandal was followed by the first energy crisis and unaccustomed restrictions on the beloved automobile. Leaders of the 1960s had been assassinated, and the nation wandered into recession and a clouded future. The goal of American striving shifted from the perfection of society to "taking care of number one."

The most immediate result of the tougher attitude of school management was that teacher strikes were more frequent, longer and ended with less satisfactory settlements. Except for the bitter 13-week battle of Ocean Hill-Brownsville in the fall of 1968, very few strikes had lasted more than two weeks during the early period of the rebellion.

Throughout the 1970s, as teacher strikes became more hard-fought and longer-lasting, the AFT and the NEA continued their warfare. It was as though two people standing in a leaky boat continued to punch each other out while the water rose above their knees.

## MEMORY TAPE: TEACHERS AND OSTEOPATHS

*It is 1966. The phone rings in my office at Chicago AFT head-quarters. "A Mr. Burns from the board of examiners," the switchboard operator announces.*

*"Could I come over and talk with you?" the man on the phone says.*

*"Sure," I answer immediately. After twelve years battling New York City officialdom, I can think of only one board of examiners: the governing body of the New York City teacher licensing system.*

*"My office is only three blocks away," Burns says. "Are you free now?"*

*I am puzzled. Why would the New York City Board of Examiners have an office in Chicago? Teacher recruitment? "Come on over," I answer.*

*When Burns arrives, it takes a few minutes before I realize that I have made a mistake. "I used to be a principal in Galesburg," he begins after we have shaken hands. I note his heavy downstate Illinois twang and wonder how he managed to get connected with a New York City official body. I ask for an explanation. Bit by bit the misunderstanding is clarified. Burns works for the Board of Examiners of the American Osteopathic Society.*

*Burns had identified the main problem facing osteopaths: lack of prestige despite high incomes. To remedy the situation, he had devised the "Osteopathic Board of Examiners," a body of approximately a thousand osteopaths which assembled once a year to formulate problems which would serve as the basis for examinations through which aspiring osteopathic doctors could be awarded special certificates.*

*Meetings in places such as Bermuda, Hawaii and New Orleans added greatly to the attractiveness of serving on the board—so did the added feature of tax-deductible expenses for attending doctors.*

*But Burns has run into problems and is looking for a new job. I explain that the union has no suitable position for him. After a few minutes of polite conversation he leaves.*

*Nevertheless, I continue to muse about what he has told me. Osteopaths and teachers are alike in their lack of status. Maybe teachers should establish their own "board of examiners." The only times AFT members get together as professionals are at the state and national conventions, and perhaps a conference or two. These meetings neither allowed sufficient time nor a favorable atmosphere for serious discussion of educational policy and professional problems. NEA meetings were somewhat better, but even they left plenty of room for improvement.*

*Maybe the AFT should hold a special "policy convention" every year or so. Later, this germ of an idea becomes the first AFT conference on "Quality Education Standards in Teaching"—QUEST.*

## THE PERFECTIBILITY OF AMERICAN SOCIETY

When I joined the union in 1940 I believed I was enlisting in an idealistic struggle. I expected that victories would be hard-fought and infrequent, and that the final goal would not be achieved in my lifetime. Nevertheless, it was a struggle in which I could participate wholeheartedly, sustained by the hope that progress would be made toward the vague goal I called "socialism." That belief in the perfectibility of American life gave meaning to my participation in the teachers union and the labor movement.

Reform was in the air in the prewar period. For reformers and radicals there were two choices: change could come through revolution and violence or through social evolution resulting from education. Those who subscribed to the latter strategy considered violent revolution immoral. It was undemocratic and self-defeating. Education was peaceful and sure, but the schools as they were constituted were far from being instruments of social reform. Education would have to be improved. Teacher unionism and the labor movement would make that possible.

I taught in a K-9 school in a slum area in the shadow of the Ford Rouge plant. The students were of Balkan and Near East backgrounds. My principal was paternalistic and indulgent. In my fourth year, after I had acquired survival skills, a few like-minded colleagues and I rewrote the seventh and eighth grade curricula. We reorganized these grades on the "core" system.

Teaching, educational reform, unionism and progressive politics were an exhilarating combination. On weekends I looked forward to Mondays so I could pick up where I had left off on Friday. Eventually, I was offered an administrative position, but I turned it down. I believed in teacher control of schools, and I was having too much fun as a member of the educational proletariat.

I was particularly influenced by the ideas of John Dewey and his pupil and associate, George S. Counts. Note the following passage from Counts's classic essay, *Dare the School Build a New Social Order?* which was published in 1932 at the close of the Hoover administration with its conservative, business-oriented policies. It was a time like the 1980s, when the country was in a deep economic crisis.

> Our generation has the good or ill fortune to live in an age when great decisions must be made. The American people, like most of the other peoples of the earth, have come to the parting of the ways; they can no longer trust entirely the inspiration which came to them when the Republic was young; they must decide afresh what they are to do with their talents. Favored above all other nations with the resources of nature and the material instrumentalities of civilization, they stand confused and irresolute before the future. They seem to lack the moral quality necessary to quicken discipline, and give direction to their matchless energies. In a recent paper Professor Dewey has, in my judgment, correctly diagnosed our troubles. "The schools, like the nation," he says, "are in need of a central purpose which will create new enthusiasm and devotion, and which will unify and guide all intellectual plans."
>
> This suggests, as we have already observed, that the educational problem is not wholly intellectual in nature. Our schools therefore cannot rest content with giving children an opportunity to study contemporary society in all of its aspects. This of course must be

done, but I am convinced that they should go much farther. If the schools are to be really effective they must become centers for the *building, not merely for the contemplation,* of our civilization (emphasis added).

Later, Counts adds, "To refuse the task of creating a future America immeasurably more just and noble and beautiful than the America of today is to evade the most crucial, difficult, and important educational task."

Dewey and Counts inspired many leaders of education during the 1920s and 1930s. Both were active in the AFT.

Only dreamers could believe that teacher liberalism could have any significant effect on public policy. The Federation was too small, the NEA was too conservative and passive and teachers' status was too low.

It was not until the postwar teacher rebellion that the concept of teachers-as-progressive-vanguard acquired a measure of credibility. By that time, teachers were so hard-pressed and so occupied with their own liberation that they had little energy left for other causes.

Dewey and Counts, with a few others, were chiefly responsible for the only major educational reform which was intended both to improve the quality of education and the nature of American society. This was the progressive education movement. Progressive education sought to substitute rational motivation of students for the usual reliance on authority and force. It attempted to take the drudgery out of learning through the use of imaginative and interesting school activities. It promoted a cooperative spirit rather than the competitiveness typifying most school situations. Impartial evaluations of progressive schools have found that pupils there learn at least as well as pupils in traditional schools.

Under the increasing pressure on schools and teachers in the post-World War II period, most schools reverted to "tried and true" authoritarian methods. With the passage of the Elementary and Secondary Education Act in 1966, it seemed that pressure on teachers would be relieved. But the act was never funded at much more than half its authorized level. That was not enough to permit basic improvements in school quality.

The changes in educational practice introduced in the 1970s and 1980s have mostly been designed to put more pressure on

teachers to make them more "productive." New electronic
learning aids have emphasized individual achievement rather
than cooperative problem solving. Most of these changes have
come from outside the classroom. Some are mere profit-making
schemes.


## REACTION RAMPANT: THE COMMISSION ON EXCELLENCE IN EDUCATION

By the 1980s even the vestiges of the teachings of John Dewey,
George S. Counts and their cohorts had been abandoned. Few
teachers were interested in educational reform; most only
wanted teachable classes, "professional" salaries, and good
fringe benefits. Given these, they were content to work within
the established managerial system.

Just as the teacher rebellion had been a part of the social
protest of the 1960s, teachers could not avoid the reaction of
the 1980s. The passage of the Elementary and Secondary Education Act in 1966 seemingly marked acceptance of a measure
of responsibility by the federal government for financing and
guiding public education. A major plank in Ronald Reagan's
presidential campaign platform in 1980, however, was a pledge
to terminate the federal role. Soon after his election victory,
Reagan reiterated his intention to abolish the just-created Department of Education, and he appointed a "National Commission on Excellence in Education" to survey the strengths
and weaknesses of the public schools and to make recommendations for improving them.

The commission performed as might have been expected,
considering the context in which it was created. In due course
it produced a report. Under the vaguely British-sounding title,
"A Nation at Risk: The Imperative for Educational Reform," the
report asserted that American education had declined dangerously in recent years, and that the nation could not compete
effectively with other countries, economically or militarily.

Specifically, it was charged that the curriculum had been
gutted, student discipline had been destroyed, teachers were
lacking in intellectual quality and that teacher initiative had
been sapped by collective bargaining. The underlying assump-

tion of the report was that the faults of American education could be corrected if teachers and policy makers only wanted to do it. No mention was made of deteriorating socioeconomic conditions, particularly in the big cities, or of the lack of progressive political leadership at all levels of government.

The remedies proposed by the commission were stringent:

Students should be required to complete three or four years of "solid" academic studies in high school— mathematics, science, foreign language, and (surprisingly) history and social science.

Student discipline should be tightened, and homework should be regularly assigned.

The school day and school year should be lengthened.

Especially effective teachers should be paid more than others—"merit" pay.

There was very little that was new in "A Nation at Risk," even though the commission had sponsored a number of position papers and research studies. Educational conservatives, such as those in the Council for Basic Education, had long inveighed against "Mickey Mouse" courses, particularly in schools of education, even though few course offerings could be said to fall in such a category. Under the slogan "Back to Basics," the conservatives had long called for greater emphasis on purely academic subjects and stricter standards for graduation.

That the commission's report provided a simplistic analysis of American educational problems hardly needed stating. Study after study had shown that the most influential determinent of academic success is socioeconomic status, yet this fundamental fact was totally ignored by the commission. The truth was that the curriculum could neither be significantly "hardened" nor graduation requirements significantly raised without, on the one hand, drastically increasing the student dropout rate, thrusting more young people into the already flooded employment market, or on the other hand, providing expensive remedial and guidance services to help students overcome learning disabilities. And additional remedial services or compensatory education was not what the presidential commission had in mind.

The other recommendations of the Commission on Excellence in Education were equally hollow. The recommendation to lengthen the school day and school year, for instance, stemmed from research indicating that children, in the lower grades at least, learn in proportion to time on task. However, the research was concerned with use of time in classroom situations, not the number of hours per day or per year spent in school. Obviously, children can spend a great deal of time in school without learning much if they are not well motivated and taught effectively. Thus, what seems perfectly logical at first glance—"the longer in school, the more they learn"—on closer scrutiny is seen to be dependent on many other variables.

There is no evidence, either, that basing salaries on "merit" would elevate the intellectual quality of teachers or increase their productivity. Merit rating of teachers is an idea which has been tried in hundreds of school districts, but few of those districts have stayed with the practice over any long period of time. There is no important school system which bases teacher salaries on merit.

The argument for merit rating of teachers advanced by the presidential commission was that the higher salaries for especially meritorious teachers would attract college graduates with high academic credentials to teaching. This reasoning seems dubious. So far as the drawing power of economic rewards is concerned, it seems more likely that graduates of high academic standing would be attracted by the normal earning expectation of a profession rather than by the incomes of a few outstanding individuals. Furthermore, the merit pay idea is simplistic. Its operating principle is that career choices are made primarily on abstract economic considerations rather than on the basis of factors intrinsic to the chosen field. It is at least possible that persons of high academic standing would choose teaching if they perceived it as a career in which they would be successful, would gain a sense of personal worth, would feel appreciated by others and would be encouraged to continue to grow intellectually.

All in all, "A Nation at Risk" was a direct attack on the public schools and teachers without practical proposals for making it possible for them to serve the needs of American society more effectively.


## THE PRICE OF DISUNITY

If either the NEA or the AFT had been seeking teacher unity the release of "A Nation at Risk" would have been an occasion for drawing together to take joint action. The report was enthusiastically hailed by all the usual critics of the schools. Newspapers, radio and television featured discussions of the report's recommendations. Under these circumstances, strong, clear reactions could have been expected from the teacher organization spokespersons. Such was not the case, however. Their reactions were defensive and contradictory. The NEA, already in irrevocable opposition to the Reagan administration because of Reagan's pledge to eliminate the newly established Department of Education, attacked the report in general, concentrating on the commission's merit pay advocacy. The AFT, which had opposed establishing the department, sought to exploit the situation for organizational advantage.

Speaking for the AFT, Albert Shanker declared that the educational excellence report deserved serious consideration by teachers. He agreed with the call for academic rigor, and while not criticizing its proposals for a longer school day and school year, he pointed out that additional funds would be needed to pay teachers for the additional time. He also said that merit pay would be all right in certain circumstances.

The Reagan administration, following its political strategy of chipping away at voting blocs considered to be in the Democratic camp, soon attempted to exploit the differences revealed by the contrasting reactions to the educational excellence report. Shanker was invited to the White House to confer with Mr. Reagan. The way for this meeting had been prepared by James Kilpatrick, the conservative newspaper columnist, who had written that the views of Shanker and Reagan were not all that far apart. Other friendly gestures from the White House included acceptance of an invitation to address the coming AFT convention, after rejecting an invitation from the NEA, and the appointment of an AFT staff member to be executive secretary of the revamped U.S. Civil Rights Commission.

In preparing the AFT convention for Reagan's appearance, Shanker said he would give the president an F + —the "F" for his performance, and the "plus" for at last making public education a national issue. Nevertheless, Shanker added that he and Reagan had a lot in common. Possibly he had in mind their mutual support of the cold war and their opposition to affirmative action and school busing to reduce racial segregation. In his address, the president emphasized his support for tougher student discipline, a declaration for which he was warmly applauded by the delegates. It is impossible to say whether Mr. Reagan succeeded in counteracting any significant teacher opposition to his policies, but his efforts must have had some effect.

The Nation-at-Risk episode clearly illustrated the harmful effects for teachers of their organizational divisiveness. A unified organization could have made a telling response to the report which would have laid the basis for actions leading to true excellence in education.

The report of the Presidential Commission on Excellence in Education not only revealed the lack of a credible national strategy for educational excellence, it also exposed the lack of such a policy on the part of the teaching profession, a lack traceable directly to the continuing warfare between the two teacher organizations.

Teachers must be given the time and encouragement to develop school-tested improvements which incorporate social goals. Educational reform must deal with the *purpose* of education. That purpose must not only include the development of the capacities of children. It must also be based on faith in the ultimate "perfectability" of American life.

## DARE THE TEACHERS BUILD A NEW SOCIAL MOVEMENT?

From the vantage point of time, the vision of John Dewey, George S. Counts and their colleagues stands up very well. The educational progressives believed that eliminating the antiso-

246                                          THE TEACHER REBELLION

cial and authoritarian practices of the schools and democratiz-
ing the curriculum would produce a new, "more perfect" nation. They were also convinced that a new progressive social
movement was needed, and that the labor movement could
form its core.

Schools are embedded in their times. A new progressive
movement would generate the environment schools need to
become truly effective. More than that, it could establish a political climate which would foster schools capable of building
the cooperative society of the future.

Liberal left movements in other countries have derived their
basic strength from their labor movements, which have been
augmented by middle-class liberals, intellectuals and Socialists. They have been built through formal party structures functioning over long periods of time. For the past hundred years,
however, the liberal left in the United States has been frag-
mented. In more recent times it has been preempted by the New
Deal, overrun by World War II and suppressed during the
McCarthy-Eisenhower days. It glowed briefly in the 1960s, only
to subside under the cynicism of the Nixon-Ford-Carter-Reagan
era.

The weakness of the liberal left stems most directly from the
weakness of the American labor movement, which in turn is
caused by the movement's peculiarities. Almost all other national labor movements are aggressive and socialistic. The
American labor movement is cautious and bureaucratic. It accepts capitalism as its fundamental economic principle, but
favors restrictions and reform to prevent abuses. The program
of the AFL-CIO is idealistic and humane, within its limitations.
Except for foreign affairs, the AFL-CIO is usually on the liberal
side, but the movement lacks a spokesperson of the stature of
Walter Reuther, John L. Lewis or Eugene Debs.

The American labor movement has more than a public relations problem, however. From its beginnings, the movement
has been strongly anti-Marxist. Marxist organizations look to
the proletariat for support. Because AFL craft unions did not
try to organize workers in mass production industries, the
Marxists formed competing, "dual" unions. Thus, the movement was engaged in its own cold war long before the cold war
became official United States policy. The AFL-CIO was the

staunchest supporter of the war in Southeast Asia, and it continues to support increased expenditures for defense and overt and covert resistance to the possible spread of communism in Latin America and other third world countries. As a result, many liberals and young people have been alienated.

There are persons closely associated with the labor movement who argue that the AFL-CIO should center its policies even farther right in order to attract more support, rather than rebuild the liberal-labor-rights coalition and improve its basic rationale and coherence. This viewpoint was put forward by Richard M. Scammon and Ben J. Wattenberg in *The Real Majority* (Berkley Medallion Books, 1970). Scammon is a political pollster who is often used by the AFL-CIO. Wattenberg is a neoconservative writer in close contact with influential AFL-CIO leaders.

Speaking to the COPE operating committee in January, 1981, Scammon warned, "We must not let the trade union movement become the caboose to the intellectuals who make scandals in Big Sur or live in Scarsdale with their parents." There was much more in the same vein (John Herling's Labor Letter, January 24, 1981). Polls agree that only a slim majority of union members voted for the Democratic candidate for president in 1980 despite their lack of enthusiasm for his opponent.

Where does this leave teachers? In spite of the difficulties, is teacher unity still attainable? Is it such a good idea, after all? As I have said throughout this book, a united teachers union under progressive leadership *could* be the strongest force in the AFL-CIO and in American society. Its more than three million members, counting nonteaching educational employees, would make it three times as big as any other AFL-CIO affiliate. And teacher unity could still be achieved in spite of the difficulties. But could such a massive organization generate the vitality to maintain a progressive program, or would it settle into the bureaucratic, minimal unionism which characterizes many American unions?

In spite of its overwhelming size, a united teacher organization might have some difficulty in forcing the AFL-CIO to shift to the left, even if that were its objective. Social policy issues which do not affect the welfare of members directly are of little moment in most unions. Officers and staff members can shape policy much as they wish. The labor movement's conservative stance on foreign policy and resistant attitude on some racial issues is supported by a neoconservative network within the labor federation. Similarly, although the NEA outnumbers the AFT three to one and has been more liberal than the AFT on most issues in the 1980s, it is not certain it could retain that orientation in a merged organization.

The problem becomes even more difficult when the kind of trade-off which would be required to achieve teacher unity is taken into account. In the event of a merger, the NEA, as the larger organization, would name the president of the new organization, but Shanker would be in charge of relations with the AFL-CIO, whatever his title. He would retain his seat on the labor federation's executive council and perhaps some day run for its presidency. Since Shanker is a key figure in the neoconservative network previously alluded to, restraining his conservative tendencies would be difficult.

Whether progressive forces in the teacher organizations should continue to press ahead for teacher unity, or whether they should wait for a new leader to emerge on either side of the organizational fence is a question which must be given careful consideration. Perhaps the magic moment has passed. Sometimes progress can only be made by going backward.


## MEMORY TAPE: A WALK ON MURRAY STREET

It is a raw, dark, snowy Saturday night in lower Manhattan in January, 1978. I am walking along Eighth Avenue a block or so away from city hall. Walking with me is Wade Cummings, a new, young acquaintance from Houston, Texas. We have just finished a pleasant dinner with other friends who, like us, have come to this desolate location for a meeting of the national executive board of DSOC, the Democratic Socialist Organizing Committee.

Cummings and I reach the dimly lit subway stop at Chambers Street. We are going to take the subway uptown to a party. I stop and ask "How about taking a little walk? I want to show you a few things."

In his Texas clothes, Cummings is not eager to stay out in the cold, but he obligingly agrees. I look at the grimy pre-World War I buildings. They reach up four or five stories, with a higher one here and there. Many of the windows have ancient gold lettering on them.

"I used to love to walk around down here," I say. "You could get anything here—hardware, boat supplies, shoes—anything. But that's not what I want to show you."

We reach the corner of Murray Street and turn left toward city hall. "Right here is where it all began," I say. "Of course it really began back in the schools and in the Teachers Guild headquarters at Twenty-third Street and Broadway, but this is where we used to hold our rallies. The outdoor ones, that is. We held the indoor rallies at St. Nick's."

Cummings looks up and down the narrow block. "Sure doesn't look like much," he comments.

"Yes, I know," I agree. "This place always looks like this on a Saturday. Nobody comes down here. But until five-thirty on week days, it is a busy place." I pause. "The police made us hold our meetings here, but we would always picket city hall for an hour or so first. We usually got along all right with the cops. They knew that if we got more money, they would get more too."

"How many teachers would come to the rally?" Cummings asks.

"In the early 1950s, we would only get a thousand or so. Then we began getting enough to put a picket line all around city hall and the park in front of it. One time we picketed all night. We called it a vigil."

"What were the rallies for?"

"Protest. That was all we could do at that time," I explain. "We were afraid to strike. But then came the first big one, April 11, 1962. We had gone out a year earlier, but it was not well supported. In 1962, though, we had more than 25,000 screaming, chanting teachers down here." I point to a spot in the middle of the block. "Here's where I parked my car," I add. "A Jeep station wagon with the public address horns clamped on top. I carried a stepladder so the speakers could climb up there. Charlie Cogen got excited and stamped his foot so hard the car roof caved in. He kept right on talking, though."

"Twenty-five thousand teachers down here?" Cummings stares through the sifting snow at the bleak store fronts.

"There were so many that they jammed this whole block, wall to wall and out into Broadway. On that day, teachers had a movement! 'Day of Dignity' a reporter called it."

We start walking back to the subway. "Were you a Socialist then?" Cummings asks.

"Oh sure. At least I called myself a Socialist. That's what it was all about."

"Do you think the teachers will ever have a movement again? The United Teachers of America?"

"I don't know," I say. "I don't know."

# Index